THE
SUCCESSFUL
FAMILY
BUSINESS

SCOTT E.
FRIEDMAN

NGP PUBLISHERS LLC

This publication is designed to provide accurate and authoritative information in regard to the subject matter covered. It is sold with the understanding that the publisher is not engaged in rendering legal, accounting, or other professional service. If legal advice or other expert assistance is required, the services of a competent professional person should be sought.

©1998 by Scott E. Friedman

Published by NGP Publishers LLC

Distributed by Prometheus Books, 59 John Glenn Drive, Amherst, NY 14228
VOICE: 716-691-0133, ext. 207
FAX: 716-564-2711
WWW.PROMETHEUSBOOKS.COM

Printed in the United States of America

01 02 03 04 10 9 8 7 6 5 4 3 2 1

Library of Congress Cataloging-in-Publication Data

Friedman, Scott E., 1958–
    The successful family business / by Scott E. Friedman.
       p. cm.
    Includes index.
    ISBN 0–9716212–0–9 (pbk.)
    1. Family-owned business enterprises—Management—Case studies.
I. Title.
HD62.25.F749 1998
658'.045—dc21   2001098260
                                          CIP

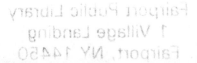

Dedication

I dedicate this book to the most important people in my life: my family, who, again, supported me while I worked long and difficult hours to complete this book.

I hope that this effort will benefit you and your family.

Other Books by Scott E. Friedman

How to Profit by Forming Your Own Limited Liability Company

How to Run a Family Business, with Michael H. Friedman

The Law of Parent-Child Relationships

Sex Law: A Legal Sourcebook on Critical Sexual Issues for the Non-Lawyer

ACKNOWLEDGMENTS

Although it is the author who gets credit for writing a book, every author knows that the book could not have been completed without the support of a variety of people. So it is with *The Successful Family Business,* which truly could only have been written with the support of many of my friends, family members, and business partners.

First, I'd like to express my appreciation to my father-in-law, Irwin Pastor, chairman of the board and president of Pepsi-Cola Buffalo Bottling Corp., for affording me the opportunity to serve as general counsel to our family business. Working side by side with my father-in-law, a leader with energy and vision, has helped me to appreciate the unique attributes of family businesses. I have come to understand family businesses far better than I ever could had I simply been either a lawyer or a family member.

I count myself extraordinarily lucky to have three other important professional mentors. My partner, Henry M. Porter, is a wealth of information on a variety of subjects, including tax law, business law, and estate planning, which he is always willing to share with his younger partner. I have also benefited from the particular support and encouragement of another partner, Gerald S. Lippes, whose combination of business and legal expertise is well known and admired. My father, Dr. Irwin Friedman, has taught me many lessons by both word and action. His patients from around the world have come to appreciate his rare combination of intelligence, work ethic, patience, and devotion. I continue to strive to match this combination in my own professional life (although I have come to accept the limits of my own intelligence and try to make do).

I would also like to thank my partners and colleagues at Lippes, Silverstein, Mathias & Wexler LLP for their continued and much appreciated support and encouragement. I am indeed fortunate to be surrounded by such consummate professionals. Special thanks to my secretary, Barbara Fitzgerald, for her expert assistance in the preparation of this manuscript.

Special thanks to Dr. William "Chip" Valutis, president of Family & Business Directors, Inc., in Buffalo, for critiquing this book and providing helpful suggestions from his perspective as one of this country's leading family business consultants.

Thanks (again) to everyone at Dearborn Financial Publishing for their work on this project, particularly Danielle Egan-Miller for her guidance and editorial suggestions at every step of the way. This book has benefited greatly from Danielle's suggestions. Thanks also to Jack Kiburz, managing editor, and Bobbye Middendorf, marketing director, for their assistance. These Dearborn professionals continue to make the publishing process an exciting and rewarding one for an author.

Finally, of course, I thank my family. My wife, Lisa, and my children, Samantha, Eliza, Julia, and Madeline continue to permit me to practice law by day and to write by night. I see their love, support, and encouragement etched on every page of this book. I see as well my wife's insights, intuition, and intelligence on these pages and know how lucky I am to count her as my ultimate "partner."

CONTENTS

Foreword   ix

Preface   xiii

Introduction   xvii

1. *Do Members of Your Family Business Argue?*
   Here's Why!   1

2. *Your Family's Not Talking?*
   Establish a Family Council   22

3. *Do Your Business Decisions Meet Family Resistance?*
   Establish a Functioning Board of Directors   34

4. *You've Reached an Agreement with Members of
   Your Family. Now What?*
   Put It in Writing!   51

5. *What Can You Do If Conflict Erupts?*
   Establish a Dispute Resolution Process   74

6. *You're Ready to Pass the Leadership Baton?*
   Here's How to Plan a Smooth Transition!   88

7. *You're Worried about Estate Taxes?*
   Here's What You Can Do!   104

8. *You're Worried about Losing Control When
   You Transfer Assets to Family Members?*
   Here's What You Can Do!   137

9. *Do You Want to Reduce Taxes and Retain Control?*
Consider Establishing a Family LLC 159

10. *What Else Can You Do to Keep Your Family and Business on Track?*
Consider These Miscellaneous Planning Techniques 176

11. *Planning for the Long Term?*
Prune the Family Business Tree! 195

Appendix A Sample Family Charter 203

Appendix B Sample Family LLC
Operating Agreement 207

Index 223

FOREWORD

Family-owned businesses have been a hot topic for consultants, lawyers, accountants, financial planners, and authors in recent years. Many have promoted their knowledge, tips, and techniques in an attempt to benefit these unique enterprises. Interestingly, for all the hype and attention, there is no indication that the alarming number of failed family-owned businesses has been reduced.

Scott Friedman has written the first book I've seen that will force the ostrich to pull its proverbial head from the sand. He makes no apologies for his perception that, without significant effort, most family-owned businesses will fail. Further still, he shows with candor and clarity why this perception is true. Make no mistake, this is not a book filled with easy solutions to difficult problems. Instead, it is a book based on research and experience that provides a way to avoid becoming a broken or failed family business.

If you are looking for a fresh, readable, candid guide for beating the odds, read on. If, on the other hand, you are looking for a quick fix or an excuse to put off dialogue or planning, don't bother. If you choose not to read further, please pass the book along to your professional advisers. The information in this book will improve the way they serve their clients' needs.

What makes this book so effective? Early in the book, Friedman challenges the reader to look at decisions, conflict, and communication differently. He writes that family or business decisions can be (1) good for both the business and the family, (2) good for business but bad for the family, (3) bad for business but good for the family, or (4) bad for both the business and the family. Once family members understand these choices and reach consensus on important priorities for their family and business, they can approach decisions or issues from a common perspective. Applying this deceptively simply model can account for significant, positive changes. This should be good news for business owners and advisers who are tired of experiencing disappointment and failure every time they try to move the family business forward.

Friedman continues by introducing the reader to some of the toughest issues faced in family businesses today. Without psychobabble or legalese, he discusses retirement, compensation, boards of directors, buy-sell and shareholder agreements, estate planning, conflict, and the selection of a successor to the firm. Chapter by chapter, he lists key issues for family business perpetuation and teaches a different perspective to use in avoiding historical failures. He shows how to tackle difficult planning issues, warns of common pitfalls, and encourages when it all feels overwhelming.

As a psychologist and management consultant, I work with many family-business clients and frequently encounter the issues covered in this book. Though I try to keep up with the multitude of legal and financial techniques available, this is the first book I have read that clearly explains what these techniques are and how they can help. On the topics of trusts, shareholder agreements, business valuation, insurance, corporate structure, estate planning, and buy-sell agreements, this book is clear and informing. And even though the amount of information is comprehensive, the reading is interesting and thought provoking. Also, interwoven throughout are fascinating case studies, informative sidebars, up-to-date legal precedents, specific recommendations, and challenging Family Business Audits.

I hope many professionals, advisers, and nonfamily managers of family businesses also will read these pages and glean the insight and tools for coping with the complexities of their positions with family businesses. Armed with this information, advisers will find fewer of their succession plans, estate plans, or buy-sell agreements sitting on clients' shelves collecting dust. And nonfamily managers will be able to exert more effective influence and make more informed decisions about their future with the family firm.

Finally, I recommend this book to all family members in business together and to those thinking of going into business together. Use chapters as discussion guides in family meetings or family councils. Adapt the Family Business Audits as road maps to your planning efforts. Set goals and objectives based on the challenges herein. I already have used the information in several chapters to teach and challenge my own clients.

In closing, I will say again that this book is not for the unmotivated or undisciplined. Once you see and understand the issues at hand, it will be very difficult *not* to take action. The statistics are clear: Only one in ten family businesses surpasses the founding generation, and the costs associated with a failed family business (emotional and monetary) are life altering. Only by heeding the counsel from books like this can you take charge and manage the destiny of your family business. I challenge you to make this book the first step on your journey to success.

—Wm. (Chip) Valutis, Ph.D.
President, Navitar Consulting, Inc.

PREFACE

Over the past decade, growth of interest in the family business has been explosive. This growth is evident in seminars, courses, professional meetings and research conferences; the emergence of research institutes and academic centers; and rapidly proliferating, specialized consulting and professional services.

Fueling the interest in family companies is the delayed recognition of family businesses as the latent core of all market economies. Even in the United States, which has the most active stock exchanges, family firms account for more than two-thirds of all U.S. companies, around 50 percent of the workforce and at least 40 percent of the U.S. gross domestic product, and as many as 78 percent of new jobs created from 1976 to 1990.

Scholars in business schools and service professionals 50 years ago were enamored with public ownership of companies and what was termed "professional" management. Big public companies were supposed to be the future, and most everyone in academia and professional organizations focused their writing on these organizations. The result was a limited understanding of how family businesses work and how important they are to the economy and society.

In the 1960s, the fledgling family business literature remained limited to a few dozen articles. These articles dissected the typical problems and social dynamics found in family firms.

The 1970s saw a heightened recognition of the distinct and often divergent family and business interests within the family business. During the late 1970s and 1980s, family and business came to be analyzed as distinct "systems." It was during this period that Tagiuri and Davis introduced the three-circle approach to understanding the family business system ("On the Goals of Successful Family Companies," *Family Business Review* 5, no. 1). Their framework explicitly integrates the

Three-Circle Model

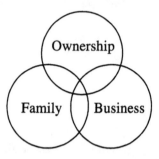

owners of family companies (and their concerns) into discussions that had previously only compared family and business concerns. This three-circle framework has become the dominant approach for the field.

Since the late 1970s, interest in family companies has increasingly focused on how they develop over time, culminating in an integrative analysis of family business development. We now have ways to understand the strengths and challenges of family companies at a point in time and the ability to predict what they will face in the future.

With each new conceptual advance in the field of family business comes a heightened ability to identify issues and prescribe solutions to these challenges. At this stage in the evolution of the field, it is broadly accepted that the mixture of family and business can either lead family companies to be highly innovative and durable, or indecisive and vulnerable to more aggressive competitors. The outcome depends on how the essential characteristics of family firms are managed. If family companies capitalize on the strengths that industrious, flexible families can bring to business, they can be difficult to beat in most marketplaces. If family firms fall victim to excessive traditionalism and family rivalry, they can be easy prey. Families in business must not only keep up with quickly changing technology and competition in their industries, they also must learn to manage the interface of family and business.

Scott Friedman, a business attorney who helps many family companies through their challenges, has crafted *The Successful Family Business* for families in business. This practical, problem-solving book is a handy family business legal reference. It also provides a sound overview of many issues facing families in business today. In my view, it is particularly useful for first- and second-generation business families with small and medium-sized companies who are concerned with succession planning, estate planning, and establishing agreements to protect the business and preserve family relationships.

As an attorney and a participant in a business owned by his family, Friedman has developed practical remedies for the daily struggles of family businesses. He understands that although business families are often in conflict, they have the ability to build some of the most successful businesses in the world. With the proper tools and understanding, families are able to deal with their day-to-day challenges and plan well into the future.

Family councils and boards of directors are two of the essential tools discussed in this book. These separate discussion groups encourage good decision making and effective conflict management in the family business. In my view, any family in business is tempting fate if it does not have a board with independent outsiders, a family council to discuss the sensitive issues that are a natural part of having a business, and rules that define rights and responsibilities in the family, management, and ownership.

Friedman provides guidelines for families to establish councils and boards and to create rules for family involvement with the business (a family charter) that will lead the company to a more successful future. Chapter 4, for instance, is a good primer on buy-sell agreements. Friedman explains that eventually someone will want to (or should) get out of the business, and if this agreement is developed early on, there will be less confusion as to how to proceed. On a related topic in Chapter 5, Friedman discusses the important process of dispute resolution in family businesses. He wisely emphasizes that families should always be working toward better communication and decision making to maximize their business effectiveness.

Although they are not easily discussed by families, succession and estate planning are fundamental for long-term family-business success. Friedman provides an easy-to-understand analysis of the legal and financial considerations in these matters. After reading this book, families will have a much better understanding of the need to discuss difficult issues early on. In Chapters 7 and 8, he provides a crisp, readable analysis of estate planning options and trusts, handling some very complex legal options in a simplified way. Those curious about limited liability companies will find a helpful explanation in Chapter 9.

Attorneys help us prepare for eventualities like death and taxes and deal with problems along the way. We can learn from their problem focus. I am delighted that Scott Friedman has added his insights and advice to this growing field and encourage the reader to take his recommendations to heart.

—John A. Davis
Senior Lecturer, Harvard Graduate School
of Business Administration, and President,
Owner Managed Business Institute

INTRODUCTION

Most businesses in this country are family businesses: restaurants, hardware stores, manufacturers, insurance agencies, and service providers. Family businesses can be very small or very large; they can be extremely successful or struggling to survive; they can be well established or recently started. They are owned by people of all races, religions, sexes, and national origins. In spite of their many differences, however, family businesses share a most important characteristic: They are owned or controlled by a family. The family owners may be few, perhaps a parent and child or two siblings, or very large and include siblings, children, grandchildren, cousins, aunts, and uncles.

Family ownership is such an important factor that its significance transcends the many differences found throughout these businesses. For example, a family-owned restaurant may be more like a family-owned manufacturer than another restaurant whose stock is widely traded on a public stock market! This book explores the significance of family ownership, how it increases the likelihood of family and business conflict, and, based on this analysis, more importantly, what can be done to minimize conflict and maximize peace and understanding within the family.

Make no mistake: Family-owned businesses are wonderful institutions that offer rich and rewarding opportunities to family members. Carefully conceived, they can provide employment opportunities to those family members who want them, returns on investments to those who own them, the psychic benefits derived from parents, siblings, and other relatives working closely together toward a common objective, and countless other benefits. From a financial perspective, family businesses can be lucrative, a fact due in part to their ability to seize upon new opportunities faster than their publicly owned counterparts, many of which have an unfortunate tendency to get bogged down in layers of bureaucracy.

In spite of these advantages, family businesses have a miserable failure rate. Statistically, approximately only three out of every ten family businesses survive beyond the founder's leadership tenure and into the second generation and approximately only one in ten family businesses successfully makes it to the third generation. The average life expectancy of a family business is approximately 24 years: the same leadership tenure period as the average founder of a family business!

As impressive as these statistics may be, they remain a poor measure of the emotional devastation that can accompany conflict in a family business. Conflict in a family business has aptly been likened to conflict in a bad marriage, and the emotional and financial stresses of a business separation can be just as painful as a nasty divorce. The stories of several actual family conflicts that have been, or are being, waged are considered throughout this book. In many instances, these are stories of fathers and sons or brothers and sisters locked in battles that have ended up in the legal system and, on occasion, on the front page of national newspapers. Sometimes, the battles are over significant business issues such as the proper deployment of company resources; sometimes over petty ones such as a perceived lack of respect among family members. The "business" of the family usually suffers as a result of such hostility and, although more difficult to measure, so too does the "family," which is almost invariably a casualty in such circumstances. Indeed, anyone who has ever worked in a family business knows that this type of business can be a pressure cooker where the slightest misstep can result in litigation and even the most innocent oversight can result in fisticuffs. What appears to outsiders to be a family blessing is, in reality, more often a family curse.

I believe that family business failures can be largely attributed to three distinct factors:

1. Disagreements over business-related decisions that create conflict among family members
2. The estate and gift tax system, which business owners and professionals commonly describe as "confiscatory"
3. General business problems that every business faces

How families can better manage these first two factors, in order to reduce the statistical failure rate of their businesses, is the subject of the balance of this book; the third factor, which is not unique to family businesses, is not.

Why do so many families argue about decisions made in their business? Why are so many family leaders incapable of developing a satisfactory plan that addresses their inevitable estate tax obligations, even if they have many years to do so? What lies behind the difficulties experienced by so many family businesses regardless of their success, their size, or their industry? How can loving family members turn against each other over and over and over again? More important, what can be learned from the mistakes of others so that the ignominious history of family business failures can mercifully come to an end?

I believe the answers to these questions ultimately lie in the chaotic and irrational manner in which decisions in family businesses are often made. Let me explain. Decisions made by *public companies* can basically have *two* consequences: They can be

1. good for business or
2. bad for business.

By contrast, decisions by *family businesses* can basically have *four* consequences: They can be

1. good for business and the family,
2. good for business but bad for the family,
3. bad for business but good for the family, or
4. bad for the business and the family.

Therefore, the odds that a decision in a family business will be acceptable are markedly lower than in a public company. This analysis is further complicated by the fact that each individual views the world in a unique way. This of course sometimes means that one family member may conclude that a particular decision is good for business and family while another family member may conclude that the same decision is bad for business and family. To some, the glass is half full; to others, it is half empty.

Aside from the fact that people view the world through their own unique perspectives, individuals involved in family businesses are frequently torn by their roles as family members and their roles as professionals. For example, as a parent, an individual may unconditionally love his or her child. As the child's employer, however, that same individual fills a role that requires his or her critical evaluation of the child on the basis of performance results. Family members understand that mistakes should be understood and forgotten; employers record mistakes for objective performance evaluations in order to guide future employment decisions. While emotions govern many family relationships, objectivity and reason are the governing forces in the workplace. In short, an individual's family role and business role often conflict, and this fact adds to the volatility of the family business.

The message of this book is simple: If a family can improve its decision-making process so that family members can more often agree that decisions are in the best interests of both the family and the business, a family business is more likely to prosper. Accordingly, any planning tool or strategy that helps accomplish this objective is useful; planning tools that ignore this objective will, ultimately, prove insufficient or even useless (which explains why even family businesses with elaborate legal structures and complex agreements are nevertheless prone to experience conflict and failure). Chapter 1 explores this concept in more detail so you will be able to understand its sweeping importance and use it to help your family business prosper and succeed.

This book not only offers a variety of techniques that should benefit any family business but, more importantly, clearly explains how and why they work. These techniques are neither too complicated to understand nor too complex for any family to implement. Properly utilized, they can help your family business minimize conflict and maximize prosperity.

This book also offers a variety of techniques designed to assist family business owners to reduce, minimize, or, perhaps even eliminate the estate and gift tax obligations that may be imposed on the transfer of their ownership interests while managing a transition of leadership control from senior family members to junior family members. Together, these techniques can help your family avoid ruinous conflict and can keep your family business from becoming another statistic of the seeming inevitability of ruinous conflict in family businesses.

These techniques—what they are, why they work, and practical suggestions designed to help you use them in your own family business—are the basis of this book. Family Business Audits are included in each chapter to help you measure your progress and to suggest possible areas to focus on. I have endeavored throughout to make this book not only as useful as possible but interesting and understandable as well. I believe that a family and its business are more likely to survive and prosper if a family—not just its lawyers, accountants, and financial planners—is familiar with the problems and suggested solutions discussed in this book. You will, therefore, find that this book is written in plain English, is readily understood even by those without advanced professional degrees, and, to the greatest extent possible, avoids "legalese" and "psychobabble." If my suggestions, or their possible applicability to your situation are unclear, please feel free to contact me. You may reach me in any of the following ways:

- By phone: 716-853-5100
- By fax: 716-853-5199
- By e-mail: SFriedman@Lippes.com
- By mail: Lippes Silverstein Mathias & Wexler LLP
  28 Church Street
  Buffalo, NY 14202

I look forward to hearing from you and wish you well with your family business!

Please contact me if you would like to receive information about The Family Business Scorecard™, a proprietary new planning tool I have developed especially for owners of family businesses that is designed to

- provide an objective analysis of the critical issues facing your family business,
- diagnose your family business health and its hot spots,
- assess the quality of your succession planning process, and
- map dynamic changes in the health of your family business to help increase the likelihood of its success!

CHAPTER 1

Do Members of Your Family Business Argue?

Here's Why!

An Introduction to Conflict

*T*hroughout this book, I use the term *family business* to refer to a business that is owned or controlled by a family. Most, but not all, family businesses also are characterized by the presence of one or more family members on the senior management team. Various estimates suggest that somewhere between 80 to 90 percent of all businesses in the United States are family owned or controlled. They range from some of the smallest businesses to some of the largest, including Wal-Mart, Ford, and Cargill. They span every industry, from manufacturing to service, from high tech to supermarkets, from cinemas to real estate developments, creating millions of jobs. Estimates suggest that most employees in the United States are employed by a family business. Family businesses are surely the backbone of the U.S. economy.

In spite of their economic importance, most family businesses fail to survive a transition in leadership from one generation to the next. Many family business failures can be attributed to unresolved conflict between family members. This chapter explores this phenomenon.

Although statistics on both the likelihood of conflict in a family business and the probability that a family business will not survive beyond one or two generations are compelling, most family business owners may spend little, if any, time planning to promote family peace, avoiding conflict, and ensuring a smooth ownership transition from one generation to the next. Psychologists, I believe, call this "denial."

Part of the reason for this phenomenon may be that most of us simply can't understand the pain that lies behind these statistics until it is too late. The agony a family experiences when its business is racked by conflict or forced into liquidation in order to raise money to satisfy estate tax obligations may never really be felt until the problem strikes home. By then, solutions may be hard to come by.

Throughout this book, I offer for your consideration accounts of several families, their businesses, and their problems. These accounts are based on information made available in public records as a result of intrafamily litigation. Far better than statistics ever could, these stories highlight the brutal reality of family businesses, which if ignored, will ultimately destroy the precious bonds of family forever.

To make sense of these family tragedies as well as the overwhelming statistical failure rate for family businesses, the next section first explains that, while each family's specific problems and their effects may be unique, their inability to successfully resolve such problems frequently can be attributed to the same cause: poor communication and consensus-building skills. I then suggest a strategy for minimizing the negative aspects of conflict by enhancing communication opportunities through use of the planning techniques offered in this book.

The Origin of Conflict

As long as a business is operating, its owners face an ongoing decision-making process. What products or services should be offered? How much should be charged? What suppliers should be used? What customers should be sought? Who, even, should make which of these decisions? The list can seem endless. The ongoing decisions that owners of a family business must make inevitably result in disagreements. Why? Each individual views the world uniquely and, therefore, often is unable to either accept or understand why someone else thinks and acts as he or she does. An inability to understand another's decision-making process on any meaningful issue may produce friction or hostility. This is especially true when individuals attribute selfish motive as the reason for another's disagreement with the "correct decision." For example, one family member may believe a decision to build a new production facility to streamline operations is great for both family and business, while another family member may think the same decision is horrendous since the facility's cost would be high and would require the family to assume an unacceptable level of debt. The fallout from disagreements like this almost inevitably spills over, resulting in stress on owners, employees, spouses, and children. In many instances, the cause of hostility may not even be remembered as a disagreement over a decision. Instead, the cause is attributed to another's stupidity, jealousy, spitefulness, etc. Ironically, like a self-fulfilling prophesy, these attributes often become justified as family members give up trying to resolve family disputes and focus instead on protecting their self-interests.

Conflict in the Smith Family

To better illustrate how conflict can develop in a family business, let's consider the following example. Tom Smith and his sister, Jane Norton, each own part of a family business, started by their now deceased parents, a chain of five movie theaters in their hometown of Buffalo, New York. Tom owns 60 percent of the business and Jane owns the other 40 percent. Tom works in the business; Jane does not. Tom has two children, an 18-year-old son, George, who dropped out of high school when he was 16 and spent the next two years backpacking across Europe, and Sally, a 32-year-old struggling artist. Having recently returned home, George wants to start working in the family business. Tom is convinced that the job will help George "grow up and become responsible." Tom believes that a decision to employ his son will not only be good for the family but, ultimately, the business as well, since "George can even be trained to run the business one day." Jane disagrees with her brother, believing instead that her nephew should complete his education and prove himself in the business world before he is permitted to join the family business. She believes that the decision to offer George a job will be bad for the family ("What kind of values do you teach the kid?") and bad for the business ("Without proper training or an education, he'll run our company into the ground"). A decision grid of Tom and Jane's differences in perspective is shown in Figure 1.1.

This same example can also illustrate how the perspectives of only four family members—Tom, Jane, George, and George's sister Sally—

FIGURE 1.1   The Decision: Whether to Employ George in the Family
Business

Tom's Perspective		vs.	Jane's Perspective	
Good for family/good for business				
				Bad for family/bad for business

could easily view the same decision in four separate ways. If we consider these four separate perspectives of the decision, our illustration
might look something like Figure 1.2.

Finally, if the same decision about whether George should be offered
employment in the family business were considered from the different
perspectives of individuals in an extended family business—one that
includes George's cousins, for example—the likelihood of differing
opinions and of conflict increase.

FIGURE 1.2   Four Perspectives on Whether to Offer George a Job

Tom		Jane	
Good for family/good for business			
			Bad for family/bad for business

George		Sally	
			Good for family/bad for business
Bad for family/good for business			

As the number of people who care about the outcome of a decision increases, the messier and more complex the disagreement—and our grid—becomes. These illustrations highlight why it can be so difficult to achieve consensus on decisions among increasing numbers of family members. Further complicating this dynamic are the often-conflicting roles a person serves as a family member or a business owner or employee. The increase in conflict in relation to the number of family members connected with a family business, combined with the conflict caused by the clash between roles individuals fill in the family system and the business system is, I submit, why conflict in a family business is virtually inevitable.

How to Reduce Conflict and Maximize Consensus

The techniques offered throughout this book are based on the premise that specific action can be taken to minimize or eliminate conflict by maximizing consensus and understanding within the family.

To see how these techniques can be practically applied and effectively used by any family, let's review the following decisions commonly made in family businesses. I will then suggest why conflict frequently results from these decisions and recommend what can be done to reduce the conflict. These recommendations are based on many of the techniques that are reviewed throughout the balance of this book.

Decisions about Whether the Company's Profits Should Be Reinvested in the Family Business or Distributed to the Owners

The origin of conflict.   Individuals' unique positions and perspectives can affect the family business in a variety of ways. For example, using our hypothetical family considered earlier, if Tom Smith married into a wealthy family, he may be more interested in reinvesting the earnings of the family business to grow the business, while his sister Jane, whose spouse is a struggling artist, may be more interested in taking as much money out of the business as possible, because the business provides little financial benefit to her. This disagreement is particularly common between family members who are active in the business and others who are inactive in the business.

Recommendation.   Tom and Jane need to agree on the mission of their family business, including their vision and objectives, as well as a broad strategy for how best to pursue these objectives. This agreement must be clear and understandable to all the family members, not simply Tom as the family business leader or the attorney who may document it and who may be unavailable (or unable) to interpret it for the family when necessary. For example, if Tom simply reinvests the business profits without considering how Jane can cash out one day, he is inviting conflict. By contrast, Jane may be prepared to accept and even support Tom's decision to reinvest all profits in the family business for five years and grow the business if the plan also includes an agreement to "go public" or buy out Jane's interest in the business at the expiration of this five-year period. This understanding may be reflected in a family mission statement defined in Chapter 2, and a shareholder agreement, discussed in Chapter 4.

Decisions Over How the Family Business Should Be Run

The origin of conflict.   For a variety of reasons, individuals have different ideas about what is good or bad for business. Some differences are due to one's risk tolerance; some individuals are prepared to "bet the house," while others would rather "play it safe." Other differences may be due to differences in judgment as a result of experience, education, or personality. Whatever the basis for the difference, a disagreement over business decisions within the family business has precipitated many conflicts. Mike, for example, may think the family company should expand into new territory. Sue thinks the business is going along just fine as it is. Mike's decision would require the business to borrow money to finance the expansion, but Sue does not want to borrow money and is appalled to learn that her personal guaranty might be required. Conflicts can become particularly unwieldy in those situations where a poor decision turns into a debacle and the family business loses a substantial amount of money. Finger-pointing in such circumstances can rise to unfathomable levels.

The case of *Johnston v. Livingston Nursing Home, Inc.* illustrates how conflict over how a business should be run can develop. In this lawsuit, Esther Johnston sued her sister, Lessie Vick, for mismanaging a nursing home they jointly owned in Alabama. Among the charges, Johnston claimed that her sister mismanaged the business affairs of the home and neglected the patients by serving poor-quality food. Not surprisingly, Johnston's lawsuit also claimed that her sister was overpaying herself and receiving unnecessary perks from the business. Vick, of course, denied the charges.

In its consideration of the claims, the Alabama Supreme Court observed that the sisters' "arbitrary differences of opinions provoked some harsh words between them and a few blows might have been passed." Although the court found that there was some justification for Johnston's claims, it concluded that neither the appointment of a receiver nor liquidation of the business were justified. Instead, the court concluded that the business could continue to function "even though there may not be mutuality and harmony in their ideas of how the business should be managed." In a passage worth quoting at length, the court noted:

> While it is true that Mrs. Vick complains that [her sister] makes herself obnoxious when she comes on the premises of the corporation, and that she is guilty of meddlesome and obtrusive acts, we conclude that such conduct . . . is no reason for excluding [the sister] from on-premise inspections . . . While [such inspections] may not be a pleasure . . . we cannot say that it would not be to the advantage and improvement of corporate management. At least, reasonable criticism by [the sister] when for constructive purposes, might be to the advantage of all concerned.

The court then ordered the matter back to a lower court for further consideration (i.e., more litigation) on several specific issues.

Recommendation.   Mike and Sue can benefit from an agreement that certain decisions should be made exclusively by Mike as the designated business leader, while other specified decisions should require Sue's approval. For example, it may be appropriate for this family to agree that Mike makes all the day-to-day decisions, including what movies are shown at the theaters. Certain other decisions, such as whether the business should invest in a new replacement screen, may be decided by a simple majority vote of the owners, while decisions that relate to such out-of-the-ordinary matters as whether to borrow money to build a new cinema complex in a new market or acquire an unrelated business that Mike believes is a good investment opportunity, should require Sue's approval. This arrangement may help confirm that a sufficient consensus on key decisions is reached. This understanding can be secured through customized bylaws, discussed in Chapter 10, or shareholder agreement that reflect the family's unique circumstances and understanding.

A Leader's Decision to Commit Extraordinary Resources to a Business Dream without Thinking Through the Constraints of Reality on the Family Business

The origin of conflict.   Historically, many family businesses have been led by a family leader whose vision for the business has not benefited from the feedback provided by an outside board of directors. As a result, a leader sometimes commits to a course of action that makes little sense, but the other family members are unable or unwilling to challenge the decision. The problem can become particularly acute when the decision proves unwise and pressure grows to abandon the course of action. The leader, perhaps anxious to prove how valuable he or she is to the family business, may be reluctant to abandon the course and can develop an irrational loyalty to the business. When a leader's personal goals cloud his or her judgment about the viability of a business, other less involved family members may become very critical. As the family business loses more and more money, the likelihood of unhealthy conflict, not surprisingly, increases.

Recommendation.   As noted earlier, an agreement could be reached requiring that decisions on extraordinary matters (expansion, borrowing, sale, continuation, or closure of business, etc.) could only be undertaken after approval of a supermajority (e.g., 75 or 85 percent) percentage of the family business owners is secured. An independent board of directors, discussed further in Chapter 3, that provides honest and informative feedback could also prove a useful reality check on the merit of the leader's dream as well as a source of comfort to other family members that significant business decisions have been carefully conceived.

Decisions by Spouses of Family Members That Are, or Appear to Be, Biased Toward Their Immediate Families

The origin of conflict.   Pressures are often brought to bear on a family business from many different directions, including spouses of family employees. A spouse, who technically may have no formal position in the family business, often wields as much, if not more, power and influence over business decisions than anyone else. For example, when Tom has to explain to his wife Sandy (who is not a board member, officer, or employee of the corporation) why Jane's daughter, Mary, who has been successfully working in the family business for 12 years, got a bigger raise than George did, Tom's role as the CEO gets more difficult. When Sandy screams at Tom if she is not satisfied with the explanation, the job, understandably, becomes impossible. Since Tom has to live with his spouse all day, every day, and is with his niece Mary only during the work week, Mary may be an easy casualty for Tom, as the CEO, to accept. Conflict commonly occurs when the CEO decides to favor his immediate family to appease a spouse and thereby incurs the wrath of the other side of the family.

Recommendation.   A mechanism needs to be established that permits spouses to understand the mission of the family business, its challenges, its organizational structure, and, perhaps most important, the basis on which decisions are made about how family members can be employed in the business and how family employees are compensated, promoted, terminated, etc. A forum that offers a spouse the opportunity to communicate his or her concerns, desires, feelings, etc., with other family members should also help reduce misunderstandings. A family council, discussed in Chapter 2, may be the best available mechanism to ensure that satisfactory channels of communication are available to everyone, including spouses, whose views are critical but who don't always have the formal opportunity to participate in an exchange of views with other family members. The common understanding reached by the family can be reduced to writing, perhaps in a family charter, discussed in Chapter 2, or in a shareholder agreement. This understanding, in turn, can be duly considered by a qualified and independent board of directors (i.e., one that is composed of family representatives and nonfamily advisers) when business decisions are made that relate to such matters.

A Leader's Decision That Any Family Member Can Work in the Family Business, Regardless of Need, Credentials, or Qualifications

The origin of conflict.   Since individuals within a family tend to view the world through their own perspectives, it is common for family members to disagree on the proper balance the family business should strike between promoting the interests of the business and the interests of individual family members. A parent, for example, may believe that his or her child should always have a job in the business with a prestigious title and generous salary, regardless of the child's ability, experience, or work ethic. Such a parent decides, in effect, to follow a course that may be good for the family but bad for the business. Another family member may believe that only qualified employees should have a job at the family business or, at a minimum, a family member must demonstrate satisfactory competence and work ethic in order to justify a fancy title, salary increase, promotion, etc. This family member, in effect, would prefer to make decisions that are good for the business but bad (arguably) for the family. The decision to create jobs regardless of need or credentials may create resentment in some owners who become upset with their poor returns on investment that they are likely to attribute to the adverse effect of an incompetent family member's lackluster job performance. If a family business is unable to financially support multiple family members who work in, or would like to work in, the business, strain in family relationships is particularly likely to come hard and fast.

Recommendation.   Family members need to reach an understanding about the essential purpose of the family business and how to balance the often-competing demands of business life and family life. For example, is the business large and prosperous enough to employ all family members, regardless of qualifications? If so, should family members nevertheless be encouraged to consider alternative careers outside the family business? What, if any, entry requirements should be established to help ensure that only qualified family members are eligible for positions in the family firm? Developing a clear understanding on these and related subjects may help establish an environment of fairness, not of fighting. Such an understanding can often be reached at a family council and reflected in a family charter or shareholder agreement.

A Decision Concerning Which Family Member Should Fill a Desired Role in the Family Business

The origin of conflict.   Some family businesses can provide incredibly rewarding and satisfying career opportunities for multiple family members. Most, however, cannot. In the typical family business, there may be a satisfying position available for a chairman of the board of directors, a president, and maybe even an executive vice president or two. Other family members, however, are forced to accept less glamorous positions with little, if any, managerial influence and accompanying satisfaction and related public recognition. Adding insult to injury, these "second-class" employees are often forced to sit back and watch as their "first-class" relatives receive public recognition for business accomplishments (which are, or are perceived to be, attributable to an ancestor anyway!) and take fancy business trips to exotic conventions that are more like luxury vacations than work or so they may seem to those not on the trip. When a first-class relative is honored in public, many second-class relatives are probably more inclined to throw a pie in their relative's face than to offer their congratulations. The turf battles for positions of influence and prestige in an environment that cannot possibly satisfy everyone's demands can be likened to a Darwinian struggle for survival of the fittest. In short, decisions about which family member fills which position are fraught with difficulty and, if poorly planned, do little to promote family peace.

Recommendation.   Family members need to reach an understanding not only about who is eligible to work in the family business but, once there, what the criteria are for advancement to other positions including, ultimately, the senior leadership position. A corollary to this recommendation is that the agreement needs to specify under what circumstances, if any, a family member may lose his or her position in the family business. This understanding can be effectively reflected in a family charter and a succession plan, discussed in Chapter 6.

Decisions That May Appear to Benefit Some Individuals in the Family More Than Others

The origin of conflict.   Decisions made by family members active in the business can be a lightning rod for conflict in the family business if other family members believe that the decision is driven by self-interest instead of family interest. The problem can be exacerbated if the decision maker is unwilling or unable to responsibly consult and communicate with family members. Poor communication typically creates mistrust among the other family members who may not understand the rationale of the successor's business decisions and may, by default, attribute selfish and greedy motives to him or her as a result. For example, if Tom decides to give himself a substantial raise and not give his niece Mary a raise at all, without having demonstrated a meaningful contribution to the family business, he may be inciting his niece and his sister Jane into conflict.

Recommendation.   Family members need to feel comfortable that a leader's commitment to acting in a fair and equitable manner is safeguarded by appropriate mechanisms that both help ensure fair treatment and create or reinforce the perception that treatment is fair. In the earlier example, if Tom's salary had been doubled by vote of a board of directors comprised of both family and respected nonfamily members, Mary and Jane may have a higher degree of comfort that the increase is deserved than if Tom had unilaterally increased his own salary without input from any other party or advisory board. Utilizing an independent board of directors can help achieve this result. In other instances, other agreements, such as employment agreements, specifying family members' obligations and time commitments to the family business, and perhaps noncompetition agreements may be advisable. These agreements are discussed further in upcoming chapters.

Decisions Affecting Who Can Own an Interest in the Family Business

The origin of conflict.   Many family businesses begin with siblings who work closely together and build a successful operation. In spite of the garden-variety differences they may have, such siblings often work reasonably well together or, at least, have learned to put up with each other. Family relationships can quickly sour, however, if the ownership structure changes and decisions are suddenly being made by other family members. For example, if Jane dies, the ownership structure in this hypothetical family business may change from brother and sister to brother and brother-in-law (i.e., Jane's widower, Lou). In spite of having no experience in the family business, Lou, whose artworks are not selling well and who is concerned about not being treated fairly, might develop an increasing interest in the family business and seek to influence the decisions required to be made. Tom may resent having a "new partner" who may be ignorant of the demands of running a business. The personalities of the brothers-in-law may clash and conflict can easily develop on a variety of matters.

Recommendation.   Families should reach an understanding about who is eligible to own an interest in the family business and how such interests are to be transferred on the occurrence of specified events. For example, the family might agree that on the death of an owner, the surviving owners have the option to buy the ownership interest from the estate of the deceased owner for a specified sum of money. The same agreement also might provide that a family owner must first offer his or her interest in the family business to other family members before he or she can sell the interest to an outsider. This agreement is often referred to as a buy-sell agreement. As discussed in Chapter 5, buy-sell provisions can be easily incorporated in a more global family agreement, like a shareholder agreement.

Decisions by Former Spouses of Family Owners, as Part of a Contested Matrimonial Proceeding, to Seek an Interest in the Family Business

The origin of conflict.   History is replete with examples of family businesses that have stumbled, faltered, and even failed because of an owner's matrimonial problems and divorce. Matrimonial law throughout the United States continues to expand the rights of spouses whose only claim to a family business is through marriage. Indeed, evidence that a spouse has been trained to operate a family business has resulted in court awards of that family business to such spouse as part of the "financial reckoning" commonly known as alimony. Such decisions, of course, are unwelcome to the family member who might never have considered the possibility of such an award. Even if the business remains in the family, the family member may need to pay the ex-spouse a substantial sum of money in lieu of an interest in the family business.

Recommendation.   A prenuptial agreement or a buy-sell agreement are commonly used planning tools that permit two people to agree how they will divide some or all of their assets if their upcoming marriage ends in divorce. Such agreements can be drafted to provide that a designated spouse can buy the other spouse's interest in the family business at a specified price in the event of divorce.

Decisions That Emphasize Conflict Rather Than Conflict Resolution

The origin of conflict.   Although business owners typically spend countless hours agonizing over their business plans, they often fail to give even the slightest consideration to the prospect of how an internal dispute may affect their family business. The odds of avoiding a damaging dispute in a family business without preplanning are small given the many events, circumstances, personalities, and decisions that any business must face. Most business disputes produce emotional strain and psychological discomfort. Disputes between individuals who have not only a business interest at stake but a family interest as well are often as ugly as the nastiest divorces. Left unresolved, disputes can also be responsible for the collapse of a family business, with the accompanying losses of jobs, wealth, and self-esteem.

Recommendation.   Many disputes can be avoided by careful planning and ongoing efforts to build consensus well in advance of any problems. The techniques offered throughout this book are designed with this objective in mind. It is, however, impossible to design any agreement that contemplates every conceivable circumstance and possible subjects of dispute, since the family business, and the individuals in it, are ever-changing and the potential causes of disputes are infinite. It is therefore advisable to select one or more dispute resolution mechanisms and incorporate them into your family agreements. Such mechanisms, discussed further in Chapter 5, can help parties resolve their differences relatively quickly, inexpensively, and, perhaps, even peacefully.

For example, Jane is unhappy with Tom's decision to build a new movie theater and thinks that, based on specified financial tests, her agreement should have been secured. Tom believes these same financial tests do not require such approval. If the family agreement lets Jane submit this question to a neutral party (the family attorney, accountant, or an arbitrator, for example), her question will be quickly and (relatively) inexpensively resolved by a neutral party.

Decisions by Family Business Owners Regarding How Their Assets Will Be Divided Among Their Heirs

The origin of conflict.   One of the most difficult decisions facing owners of family businesses is how to plan their estates. The need for such a plan in the first place, of course, is almost self-evident in the face of federal estate tax rates that rise as high as 55 percent of an owner's taxable estates. The difficulty usually comes in determining how an owner's assets should be divided among his or her children, some of whom may be active in the family business, and others who are not. Simply distributing the family business to the children who are active in the business is usually an unattractive solution, since the business often represents a disproportionately large percentage of the owner's assets. Alternatively, distributing ownership interests to all the children and leaving them to figure out what to do is often unattractive as well in light of our premise that such children, with different financial and other interests, will ultimately disagree on decisions affecting the business. Nevertheless, many family business owners, perhaps unaware of their options, either effectively "disinherit" their children who have pursued a career path unrelated to the family business or, alternatively, force their children who are active in the business to work with, and answer to, their siblings, who often have no clue as to the difference between a good business decision and a bad one. Either decision usually will cause resentment among one or the other group of children and, so it seems, its occurrence comes sooner rather than later.

Recommendation.   Family business owners can take advantage of a wide variety of techniques to help transfer assets from one generation to another with a minimum of adverse tax consequences while ensuring that management control is allocated to those individuals most capable of running the business in the future. Such techniques include the use of voting and nonvoting stock, common and preferred stock, trusts, shareholder agreements, and family limited liability companies. Ultimately, such transfers, discussed in later chapters, can be completed with a buyout of the nonactive family members by the active family members at a fair price, thus providing the active members with the control over the business they seek and the inactive members with cash compensation to ensure equitable treatment of all the family members.

Decisions about Who Is to Replace a Leader in the Family Business Who Unexpectedly Becomes Ill or Dies

The origin of conflict.   Family business leaders commonly ignore the task of planning for their ultimate withdrawal from the family business. Unfortunately, this is one of a leader's most important job assignments and, left ignored, it almost surely will result in conflict. If a family has not had the opportunity to plan for the ultimate transition in leadership authority and reach a consensus on the best plan prior to a leader's death, a successor leader will be chosen who may not have the blessings of his or her family. Those family members who were not selected as the successor may harbor resentment and jealousy against the new leader. They may, for instance, disagree with the direction the new leader believes the business should take and struggle to gain (or hold onto) control of the business. Such struggles may take years to rise to the surface but, inevitably, they are sure to do so.

Recommendation.   Family members need to agree on who should replace the current business leader at the appropriate time. This often entails reaching an understanding about the selection criteria, training, transition process, and a backup plan in case the designated successor is not prepared due to the premature illness or death of the current leader. The agreement can be reflected in a succession plan.

A Senior Leader's Decision to Retain a Leadership Role in the Family Business Beyond a Reasonable Period

The origin of conflict.   Many leaders of family businesses are reluctant to pass the baton to a qualified successor when it is clearly appropriate to do so. These leaders may be unwilling to relinquish control of the business for a variety of reasons, including fears that they will lose their "heroic status" within their families, they will lose their identities within their families or communities, or perhaps they have a need to demonstrate their value and worth to their communities and families.

Financial concerns may also make it difficult for a leader to abdicate control. For example, Tom may find it difficult to relinquish control of the family movie theater business to his niece Mary if he has not built an adequate nest egg to comfortably fund his retirement. When the financial demands on the family business are increased at a time when they should be reduced in order to have sufficient funds available to compensate, and so retain, qualified young workers in the family business, conflict is not far away.

Recommendation.   The family needs to recognize that a transition in leadership is an inevitable consequence of human mortality and it is better to accept this fact and prepare for it appropriately with a succession plan, a retirement plan, and an estate plan (discussed further in Chapter 7) than it is to ignore this fact and leave the transition to chance. In many instances, a senior leader can gradually transition management control of a family business to junior family members over a period of time to help ensure that he or she has adequate financial support and that the junior family member has demonstrated his or her competence to fully assume management control.

Decisions Made by Siblings When Their Parents Are Not Around to Act as Referees

The origin of conflict.   Subjects of potential disputes between siblings (which may range from job titles, compensation, perks, favoritism of branches, etc.) that may remain dormant when parents are around to supervise such relationships, may become subjects of substantial dispute when the parents are no longer around to arbitrate or dictate solutions. The problem becomes particularly acute when one or more siblings are active in the family business and familiar with its operations and other siblings are inactive in the business and, perhaps, are ignorant of operational issues.

Recommendation.   Family members need to agree on mechanisms that balance the need to empower siblings who are active in the business with the interests of family members who are inactive in the business. The promotion of family peace through the balancing of the interests of family members who wish to participate in and benefit from a family business often can be secured through a variety of mechanisms, including a family limited liability company, discussed in Chapter 9.

Decisions That Result in the Number of Family Members Who Own an Interest in the Family Business Being Increased, Not Decreased

The origin of conflict. Historically, it seems to have been commonplace for families to give little thought to the long-term direction of their family business. If there were children, grandchildren, and maybe even great-grandchildren who were interested in working in and perpetuating the business, such individuals may all have had the opportunity to do so. The permutations of possible family relationships in such businesses can quickly become unwieldy, especially if spouses are included in the calculation. Haphazardly grown, the family business tree can quickly resemble an overgrown redwood. Logically, the likelihood of unmanageable conflict arising in such circumstances is high.

Recommendation. Family members need to agree on how to limit the number of family members in a family business in order to make the decision-making process work efficiently and to allow consensus to be more often reached. Contrary to the laws of nature, where the stately redwood tree may have the best chance for long-term survival, the family business tree with the best chance of surviving more closely resembles the small sapling. To accomplish this objective, the family business tree must be pruned, as explained in Chapter 11.

The Psychology of a Family Business

The model for family prosperity outlined in this chapter represents the starting point for keeping the peace in any family business. By recognizing the common causes of conflict through proper education and sensitivity to the interests of other family members and participants, family members can utilize a variety of techniques and mechanisms to develop and build consensus, understanding, and, ultimately, agreement. In order for this model to work as efficiently as possible, two critical psychological assumptions must be satisfied:

1. Family members must be capable of behaving rationally.
2. They must be willing to do so.

These assumptions are based on the premise that individuals with open minds generally are capable of reasoning through disputes, making fair decisions, and acting accordingly. In the real world, these assumptions are often correct; sometimes they are not.

Professional psychologists have made remarkable inroads in understanding the complex web of influences that drive individuals to act irrationally at times. Such professionals can often explain why family members seem incapable of developing a common view of the world and, instead, develop extreme levels of hostility for each other. Psychologists, for example, may recognize that what appears on the surface to be a conflict based on the merits of a plant expansion may have less to do with the need for an expanded facility and more to do with a business leader's delusions of grandeur and consequent need to build a business monument for the world to admire. The identical argument in another family may be generated by a child's subconscious decision to humiliate a father for childhood wrongs committed against him or her and, so, prove to the father that his idea for a new plant is wasteful. The possible psychological dysfunctions to which all individuals are susceptible are difficult to conceal in a family business setting and often bubble over, out of control. When reason gives way to emotion, and love to spite, consensus building and agreement may be difficult or impossible to secure.

Because of the critical role qualified professional psychologists and consultants are able to play in resolving such dysfunctions, I encourage members of any family business to consider retaining their services; their contributions can be priceless. Alternatively, if all efforts to build consensus are unsuccessful and family members are more interested in fanning the flames of conflict than smothering them, the only solution may be to get rid of those family members, through a peacefully negotiated buyout or through less peaceful means. In those cases where litigation is necessary, the best advice I can offer is to retain a good trial lawyer!

Family Business Audit

1. Are two or more family members working in your family business? If so, how are decisions that affect the business and the family made?

2. Are decisions made according to neutral standards that are acceptable to all family members?

3. Are decisions for routine matters made in the same way as are decisions for extraordinary matters?

4. Are siblings in your family business capable of working together without having a parent referee their actions?

5. Do spouses have a forum within which they can express their ideas, interests, and concerns to all family members?

6. Are employment decisions made on the basis of family status or qualifications?

7. Are there legal restrictions on who can own an interest in your family business?

8. Is your family business protected in the event of an owner's divorce?

9. Does your family business have a conflict resolution mechanism in place?

10. Does your family business have an estate and succession plan that is capable of
    - efficiently transferring assets to minimize estate and gift taxes,
    - treating all family members equitably (if not equally),
    - providing senior family members with sufficient assets to fund their retirement years, and
    - transitioning management control of the business from senior to junior generation in a way that is generally acceptable to the family?

CHAPTER 2

Your Family's Not Talking?
Establish a Family Council

*M*any of the suggestions contained in this book rest on the premise that an open and explicit dialogue among family members is preferable to the informal and often secretive dialogue that, unfortunately, often predominates in family businesses. Through communication comes understanding and thereby, perhaps, even agreement. The more often family members can reach understanding and agreement, the greater is their likelihood for success.

The importance of effective communication in a family business is hard to overestimate. Unlike a typical business, where employees are often able to leave their work at the office, a family member working in a family business rarely has that privilege. Instead, work is discussed at all times of the day. Dinnertime, evening, weekend, and holiday party conversations often covers little else than yesterday's, today's, or tomorrow's events at the office. Those family members not actively working in the business may often feel more like outsiders than a part of the family.

Although there generally is no shortage of communication itself, the communication patterns found in a typical family business are, nevertheless, imperfect. Dialogue is often secretive and selective; family members may speak to only a few other family members, or not all, and the subjects of their discussion are often kept from the other family members. For example, much like tattle telling that young children seem to relish, a sibling's mistake at the office may be anxiously reported to a parent but never once mentioned to the culpable party for possible correction or educational value. Alternatively, a daughter who would like to work side by side with her brothers in the family business, but who has never been encouraged to do so by her family, may be unsure of how to express her pent-up resentment for being treated like a second-class citizen. These and other similar patterns of miscommunication tend to enhance the likelihood of conflict in the family business.

Family members who can openly communicate with each other are more likely to understand each other and, with their common understanding, work out their differences more effectively than those families who communicate poorly. The family council is an increasingly recognized technique to facilitate open and healthy communication within a family. The first part of this chapter discusses how your family can design and establish its own family council to promote effective channels of communication in your family and family business. Later in this chapter, I suggest a variety of tools that a council can be instrumental in developing for the benefit of a family and its business.

How to Design Your Family Council

A family council is a mechanism many family businesses are increasingly utilizing to ensure the existence of a satisfactory forum for family communication. The council is designed to facilitate discussion and decision making on any number of important issues for the family and the business. It is a vehicle designed to ensure that all family members have an opportunity to express themselves and voice their opinions about issues of importance.

How a Family Council Works

The purpose of a council is to facilitate free and open communication between family members. Accordingly, a well-working council can be an effective forum within which to consider any variety of issues that a family may want or need to address. For example, councils can be used to discuss the future direction of the family business, the employment opportunities that the family business might offer family members, or what criteria family members must meet to be eligible to work in the business. A council can be a forum for sharing and addressing jealousies, hurts, rivalries, or conflicts; and for discussing problems, accomplishments, dreams, concerns, and fears. A council can even be a forum for addressing all those "decisions" examined earlier in Chapter 1—and more. As discussed later in this chapter, it can help a family develop a value statement, a strategic plan, a mission statement, and a family code of conduct. Indeed, every single planning technique noted in this book can (and perhaps should) be discussed and considered at a council meeting. Ultimately, a well-designed council can facilitate common understanding on any subject of importance to members of a family.

Many families have found that the communication process fostered by a family council can help strengthen family bonds and preserve important traditions. The ongoing communication process also enhances family members' level of understanding (and sensitivity) for each others' concerns. Often, the mere act of establishing a council sends an important message to those disenfranchised family members that old fashioned notions about how the family business should be run are gone.

Using the Council to Minimize Family Conflict

Well-designed councils can help a family minimize intrafamily conflict and hostility. By establishing an effective forum for communication, a family can often better understand, and then resolve, problems before the problem becomes magnified and gets out of hand. For example, family members can share and learn facts and circumstances with and from each other that may enable them to make decisions with due sensitivity to the circumstances of particular family members. A family that understands that a member may have marital problems may be more sympathetic to sloppiness on the job than if they are unaware of such problems. Alternatively, a council can prove an effective tool for family business leaders to clarify business decisions that may have been misunderstood by family members unfamiliar with the background of the decision. For example, family members may be unhappy with a business leader's decision to invest a large amount of money in new equipment. If the leader can explain to those family members that the family business's customers insisted on a speedier delivery date, which the new equipment will ensure, or they would move their business elsewhere, the misunderstanding may turn to appreciation for the leader's quick and decisive action.

A council can also help by serving as a vehicle to mediate personality and other conflicts that inevitably arise within all families. For example, a brother, upset with his sister for squelching his pet project, may find that the sister had a legitimate bigger picture reason for doing so, and was not simply showing her brother who was the boss.

Finally, a council should prove valuable for those family members who historically have felt like outsiders looking in. This group may include family members who are not active in the business on a day-to-day basis or spouses who have their own opinions about how the business should be run but have no one to share their opinions with other than their own spouse. These and other family members who historically have not been assured an opportunity to talk about, and listen to others talk about, the business, may find a council a welcome forum. In short, an effective and well-designed council can foster strong and meaningful channels of communication within a family that can help ensure the family bonds remain strong and supportive.

How to Design an Effective Council

Family councils can be structured in a variety of different ways and families are well served by adopting a form that works best for its particular situation. Because of the difficulty that some families may experience in establishing a formal channel of communication, particularly when healthy communication has been largely absent, it is often a good idea to use a professional facilitator, such as a trained psychologist, to help establish a council. Such a facilitator can be especially effective in introducing the council concept to a family at a retreat. The following four suggestions for establishing an effective council are offered for your consideration.

1. Membership in the council should be open. Unlike a corporation's board of directors, which, as discussed in Chapter 3, typically should not include all family members, the premise for membership in a family council should be openness and inclusiveness. Since the council is a vehicle to ensure that all family members have access to effective channels of communication, the council usually works best when it is open to all family members who have reached a minimum age, perhaps age 21. Therefore, active and inactive members who own an interest in the business, and their spouses and children (if old enough), are all likely candidates for membership. Nonfamily members may be appropriate guests of the council from time to time to address particular subjects of interest. Ordinarily, nonfamily members probably should not be regular council members so that the family may more freely address confidential family issues without concern for appearances in front of nonfamily members. For example, a parent may be upset with his or her son for buying an expensive house that he simply cannot afford. A discussion of the parent's feelings, and the need for fiscal prudence by all family members, may be more comfortably handled at a council meeting than a director's meeting.

2. Designate council representatives for the board of directors.   All council members should not be involved with the business! Instead, the council should designate one or several of its members who, in turn, may serve on the family business's board of directors. This ensures that the family perspective is duly considered, but does not dictate when and how the family business's business decisions should be made. This permits governance of the business to remain in the hands of capable business leaders and not exclusively with the family, who may be well intentioned but nevertheless unsophisticated in the world of business. In effect, the family council serves as an advisory board to the family business. A well-functioning council can help push any family and its family business beyond traditional and conservative thinking by serving as a spark for creativity and innovation and, thereby, perhaps, helping a family business become or remain prosperous in what has become an extremely competitive world.

3. Don't be afraid to start slowly.   Families that have not historically emphasized the importance of open and candid communication may have some initial difficulty in opening discussion on important, yet sensitive, subjects. Many families have found that by first addressing relatively noncontroversial matters, they can pave the way for later discussion of the hard subjects. Typically, a good way to begin a dialogue is to have one or more senior family member review the history of the family business for all of the other family members. This review can help remind family members of the original vision the leaders had for their family and the business. It may be desirable to retain the

FIGURE 2.1 Council Ground Rules

Rule #1: Council members agree to remain focused on the meeting agenda and avoid straying from the topic at hand.

Rule #2: Council members shall be supplied with relevant information so they can make informed decisions on matters of interest.

Rule #3: Council members are encouraged to be honest and, as appropriate, consider the use of anonymous communication from time to time if necessary to address particularly sensitive subjects.

Rule #4: The council and its members agree to follow up their decisions with appropriate action.

Rule #5: Council members acknowledge that good communication starts with good listening and, so, agree to work on listening to each other.

---

services of a professional to help facilitate early council discussions. Psychologists and consultants experienced with family businesses may be particularly adept at breaking down long-established communication barriers that might otherwise stymie a council's effectiveness.

4. Establish ground rules for your council.   Effective councils often have ground rules that are designed to ensure that all family members understand how the council operates. These rules may specify which member shall lead the council and what the leader's responsibilities are, such as, for example, determining an agenda and scheduling regular council meetings. Whether the leadership position should be rotated can also be set forth in the ground rules.

In order to be successful, a council must meet on a *regular* basis; it is not a one-time family reunion or retreat. The family may wish to specify in its ground rules when meetings are to be held in order to emphasize this regularity. This expectation of having a regular forum is essential, since the family and the family business are constantly changing and evolving, requiring constant communication and updating.

While every family should consider which ground rules work best for its council, the ground rules in Figure 2.1 may be useful.

Other rules also can be developed as each family sees fit. Indeed, some families find that they are better served by utilizing a more informal council, where families meet when there is a reason to and the agenda is loose, not fixed. The relative formality of your council is probably best determined in conjunction with your family and its professional advisers.

Family Business Audit

1. Are family members encouraged and able to openly express their opinions, concerns, suggestions, etc., to all other family members?

2. Does your family business have meaningful channels of communication that permit all family members to communicate with each other?

3. Is membership in your family council generally open to all family members?

4. Does your council have sensible guidelines?

Creative Uses for Your Family Council

The only limits on a family council's usefulness may be the creativity of the family and its advisers. Implementation of many of the planning techniques discussed in this section can be the culmination of decisions reached through council discussion. It usually is desirable to record the understandings and agreements a family reaches in council meetings in appropriate documents signed by the various family members. This creates a record that can guide the family in making future decisions. The balance of this chapter considers how a family council can be used to develop four specific planning tools:

1. A family mission statement
2. A strategic plan
3. A code of conduct
4. A family charter

Properly utilized, each of these tools can significantly help a family maintain peace and prosperity for its family business.

Mission Statement

A mission statement is ordinarily a relatively short statement that ideally serves to encapsule the philosophy and expectations of a business and its owners. A mission statement can be advantageously developed by a family council and used by a family and its business for this purpose as well as to help a family focus on how its own unique formula for success and family consensus can be enhanced. For example, a mission statement may force family members to acknowledge the simple reality that a family business is not merely a business, but, rather, is a family business. By doing so, the family may reach a broad understanding that it is important to make decisions that emphasize not only individual and business interests but also decisions that set an overriding tone emphasizing family values, family harmony, and personal and business growth in a positive direction. A sample mission statement might read as follows:

Family members are encouraged to be responsible and productive members of our community by

1. working hard at business,
2. working hard at continuing their education,
3. working hard to ensure their health,
4. working hard at understanding each other, and
5. playing hard when appropriate.

By working hard, we will be successful as a business and as a family!

Although the mission statement itself is often short and devoid of specific guidelines, once agreed on, it can serve as the basis for guiding the development of other documents that do offer such guidelines, such as a code of conduct, family charter, or strategic plan. Some of these other tools are discussed in this section.

Strategic Plan

A strategic plan or business plan can be helpful in clarifying the direction of the family business on a variety of fronts. The plan may address a variety of subjects, such as how the business intends to respond to changing consumer demands, the long-term benefits of plant relocation or expansion, and the advantages of strategic acquisitions or dispositions of other businesses or company assets. Developing a strategic plan may instill a level of confidence among family members that their investment remains a good one; failure to develop and share such a plan may create the impression, deserved or not, that the business is much like a ship without a rudder and decisions are being made on an ad hoc basis instead of on the basis of a sensible long-term vision.

A family council can be an ideal forum within which to either develop a vision and plan to pursue that vision or it can simply be a forum within which to share with the entire family what that vision is and how it has been developed in conjunction with the assistance of outside advisers or directors. Having a plan and sharing that plan engenders trust and confidence in the business leadership; ignoring the development of a plan, or failing to share it with family members, engenders mistrust and suspicion.

Family Code of Conduct

Families may find it useful to formalize a code of conduct that establishes certain rules for behavior within the family business. Such a code can help ensure that a minimum level of courtesy and common decency exists within the business. A code of conduct may encompass a variety of subjects, from rules encouraging direct communication between family members (instead of "triangulated communication," where family members communicate only indirectly through an intermediary) to, perhaps, a dress code. While family members must still be able to reach agreement on the contents of a code of conduct, once agreement is reached, it will, presumably, reduce the likelihood of unhealthy disagreement on the subjects of the code.

A code of conduct might help avoid conflict between a father and son about, among other things, whether the son should grow a beard while working in the family business. In the case of *Duhon v. Slickline, Inc.,* a father refused to do any sales work for his family business until one of his sons shaved his beard. The father's position was based on his concern that his son's appearance would set a bad example for the company's other workers, who also seemed to be growing beards and long hair. The father believed that the workforce would be unpresentable to potential customers, who would take their business elsewhere. In response to his refusal to do any work, the sons terminated their father's job at the family business. The father then brought a lawsuit for wrongful termination of employment. The Louisiana Court of Appeals, in affirming a lower court's determination that the father had been wrongfully terminated, noted:

> It is also important to observe that the plaintiff [the father] held a position of authority with Slickline, Inc. While we may disagree with the position taken by the plaintiff on the issue of his son's beard, the record makes clear that the plaintiff, by virtue of his position, was entitled to have some input into policy-making, a function apparently shared with his sons. Thus, the plaintiff's strong stand on the issue, in our view, is not in the nature of subordination, but rather a policy conflict with whom he shared authority.

Family Charter

By contrast to a mission statement, which is typically philosophical in nature and general in content, a family charter is often pragmatic in nature and specific in content. It is created with an appreciation for the need to establish very specific guidelines and rules that can govern the interrelationships between family members with each other and the family business. Given the relative specificity with which a charter can be used to regulate such relationships, it has come to be thought of as a sort of constitution for the family business.

Although charters can be creatively designed to serve an infinite variety of purposes, they are most often used to set forth decisions on such matters as the following:

- Ground rules for entering, participating, and remaining in the family business
- Ground rules for distributing ownership interests and profits
- Guidelines for succession
- A code of conduct

Many charters also include specific provisions on such issues as what preparation (education, experience, etc.) is required in order to join the business, how titles and authority are determined, how job performance is to be evaluated, and the consequences of inadequate job performance.

The premise of a charter is that decisions on certain critical issues should be reached and then broadly disseminated to the family to ensure understanding and minimize conflict. If, for example, the family agrees that a college degree and work experience outside the family business is required of any family member who wants to work in the family business, family members can plan their futures accordingly. Such a requirement may not only help ensure that only properly qualified individuals work in the family business, but it will rationalize the entry process so that the family can better understand why one member holds a position but another member cannot. Even complex issues such as how the business should respond to family members in financial crisis or who are going through a divorce can be addressed in a charter.

To be of maximum effectiveness, a charter must not merely reflect that the family has reached an agreement on a particular subject. For three reasons, that agreement needs to be reflected in writing:

1. If the agreement can't be set forth in writing, it may be due to the fact that the family members have different interpretations of the agreement. If that is the case, the family may need to revisit the subject of the disagreement until everybody agrees on the decision.
2. A written agreement serves as the best reminder of what the actual agreement was, especially since memories in families tend to be short!

3. A written document can better serve as a guide for the family over generations and helps build a tradition for certain decisions. A sample family charter is set forth in Appendix A.

The family charter can exist as a separate stand-alone document or, alternatively, can be incorporated into the co-owners' agreement. Either way, the charter can create a clear record, which a family can use to accomplish the following:

-   Reflect key decisions on any variety of subjects of importance to the family or its business.
-   Serve as a guide to develop a process for making future decisions.
-   Help avoid disputes from occurring or, when they do occur, help the family resolve them quickly and peacefully.

Recommendations

The absence of adequate channels of communication is a common source of family conflict. A family council is a valuable tool, designed to promote communication by and among family members. The council can be structured to facilitate communication with the board of directors, members of which might not be part of the family council but who certainly should be aware of the family's feelings on a variety of subjects. The family council also can be useful for developing a variety of ancillary planning tools, such as a family mission statement, a strategic plan, a code of conduct, and a family charter.

Family Business Audit

1. Has your council developed a mission statement?

2. Has your council developed a strategic plan for your business?

3. Has your council developed a code of conduct for family members?

4. Has your council developed a family charter?

CHAPTER 3

Do Your Business Decisions Meet Family Resistance?

Establish a Functioning Board of Directors

*T*he classic model of governance within a corporation may be the most formal management structure recognized in business laws throughout the United States. Under this model, a business is owned by shareholders (sometimes referred to as *stockholders*), managed or supervised by directors, and operated on a day-to-day basis by officers. Properly utilized, this model can provide significant benefits to any family business, regardless of its technical legal form.

After first examining this general model of corporate governance, I suggest in this chapter the importance of a family business utilizing nonfamily directors in operating its businesses. The suggestion is made for two important reasons:

1. The first reason is the traditional rationale that such outsiders can contribute a necessary degree of business competence to the board to enhance the quality of its decisions. This rationale continues to make sense and is considered later in this chapter.
2. Outside directors also can be useful to minimize the conflicts of interest that exist among different family members. Properly understood and utilized, the use of nonfamily directors can be an important planning technique for your family business!

The Model of Corporate Governance

The classic model of corporate governance is based on the conscious separation of ownership from management. The purpose of this separation was to craft a structure that permits owners to invest in a business without having to devote all of their time and resources to overseeing its operations by establishing a management team to perform that function. The theory is based on the need to delegate management authority while preserving management accountability. In this model, ownership resides in the shareholders while management resides with the directors and officers. A discussion of the roles of these different groups follows.

Shareholders

Shareholders are the owners of a corporation. Only they are listed on the corporation's records as owners and, as such, can receive cash returns if the business is profitable or lose their investment if the business is not. If the value of the business increases, the increase belongs to the shareholders; if the value decreases, the loss belongs to them as well.

By state statute, shareholders in a corporation generally vote in proportion to the number of shares they hold; typically, one share of stock is accorded one vote. Generally, like a democracy, action by the shareholders is taken by the affirmative vote of at least a majority of the shareholders. It is possible, however, for regular corporations to modify this basic structure by creating an almost unlimited variety of different types of stock such as, for example, preferred stock or nonvoting stock. These different stock types can be useful to help fulfill particular objectives relating to *priority* of economic returns for different owners and *control.* For example, a corporation may have preferred stock that entitles a preferred stockholder to a fixed, but limited, return on his or her investment (e.g., 12 percent of the face value of his or her stock certificate). Preferred returns must ordinarily be paid before the common stockholders receive any stock distributions or dividends. After satisfying its obligations to preferred stockholders, all of a corporation's remaining earnings can be distributed to common stockholders, subject only to otherwise applicable limitations designed to prevent the corporation from unfairly depleting its capital to the detriment of its creditors.

A corporation also may have stock with different voting rights, such as, for example, voting stock and nonvoting stock. These devices often are used to allocate control within a corporation in a variety of ways other than the one share, one vote formula.

As a practical matter, shareholder voting rights may be only infrequently exercised. Instead, shareholders generally play a relatively passive role in the management of a corporation and their vote is typically required only in those instances where extraordinary business decisions are being made. For example, a typical corporation may only require a vote by its shareholders if it is considering merging, selling most of its assets, liquidating, or going public (i.e., offering company stock to the public). In effect, corporation law generally reserves for shareholders the opportunity to consider and vote only on the big issues affecting their business.

Since shareholders usually vote only on fundamental business decisions, they usually don't vote on nonfundamental decisions, including most day-to-day business matters affecting the corporation. Instead, such decisions are made by the corporation's directors and, to the extent of the directors' preference, by the corporation's officers. As a result, perhaps the single most important decision shareholders must vote on is who should serve as their directors to oversee the management of their corporation. Electing high-quality directors can help ensure high-quality decisions and, so, a business's financial success. Electing incompetent or unqualified directors can result in poor decisions that precipitate the decline of a business.

Directors

Directors are generally responsible for managing or overseeing the business and affairs of a corporation; they make the decisions on all but the most fundamental matters reserved for the shareholders. Significant types of decisions made by directors include decisions to do the following:

- Expand product lines or territory.
- Build a new plant.
- Approve a budget.
- Pay dividends.

In furtherance of their decision-making responsibility, directors are given significant latitude and authority to pursue their primary objective: the maximization of corporate profitability for the benefit of the shareholder.

> *The directors' responsibility to maximize shareholder benefits was noted by the Michigan Supreme Court, in the case of Dodge v. Ford Motor Company, where it stated:*
>
> *A business corporation is organized and carried on primarily for the profit of the stockholders. The powers of the directors are to be employed for that end. The discretion of directors is to be exercised in the choice of means to attain that end, and does not extend to a change in the end itself, to the reduction of profits, or to the nondistribution of profits among stockholders in order to devote them to other purposes.*

Because most businesses are complex, their management is time consuming. Therefore, after establishing a corporation's policies and direction, directors then often function more like monitors than managers and delegate actual day-to-day management responsibility to officers, who are charged with carrying out these policies and directions.

Officers

Officers, who are generally employees of the corporation, have that degree of authority to act on behalf of the corporation delegated by the corporation's directors. The authorization may derive from the corporation's bylaws, specific resolutions of the directors, or common-law agency principles. States ordinarily require by statute that a corporation have at least one president, one secretary, one treasurer, and one or more vice presidents. These different positions can be, and (at least in family businesses) often are, filled by the same individual. Officers serve at the pleasure of the directors, who may remove officers with or without cause at any time. Even officers with employment agreements can be removed from their office by directors, although a wrongful removal might result in that officer having a separate claim for breach of employment agreement.

The Origin of Conflict in Corporations

In spite of its common use, the corporate model of governance may actually foster the development of conflict in a family business! Indeed, many families may spend thousands of dollars establishing a corporation but, in doing so, unwittingly sow the seeds for later conflict and even family destruction by ignoring the psychology of conflict in the process. I'll explain how in this section.

The Practice of Establishing "Family Boards"

As a matter of practice, family businesses commonly have the same individuals filling the roles of shareholders, directors, and officers. In some instances, a family member may be the only director and may fill *all* of the officer positions. Many states specifically authorize this structure by permitting corporations with fewer than a specified number of shareholders to name one individual to fill these various roles. Perhaps more common still is the practice of electing only family members to directorships. In this scenario, while all family members are not necessarily board members, all board members are family members.

In spite of its prevalence, the practice of filling board directorships with only members of a family is not well conceived and often results in disaster as a result of one, or a combination of, the following three factors:

1. Directors are regularly called on to make difficult business decisions that require a high degree of sophistication. A family member who lacks appropriate experience or education will be unable to intelligently evaluate the available options to make the best possible decision. As a result, critical business decisions are left in the hands of board members who are incapable of professionally and competently evaluating these options. For example, a decision to build a new plant or to buy expensive equipment without understanding how to interpret the business's financial statements, including cash flow and debt service expense, market share, interest rates, and market forces, is a disaster waiting to happen.

2. Family members are often reluctant to criticize other family members, especially a parent or sibling. If a parent thinks a million-dollar piece of equipment is essential to the business, it is often difficult for children to go to the mat and oppose that decision. If the children lack an adequate education or relevant business experience, this reluctance to criticize may be especially pronounced.

3. Shareholders and directors often have certain inherent and fundamental conflicts of interest with each other. Decisions that may benefit a director may adversely affect a shareholder. This last factor, which is not always well recognized, may be the most important in explaining the high incidence of conflict in family businesses.

Shareholder and Director Conflict

The practice of establishing family-only boards of directors can create problems within the family because an inherent conflict often exists between the interests of shareholders who are not directors (non-management shareholders) and shareholders who are (management shareholders). For example, management shareholders may be more interested in maximizing their compensation (which means taking the profit and splitting it with less than all of the shareholders) instead of maximizing dividends (which means taking the profit and splitting it with all shareholders). Obviously, if profits are split up among more parties, the directors' cuts usually will be less! Management shareholders may believe their hard work justifies their enhanced earnings more than an inactive shareholder is entitled to a dividend. By contrast, the non-management shareholders may believe that management shareholders are already overly compensated for a position they don't even deserve.

A management shareholder's belief that he or she is entitled to premium compensation commonly spills over into the area of job perks. Specifically, the management shareholder may believe his or her activity on behalf of the family business requires him or her to attend several business conventions every year. To the shareholder such conventions are a matter of desirability if not business necessity. By contrast, nonmanagement shareholders may view such conventions as the equivalent of a luxury vacation. Similarly, an appropriate company car to a management shareholder may be an extravagant luxury car to nonmanagement shareholders. Exacerbating the conflict may be a belief by management shareholders that their nonmanagement counterparts don't deserve comparable perks!

The difference in interests and perspectives between management shareholders and nonmanagement shareholders may potentially surface in every decision that directors make. For example, management shareholders may feel it imperative to construct a new office building that will allow them to operate more efficiently and, so, build for the future. By contrast, nonmanagement shareholders may feel the cost of a new office building is not only unnecessary, but indeed, a wasteful extravagance—a monument to the egos of the business leaders!

Beyond the management shareholder's focus on current salary and perks may be a focus on future salary and perks. Management shareholders tend to focus on empire building by making decisions that maximize business growth. Why? Perhaps for several reasons: Being a director of a bigger firm may justify a bigger salary. Also, there is an enhanced element of job security in bigger firms that presumably are less likely to be taken over or go bankrupt than is a smaller firm. Finally, there is the ego satisfaction associated with being a director and manager of a big business. As a result, it is not uncommon for management shareholders to focus on growing the business through decisions that require profits to be reinvested instead of deciding to pay out profits in the form of dividends. By contrast, nonmanagement shareholders may be more interested in distributing profits in the form of dividends. Neither group is necessarily right or wrong. It is, very simply, often a difference in perspective.

As a result of these divergent interests, the decisions made by management shareholders may be at odds with the interests of nonmanagement shareholders. The problem often is exacerbated by poor intrafamily communication, so that, even if there is no actual conflict of interest between these two groups of shareholders, the nonmanagement shareholders may perceive the existence of such a conflict, doubt the motives behind the family directors' decisions, and believe their interests are being impaired. This perception frequently results in conflict and hostility.

Checks and Balances in the Corporate Model

The possibility that directors may abuse their positions of trust and management responsibility has not gone unnoticed by the legal system. In fact, recognizing both the important role directors play in the management of a corporation, and the incentive to abuse the trust bestowed upon them by shareholders, corporate law has established certain standards of conduct that directors are required to satisfy in fulfilling their obligations. These standards of conduct are commonly referred to as fiduciary duties and, in one form or another, are part of the jurisprudence of every states' corporate law. Among the most important of these duties are the duty of care and the duty of loyalty.

Duty of care. Directors are required by law to discharge their duties in good faith and with the same degree of diligence, care, and skill that prudent men would exercise under similar circumstances in their personal business affairs. The purpose of the duty, it would seem, is to encourage directors to be cautious when exercising their decision-making authority on behalf of a corporation. Having delegated management responsibility away, the shareholders should have some degree of confidence that they remain protected from arbitrary and capricious conduct by the directors who serve them.

As is often the case, the theory behind the duty of care works only imperfectly in the real world. Courts have repeatedly stated that they don't want to be in the business of second-guessing all the various business decisions that directors make every day. Nor could they if they wanted to, since courts may have no more business expertise than do the directors whose decisions they are reviewing. In practice, therefore, directors are given a great deal of leeway in satisfying the obligations imposed by this duty of care. This judicial position forms the basis for the "business judgment rule," discussed later in this chapter. As a result of the business judgment rule, the duty of care is most frequently found to have been breached where the evidence suggests that a director has acted in bad faith, has been grossly negligent, or had a conflict of interest with the corporation which he or she failed to disclose to the shareholders.

Duty of loyalty.   Perhaps the most important fiduciary duty directors owe to their corporation and its shareholders is the duty to be loyal. This duty has been interpreted over the years in a manner designed to prevent directors from doing the following:

- Making unfair deals with the corporation to their personal advantage
- Seizing business opportunities that would be of interest to the corporation, for their own personal advantage
- Unfairly competing with the corporation through, for example, the misuse of proprietary information, trade secrets, etc.

In the case of *Miller v. Miller,* the Minnesota Supreme Court considered a claim brought by one brother against another brother for allegedly misappropriating a business opportunity for personal use that the plaintiff believed belonged to the family business. In a passage worth quoting at length, this court explained the applicable legal restrictions on the use of business opportunities for personal advantage as follows:

> . . . we acknowledge the well-recognized, common-law principle that one entrusted with the active management of a corporation, such as an officer or director, occupies a fiduciary relationship to the corporation and may not exploit his position as an "insider" by appropriating to himself a business opportunity properly belonging to the corporation. If such business opportunity is usurped for personal gain, it is equally well recognized that the opportunity and any profit or property acquired becomes subject to a constructive trust for the benefit of the corporation . . . This principle, usually referred to as the doctrine of corporate opportunity, is derived essentially from fundamental rules of agency concerning the duty of utmost good faith and loyalty owed by a fiduciary to his principal and also from the law of constructive trusts embodying equitable principles of unjust enrichment.

The Corporate Model's Failure in Practice

The model of corporate governance outlined in this section works particularly well for large publicly owned corporations, whose hundreds, thousands, or millions of shareholders are so numerous and diverse that centralized management is a practical (not simply legal) necessity. This same model, however, often works only imperfectly in family businesses and, in many instances, may cause conflict and precipitate failure. The model's failure may largely be based on the premise underlying the business judgment rule.

The business judgment rule, as noted earlier, is based on an accepted judicial tradition that courts are neither in a position to consider the merits of a director's business decision nor (if they could) would it be fair for them to do so. Essentially, the courts recognize that their expertise is in interpreting laws, not in running businesses, and they should not substitute their judgment for those who are running businesses. Moreover, the courts understand perfectly well that when they review a business decision, they do so with the benefit of 20/20 hindsight. Since directors and officers make their decisions without this same benefit, it is neither fair nor appropriate to judge a decision simply on results that stem from decisions made without the benefit of such hindsight. Thus, if a director can establish that he or she has satisfied his or her fiduciary duties to the corporation and its shareholders, the director will get the benefit of the doubt that the business aspect of his or her decision was appropriate.

In the case of *Hunter v. Roberts, Throp & Co.,* the Michigan Supreme Court explained the reluctance of a court to substitute its judgment for that of a director in the following passage relating to the merits of declaring a dividend:

Whether a corporation can safely make a dividend involves the exercise of knowledge and judgement, and the power of deciding this question should not be taken away from the directors, and assumed by the courts, unless it clearly appears that the directors have mistaken their legal duties. *Any other rule would lead to the frequent intervention of the courts, to the substitution of the court for the board of directors, and in very many instances, would prove disastrous to the best interests of the corporation and its stockholders and the business of trading and manufacturing would be seriously hampered and retarded. . . .* [Accordingly], courts of equity will not interfere in the management of the directors unless it is clearly made to appear that they are guilty of fraud or misappropriation of the corporate funds, or refuse to declare dividends when the corporation has a surplus of net profits which it can, without detriment to the business, divide among its stockholders, and when a refusal to do so would amount to such an abuse of discretion as would constitute fraud or breach of that good faith which they are bound to exercise toward the stockholders. [Emphasis added]

The protection offered officers and directors by the business judgment rule is broad—so broad, in fact, that it is extremely difficult for a shareholder to challenge a director's business judgment unless there are egregious facts that challenge not merely a director's judgment but integrity as well (such as a director having a conflict of interest with the corporation). One leading authority colorfully describes the breadth of a director's discretion as follows:

The search for cases in which directors of industrial corporations have been held liable in derivative suits for negligence uncomplicated by self-dealing is a search for a very small number of needles in a very large haystack. Few are the cases in which the stockholders do not allege conflict of interest, still fewer those among them which achieve even such partial success as denial of the defendant's motion to dismiss the complaint. [Emphasis added] [Bishop, "Sitting Ducks and Decoy Ducks: New Trends in the Indemnification of Corporate Directors and Officers," 77 *Yale LJ* 1078, 1099 (1968)]

In summary, decisions by directors tend to spell trouble for corporations or their shareholders when

- made by inexperienced or uneducated individuals, who
- may be reluctant to openly criticize another director (who may be a sibling or parent), and

- who may have a different perspective (if not a conflict of interest) on what's good for the family and the family business than does a shareholder who is not active in the business.

The business judgment rule is a judicial attempt to strike a fair balance between the recognized need to protect shareholders (whose interests sometimes conflict with the interests of their directors) and the need to let directors do their job without constant second-guessing. Given these competing interests, the incompetence of many directors, and the myriad related psychological factors, judicial efforts to strike a satisfactory balance between these interests are often unsuccessful and shareholder frustration with this process often erupts in conflict.

How to Use the Corporate Model Effectively

In spite of its problems, the corporate model does offer a structure, which, I believe, can be beneficially adapted for use by families for their family businesses. This model's emphasis on the merit of the delegation of decision-making authority remains more appropriate than ever in today's complex and fast-moving business environment. The problem, in short, is not in the delegation of authority but in *whom* the authority is delegated to.

The solution to the problems noted earlier is, I suggest, fairly straightforward: eliminate the delegation of authority to only family members. Instead, families should consider constituting their boards with three separate classes of directors:

1. Senior family leaders who occupy executive roles in the family business
2. Family members who serve as representatives of the family council
3. Nonfamily members who have demonstrated business experience, acumen, and success

The senior family leaders merit board representation because, presumably, they control ownership and management of the business. One or a few representatives from the family council can help ensure that acceptable channels of communication exist between the business and the family, as noted in Chapter 2. The benefits of having nonfamily members serve on a board of directors is considered in the following section.

Benefits of Nonfamily Board Members

Perhaps by now, the rationale for an adviser's traditional advice to their family business clients that they consider including one or several nonfamily members on their boards of directors is apparent. Such "outsiders" can help ensure that the board has access to technical business competence that might be missing on a family-only board. It almost goes without saying that good business advice and counsel are precious commodities that should be actively solicited whenever possible.

Outside directors also can lend credibility to decisions reached by the board by supporting decisions on the business merits and rejecting decisions made on the basis of actual or perceived conflicts of interest. In an environment that includes neutral directors, shareholders should feel more comfortable, for example, that a decision to build a new office building, undertake an expensive plant expansion, or acquire a new business, is, indeed, a prudent business decision (if not a business necessity) and not merely a monument to their business leader's ego. In short, outside directors not only increase the quality of a board's decision making, they also increase the fact and perception of fairness and accountability.

For the reasons considered above, it may be particularly useful to ensure that nonfamily board members are actively involved in the following areas to ensure that decisions are made competently and fairly:

- Playing an active role in the selection of a successor to avoid the impression that a candidate's selection was based on inappropriate favoritism
- Approving transactions that directly or indirectly benefit some family members more than others
- Reviewing the compensation of family employees
- Reviewing financial policies, including decisions relating to the payment of dividends, the reinvestment of earnings, etc.

By filling these roles, outside directors can help ensure that the corporate model of governance is, after all, a model for prosperity!

Suggested Criteria for Nonfamily Directors

In light of the important role nonfamily members can play on a family business' board of directors, the family's decision as to who should fill this role is a critical one. Although prospective candidates need to be considered on an individual basis, I recommend that you ask at least the following five questions:

1. What kind of business and management experience does the candidate have?   Include his or her previous experience serving on other boards when you answer this question. All things being equal, it's probably better to have a director with 20 years of business experience than one with no experience.

2. Will the prospective candidate have sufficient time to devote to the business?   The brightest individual in the world will be of little help if he or she is too busy to prepare for and attend board meetings. Accordingly, it is important to have a candid discussion with the candidate about his or her availability to serve on the board.

3. Does the candidate have a potential or actual conflict of interest with the family business?   A family may be familiar with another successful business in its industry and want to tap its leader for a directorship. Depending on the industry, it may be practically impossible for the two businesses to ever compete with each other, in which case the candidate may be worth considering. On the other hand, if that leader views the family business as a potential acquisition target or competitor, the choice could be disastrous. Once a director is selected, you can (and should) plan on their having access to all of the most confidential information about the family business. If that is a concern, keep looking!

4. Is the potential director's personality compatible with all or most of the personalities of the other directors? While it is often helpful to have different viewpoints, it is not necessarily helpful to have directors with different, conflicting, personalities. If an individual is unlikely to mix well with family members and other directors, keep looking!

5. Is the prospective director willing and able to dedicate himself or herself to the job?   If someone has all the time in the world to help, but isn't motivated to help, the prospect is a poor one. Sometimes, it is necessary to pay for the dedication by establishing directors' fees as compensation for board service. Again, this is a matter that can be considered by each family business as necessary.

The Model beyond Corporations

The management structure of a business legally depends, of course, on whether the form of the business is a proprietorship, partnership, limited liability company (or LLC), corporation, or other entity. For example, a sole proprietorship is owned, managed, and (occasionally) even operated by a single individual. A partnership is a business that is owned by two or more partners who are generally free to determine how their management structure will be established. The same is true with an LLC, which can be flexibly managed by its members or managers.

In spite of this variety, each of these alternative business forms can adopt the model of business governance recommended above and use it in a practical manner. The key is to involve family business leaders, family council leaders, and qualified nonfamily members as the particular structure permits. For example, the owner of a proprietorship could still involve other family members and outsiders as advisers or consultants. While they technically may have no legal role in the business, they can still serve the same functions. An LLC could utilize these individuals as managers. (For more information on LLCs, see Chapter 9.)

In short, don't get hung up over form; there should always be a way to accommodate this recommended structure in *any* business. Indeed, the structure can be designed to provide that the board of directors, or its equivalent, have certain advisory duties apart from any legal duties it may or may not have. Again, this is a subject that should be considered on a case-by-case basis. However structured, a capable and balanced board of directors is a significant salvation tool that can help add competence and credibility to business decisions and benefit all family businesses.

Recommendations

Family businesses too frequently rely exclusively on family members to fill the role of directors. This reliance not only limits the expertise the family can tap in making complex business decisions, but can create a sense of concern and suspicion among family owners who are inactive in the business that these directors are making business decisions primarily to further their self-interests at the expense of the inactive owners. By utilizing qualified outside directors, the family avoids these two problems.

Nonfamily directors should be selected on the basis of their expertise, their availability, and their willingness to serve the family. Compensation for board service is usually appropriate, the amount being a function of such factors as community standards, reputation, expertise, time expended, etc. Family directors should ordinarily include the largest owners as well as one or several designated representatives from the family council to ensure that the family's positions can be expressed but do not necessarily override the correct business decision. Board membership can be rotated periodically to help cultivate the existence of fresh perspectives on the board. The model of board representation was developed in the corporate context but can certainly be applied to other business forms, such as general partnerships, limited partnerships, and limited liability companies.

Family Business Audit

1. Does your family business have nonfamily directors?

2. Do nonfamily directors play an active role in the selection of a successor?

3. Do nonfamily directors play an active role in approving transactions that indirectly or directly benefit some family members more than other family members?

4. Do nonfamily directors play an active role in reviewing the compensation of family employees?

5. Do nonfamily directors play an active role in establishing or reviewing your company's financial policies?

6. Do your nonfamily directors have appropriate business and management experience to contribute to your family business? Do they have sufficient time to devote to your business? Do they have compatible personalities?

CHAPTER 4

You've Reached an Agreement with Members of Your Family. Now What?

Put It in Writing!

*M*any of the planning techniques recommended in this book reflect the combined importance of establishing effective channels of communication (in order to build understanding and consensus) and documenting those understandings (to enable family members to guide future decisions within the family business). In this chapter, I consider perhaps the most important of such documents, the shareholder agreement.

Technically, a *shareholder agreement* refers to an agreement among owners of a corporation. A similar agreement among partners in a partnership would be referred to as a *partnership agreement* and, among members of a limited liability company, an *operating agreement.* The subjects and recommendations of this chapter are intended to be broadly, not technically, construed to be generically applicable to agreements that family owners can reach with respect to the operations of their businesses, regardless of the actual legal form of such business. In those instances where a recommendation is only applicable in a particular business form, that limitation is appropriately noted.

Agreements reached by family members can cover an infinite variety of subjects and, so, a well-drafted shareholder agreement could literally serve an unlimited variety of purposes. Indeed, virtually any agreement reached at a meeting of the family council, business owners, or directors-advisers might be appropriately incorporated into a shareholder agreement. Recognizing this opportunity to creatively and expansively use such an agreement, there are, nevertheless, several particularly valuable purposes served by shareholder agreements that, due to their importance, deserve particular attention. These purposes are the subject of this chapter.

Perhaps the most important purpose served by a shareholder agreement concerns the regulation of entry into, and exit out of, the family business ownership group. By permitting individuals with different financial needs and business philosophies to exchange their ownership interests in family businesses for cash, the company minimizes the likelihood that such individuals will battle with other owners who may have contrary philosophies or differing financial interests. This subject is typically addressed in buy-sell provisions or, reflecting the importance of this subject, the shareholder agreement itself may even be referred to as a buy-sell agreement.

The first part of this chapter is devoted exclusively to buy-sell agreements, because of their critical role in ensuring family peace and prosperity. The balance of this chapter continues with a discussion of a variety of matters that might also be appropriately included in a shareholder agreement, including subjects ranging from agreements on the management of a business to capital contribution requirements. As with the other recommendations contained in this book, you should consider these provisions in consultation with your advisers to ensure their suitability for your unique situation.

Buy-Sell Agreements

One of the most important functions that a shareholder agreement can serve is to ensure that ownership of a family business remains within the family by restricting the eligibility criteria for ownership and providing standards pursuant to which ownership interests can be transferred and corresponding restrictions on when transfers are restricted. Several common scenarios may prompt owners to seek to transfer their ownership interests or acquire that of another. These include voluntary scenarios, in which existing owners desire to cash out, perhaps, for instance, after retirement or resignation. There are also involuntarily scenarios, in which owners or their estates are forced to cash out, perhaps as a consequence of an owner's death or disability.

Shareholder agreements are often used to regulate which of these transfers are permitted and the terms and conditions by which permitted transfers can occur. In short, properly structured, these agreements establish rules for when those family members who want or need to cash out (the sellers) can do so and corresponding rules that ensure that those family members who want to retain ownership and management control over the business (the buyers) can do so as well. For this reason, agreements with provisions regulating this subject matter are often referred to as *buy-sell* agreements.

The buy-sell agreement can most usefully be understood by reference to the causes of conflict in family businesses. Specifically, a well-drafted agreement should be prepared to reflect that

- certain critical events inevitably occur in the life of individuals and their families, and
- such events can change the various perspectives family members have on their roles (and the roles of others) in the family business.

As a result of such a change of perspective, it often becomes desirable or necessary to simultaneously change the ownership mix within a family. For example, if a shareholder begins competing with the family business, the remaining shareholders presumably might want the option to buy out that shareholder's interest in the family business to avoid future conflict. A buy-sell agreement can facilitate that objective. Alternatively, if a shareholder dies, the surviving shareholders might not want the deceased shareholder's spouse as an owner and that spouse may be more interested in having cash than the stock certificate transferred to his or her name. A buy-sell agreement can facilitate that objective as well. These and other events can be built into any buy-sell agreement to promote family well-being by triggering the mutual and simultaneous obligations of one or more family members to sell their ownership interests in the family business and of one or more family members to buy those interests.

After first considering the purposes of a buy-sell agreement in some detail, this chapter examines the major issues that should be included in a well-drafted buy-sell agreement. The failure in practice of many traditional buy-sell agreements is also reviewed and suggestions for ensuring that your agreement works both in theory *and* practice are also provided.

The Purposes of a Buy-Sell Agreement

A buy-sell agreement is ordinarily designed to fulfill a number of purposes that may be most easily understood by considering the perspective of the buyers and sellers. Why, for instance, would an owner of a family business be interested in cashing out and another family member be interested in paying for that same interest?

From a seller's point of view, a variety of critical events may make it more desirable to have cash than an ownership interest in a family business. For example, if an owner becomes disabled, retires, or terminates his or her employment with the family business (voluntarily or involuntarily), he or she may be more interested in cashing out than retaining an investment interest in the business. Also, if the owner dies, his or her family may be more interested in cashing out to help pay for estate taxes and to replace the cash that the deceased owner previously took out of the business as employment compensation. These and other events can be used to specify the circumstances in an agreement pursuant to which the terms of a buy-sell agreement are *triggered*. In short, a buy-sell agreement can benefit family members who want or need to sell their ownership interest in their family business in the following ways:

- Ensuring the existence of buyers for their stock (i.e., it creates a market for their stock where one otherwise might not exist).
- Ensuring the existence of necessary liquidity to pay taxes and other expenses associated with death.
- Providing a mechanism for transferring accessible wealth to family members more efficiently than through the payment of dividends.

In addition, there usually are reciprocal advantages to individuals who would like to purchase a selling family member's stock on the occurrence of the same trigger events provided for in the buy-sell. For instance, a buyer may not want to be partners with the heirs of a deceased owner. Such heirs may be incapable of or not interested in contributing to the family business but, nevertheless, as owners, they may expect a return on their investment in the form of salaries or dividends. By acquiring their ownership interests, the buyer eliminates potential friction with these heirs. Also, a buyer may have a "right of first refusal," which guarantees him or her the right to buy another family member's ownership interest in the business before it can be sold to an outsider who, potentially, would be unfriendly or hostile to the remaining family members. In short, a buyer can benefit from a buy-sell agreement in the following ways:

- By maintaining control of the family business
- By avoiding unwanted owners
- By eliminating potential friction or conflict with family members who, previously inactive in the business, might be forced to become active if they needed money as a result of lifetime events or circumstances

In order for a buy-sell agreement to satisfy the respective interests and objectives of both potential family buyers and sellers, several critical issues need to be considered and resolved:

- Who is eligible to be a buyer?
- What trigger events require the buying and selling of ownership interests within the family business?
- How is the price for the sale to be determined?
- How will the interest be paid?

The following section explores these critical questions in detail.

Potential buyers.   One of the most basic tasks in crafting a buy-sell agreement is deciding who will be permitted to buy a seller's ownership interest. This decision's importance is largely due to the following two underlying questions:

1. Which family members can "qualify" to become buyers through criteria such as bloodline, capability, interest, etc.? These issues are often best addressed in family councils and appropriately discussed with family advisers, including nonfamily board members.
2. How can available funds be most efficiently used to minimize applicable taxes?

It is to the second question that we now turn. A buy-sell agreement can be structured to provide that the buyer of a seller's stock will be one of the following:

- The business itself (in which case the agreement is referred to by professionals as a *redemption agreement*)
- Individual family members (in which case the agreement is referred to as a *cross-purchase agreement*)
- A combination of the two (in which case the agreement is referred to as a *hybrid agreement*)

Each of these choices offers a variety of advantages and disadvantages. A redemption agreement permits the business to use its funds to acquire an individual's ownership interest. This arrangement may be more advantageous for family members, who, in a cross-purchase agreement, would be individually required to save sufficient funds to purchase a seller's ownership interest or, if applicable, an appropriate life insurance policy. A corollary benefit to this advantage, of course, is that owners need not rely on another family member's ability to save enough money to satisfy their financial obligations imposed by the buy-sell agreement but, instead, can look to the family business's deep pockets to satisfy such obligations. In addition, if an individual's applicable income tax bracket is higher than that of the business, more after-tax dollars are spent by an individual to fund applicable purchase obligations (so it may be cheaper for the business to make the payment). In limited circumstances, a deceased owner's interest in a family business can be purchased by a corporation and avoid dividend treatment, thus minimizing the applicable tax consequence for the owner's heirs. Finally, a redemption agreement may be more manageable than a cross-purchase agreement where there are multiple owners, since the family business can simply acquire one policy on the lives of specified multiple owners. In a cross-purchase agreement, by contrast, if each owner were required to secure life insurance policies on other owners, many more policies would be required.

A redemption agreement may, however, pose certain disadvantages that need to be considered. For example, a business may be legally prohibited from purchasing an owner's interest in its business if the purchase renders the business insolvent or without sufficient "capital surplus." In this circumstance, the entire buy-sell plan could possibly be voided as illegal. Also, if the business acquires an insurance policy to help fund the payment obligation, the policy is a business asset and, as such, needs to be included in determining the value of the business.

The higher valuation can, as noted in Chapter 7, be counterproductive with respect to the goal of minimizing estate taxes.

Although it has certain disadvantages, some of which have been noted, cross-purchase agreements also have a number of advantages to commend their use. In this arrangement, buyers of a seller's ownership interest may receive an increase in the tax basis for the shares they acquire. On a later sale, this increased basis may reduce then-applicable capital gains taxes, an obvious financial benefit. In addition, the money that individuals have set aside to fund their purchase obligations under this form of agreement, including insurance proceeds if applicable, ordinarily are not available to satisfy creditor claims. Life insurance policies acquired by a business to fund a redemption agreement, by contrast, are subject to creditor claims. Unlike some forms of business, individuals are not subject to capital surplus and solvency restrictions. These rules are complex and should be considered with your professional advisers.

Because of the respective advantages and disadvantages of both the redemption and cross-purchase form of agreement, consider using a hybrid agreement. In this form of agreement, the business might have the first option to acquire a seller's ownership interest and, if the business declines to do so, the individual owners are then given the option (or are required) to purchase the seller's interest. This form of agreement provides the family with the opportunity to postpone its decision as to the most favorable means of acquiring the seller's interest until the actual occurrence of an applicable trigger event. Since this event may take place at any time after reaching the agreement, and a family's circumstances can change dramatically over time, this added flexibility often is a welcome benefit to family members and deserves careful consideration for every family business.

Trigger Events

The premise of a buy-sell agreement is that ownership interests in a particular business are required to be bought and sold upon the occurrence of particular events. It is therefore important for a family to consider which events it believes should serve as triggers. The most commonly used trigger events are an owner's

- death,
- disability,

- retirement,
- termination of employment,
- divorce,
- competition with the family business, and
- pledge of his or her ownership interest in the family business or bankruptcy.

Trigger events should be designed with both the family and business interests in mind. For example, a former employee who now competes with the family business has a direct conflict of interest with the family business and its owners. In this circumstance, it is usually advisable to acquire any ownership interest the former employee may have in the family business. Similarly, a retired employee who maintains an ownership interest may also have a conflict if he or she is interested in the family business adhering to a conservative fiscal policy so that the business could pay the employee's retirement while the active owners may prefer a more aggressive fiscal policy to continue growing their business. The spouse of a deceased employee or owner also may have opinions as to how the family business should be run that are at odds with those of surviving owners and current management. In these and other circumstances, common sense suggests the possibility (if not likelihood) that new owners and existing owners in new and different situations may have particular reasons for objecting to the goals and objectives of other existing or surviving owners. In such circumstances, family members may be better off by selling or buying their respective ownership interests as appropriate. If the occurrence of an event might increase the likelihood of conflict in your family, it may be appropriate to make that event a trigger in your buy-sell agreement.

In certain circumstances, it also may be desirable to include particular trigger events in a buy-sell agreement that have come to be known as *tag-along* and *drag-along* provisions. A tag-along provision is designed to protect owners with minority interests in family businesses by preventing majority owners from selling their interests in a family business without also arranging for the sale of the minority owners' interest at the same price. By contrast, a drag-along provision permits majority owners to compel minority owners to sell their shares in the family business so they can't hold out in order to "greenmail" the parties to pay them a premium sale price above the other sellers. You may wish to consider the merit of these provisions in consultation with your advisers.

Finally, courts may disregard an agreement with unreasonable restrictions on the transferability of ownership interests for public policy reasons. For this reason, buy-sell agreements often are drafted to require owners who have identified prospective third-party buyers to first offer to sell their interest to the business or other specified family members. By providing a right of first refusal, families should eliminate any question about the unreasonableness of the restraints on transferability while ensuring ownership of the family business remains in the family.

Establishing the "Buy-Sell Price"

Establishing the price at which family members buy and sell each other's ownership interests in the family business is one of the most important decisions to be made when drafting a buy-sell agreement. Unfortunately, there is no simple way to do this, due to the inherent difficulty of valuing ownership interests for which there is no public market. As a result, this most important subject is wrought with difficulty and potential conflict. An inability for family members to reach consensus on this subject can also create a reluctance for a seller to sell (if the price is too low) or a buyer to buy (if the price is too high). In such cases, family members often wind up remaining co-owners of a business when the family members' individual circumstances suggest they should separate. Unable to disengage in a mutually agreeable manner, such family members often become increasingly intolerant of each other and may wind up disengaging later by a court order.

A number of alternative valuation methods have developed over time, each with potential advantages and disadvantages including:

- Using a predetermined fixed value (which is easy to apply but routinely inaccurate since a business's value is rarely fixed and usually changes)
- Using book value, or assets minus liabilities (which is also easy to apply but, since it does not take into consideration market appreciation or depreciation in asset value, is still relatively inaccurate)
- Using one of several formulas (which requires that difficult judgments be made on appropriate data to enter into the formulas)

- Capitalizing earnings, or multiplying earnings by an appropriate factor (which, again, requires agreement on what data and factors are appropriate)

While a detailed consideration of these and other valuation methods is beyond the scope of this book, two observations are in order:

1. It is usually more complicated to determine the value of a typical family business than it is of other businesses because family employees' compensation and job perks are often above market.   Mechanical application of most valuation methods therefore will result in a below-market valuation, since earnings have been artificially depressed. In these cases, it is often appropriate to adjust the family business's financial statements to reflect reasonable compensation levels prior to valuing the business. For example, if a business has earnings of $2 million after paying family members compensation of $2 million, perhaps the value of the business is more appropriately determined by assuming the real earnings are $3 million, since compensation in the absence of family obligations would only be $1 million.

2. Complex tax rules need to be considered in establishing a business's value under a buy-sell agreement.   The purpose of these rules, essentially, is to ensure that the buy-sell agreement operates much like an arm's-length business transaction between strangers and not a cleverly disguised attempt to pass ownership to the owners' heirs. Without this requirement, the most efficient estate planning technique for family business owners would be to simply value their family business at $1 and then gift or will it to their heirs. The requirement that a business's value be tied to a fair market value helps ensure, of course, that the government doesn't lose its share of gift or estate tax revenue on the transfer of a family business by simply establishing an artificially low value.

Another important factor to consider when seeking to establish the sale price in a buy-sell agreement is what if any adjustments should be made in the event that the buyer later becomes a seller and sells the family business for a price substantially in excess of what he or she bought it for. Should a part of the price be shared with the family member who sold his or her interest at what may appear to be a discounted price? This scenario has prompted many families to provide comfort to selling family members by including what is commonly referred to as a *look-back provision* in their buy-sell agreements.

The Look-Back Provision

A constant theme throughout this book is that family members have an inherent conflict of interest with respect to their interest in a family business and mechanisms need to be established to minimize the unhealthy effects of unharnessed suspicion, which can otherwise give rise to conflict. In this instance, while it certainly is the case that a family's best interests are served by establishing a buy-sell agreement, many families may be reluctant to do so. Why? The answer may, in part, be due to distrust family members have for other members. Specifically, an owner may be concerned that if he or she were to sell out, the family would turn around and sell the business for what it's really worth—which, of course, would be a lot more than they would pay their family for it! Given the inherent difficulty involved in establishing an accurate value for a family business, this concern may, at least sometimes, have merit. Numerous cases have been litigated over the years in which one family member accuses another of fraudulently consummating an intrafamily purchase and thereafter selling that interest outside the family at a steep premium.

A solution to this concern may be to include a provision in the buy-sell agreement that specifies the following:

- If the buyer becomes a seller within a specified time period and
- sells the business in excess of a specified amount of money on that sale, then
- a percentage of that excess money is to be shared with the original seller.

In order to design an agreement that provides comfort to an original seller while treating the original buyer (who assumes a substantial degree of risk associated with continuing ownership of the business), consideration should be given to limiting the look-back period to a reasonable period of time (which may be three, four, or five years or longer, depending on particular circumstances) and gradually reducing the percentage of the excess payment price, which the original buyer is required to sell if he or she becomes a seller (say, in year one, 100 percent of the excess is split pro rata among the prior owners; in year two, only 80 percent of the excess is split, etc.). Such limitations are designed to recognize the contribution the original buyer may have made to justify the increased price on a later sale as well as the risk assumed in running the business. No particular formula is correct and each family will, no doubt, have its own thoughts on what a fair look-back provision might look like. Nevertheless, the concept can often go a long way in reducing or minimizing concerns that otherwise might stand in the way of consummating an intrafamily sale of ownership interests in the family business.

The case of *Obermaier v. Obermaier* illustrates the usefulness a look-back provision might play in clarifying a buyer's and seller's understanding about the fairness of a purchase price and, so, help to avoid litigation. This case involved a claim by Alfred Obermaier against his brother Norman. The brothers had worked together for many years, Alfred contributing engineering services and Norman contributing management services. After their parents died, the brothers succeeded to ownership of the stock in the company including, in part, through a trust for Alfred of which Norman was a trustee.

The brothers did not get along well and, after their father died, Alfred developed a drinking problem that hindered his ability to contribute to the business. The brothers eventually decided to retire and sell their business. As a result of his management position and his brother's declining involvement in the business, Norman and his attorneys dealt with all of the prospective buyers. Early negotiations to sell the business for $8 million (plus a ten-year consulting contract to Norman) collapsed following a prospective buyer's failure to secure adequate financing. Thereafter, Norman offered to buy Alfred out. Alfred, in turn, countered and offered to buy Norman out. After Norman convinced his brother that no one in the company would work for him, Alfred agreed to sell his interest to Norman for $4 million, $800,000 of which was immediately payable and the balance over time in installments. In reaching their agreement, Norman told Alfred that he would not look for another buyer for at least a year.

Prior to closing his deal with his brother, Norman received a call from another suitor expressing interest in buying the family business. Several months later, Norman completed the sale for $6 million *plus* the buyer's assumption of the remaining payments due Alfred. In short, Norman wound up with approximately $2 million more than did his brother. Upon learning of the sale and his brother's additional profit, Alfred brought suit seeking one-half of the incremental purchase price Norman had received, claiming Norman had violated his fiduciary duty to disclose all information relevant to the stock sale.

Norman denied he had breached his fiduciary duty to his brother, instead claiming that he neither concealed nor misrepresented any facts and that a purchaser of stock has no duty to disclose the possibility of a future sale. Norman also contended that his brother had been represented by his own attorney and had secured an independent valuation of the business.

The Illinois trial court rejected Norman's defenses and awarded Alfred $1.1 million in actual damages, $250,000 in punitive damages, and approximately $240,000 in interest. Norman then appealed to the appellate court of Illinois, which again rejected Norman's claims. In agreeing with the decision of the trial court, the appellate court concluded that Norman had indeed failed to adequately apprise his brother of relevant information concerning the sale and that, as a result, the damages award to his brother was justified.

The lessons from this case are clear: When dealing with family co-owners, it is usually safer to err on the side of providing too much information than not enough information and family interests are often well served by incorporating look-back provisions in intrafamily sales.

Funding the Purchase Price

The finest buy-sell agreement in the world is completely useless if there are insufficient funds available to permit the buyer to pay the seller the price established under the agreement. The difficulty many families have experienced in funding their agreements is not only due to the difficulty of raising necessary funds but the impossibility of predicting when trigger events may occur and, so, planning with certainty for when the family will actually need funds to satisfy payment obligations under the agreement. Some trigger events may occur during an owner's lifetime; others may occur on an owner's death. Most trigger events may never even occur! While this imperfect information makes planning difficult, it remains imperative for family members to determine how their purchase-price obligations will be funded if and when a trigger event does occur in order to avoid being caught unprepared.

There are essentially two basic approaches to funding a buy-sell agreement:

1. Establish a sinking fund within the business or family.
2. Procure life insurance, which can be used to fund obligations incurred on a family member's death.

A sinking fund, of course, is simply a savings plan, either within the business or by individuals. While it's great to save, it may be difficult to adhere to the discipline required to save enough money to fully fund a buy-sell agreement, especially when there are so many ways to spend money! In addition, money that is allocated to a sinking fund is money that is paid with after-tax dollars.

Ordinarily, a buy-sell agreement can be funded most efficiently with insurance *if* the buyout is triggered by an owner's death. While premiums are paid with after-tax dollars, an insurance policy provides a lump-sum payment that should be income tax–free. Many qualified insurance professionals are available to assist families in acquiring appropriate insurance coverage to help fund these agreements. Only one recommendation, therefore, is offered here. Very simply, consider the merits of purchasing term insurance instead of permanent insurance for your buy-sell agreement. Many business relationships end long before anyone's death, so the need for permanent insurance may never materialize. Since term is cheaper than permanent insurance, why spend money for a trigger event that may be unlikely to occur? In addition, since there may be less variance in the premium cost from one family member to another with term premiums, there may be less resentment among family members who qualify for the cheaper premiums as a result of age, health, etc.

Permanent insurance, of course, is and remains an important planning tool for personal estate plans and its use for that purpose should always be considered in consultation with your professional advisers.

In considering the funding aspect of a buy-sell agreement, two critical decisions have already been considered: how much should be paid (i.e., what value should be used to set the buy-sell price) and what can be done to ensure that sufficient funds will be available to ensure that the price can be paid. A third factor may, upon reflection, actually be the most important of all: What are the terms and conditions of payment? This subject is considered in the next section.

Payment Terms and Conditions

The importance of the terms and conditions of payment obligations established under a buy-sell agreement may best be illustrated by considering the following hypothetical comparison. In one family, an event triggers application of a buy-sell agreement. As a result, a buyer is required to pay a seller $500,000 cash within 30 days. In another family, a similar event triggers a similar buy-sell agreement, although in this case, the buyer has the option of paying $500,000 over a five-year period and need only pay $25,000 within 30 days. Same price, different terms, different conditions—Remarkably different transactions!

To avoid potential ambiguity and misunderstanding, a buy-sell agreement should be drafted with due consideration to the terms and conditions that will be applicable to a buyer's payment obligation. For example, will a lump-sum payment be required or will credit be extended to the buyer? If credit is extended, it is important to specify terms of the credit, including the following:

- Applicable interest
- Length and amortization of the payout term
- Security arrangements to back up the payment obligations
- Restrictions, if any exist, that apply to the buyer when the payment obligation remains outstanding

The importance of the first two items is self-evident. The other items deserve close attention.

Security arrangements.   If a buyer is required to use credit to pay the purchase price established under a buy-sell agreement, it may be appropriate for a seller to insist on receiving security protection similar to what other traditional lenders may obtain from borrowers. Two important avenues of protection should be considered by family members. The first is establishing reasonable security arrangements, which may require the buyer to furnish the seller with the following:

- A personal guarantee
- Statutory security interests in specific collateral, such as a mortgage
- An escrow agreement, which establishes a segregated pool of funds that the seller can access in the event of a buyer's breach of payment obligations

While these traditional tools may offer some peace of mind, if the family business's operations run into difficulty, they may, in practice, become irrelevant.

Restrictions.   Perhaps the most important protection a seller can look to from a buyer who pays the buyout price over time is to impose restrictive covenants similar to those that would be included in a typical credit agreement between the buyer and the buyer's bank. Such restrictions may serve to do the following:

- Limit family members' salaries and the payment of dividends.
- Limit loans permitted from the family business to individual family members.
- Limit capital expenditures that can be made by the family business.
- Limit borrowing from other lenders beyond a specified amount.
- Otherwise limit the ability to run the family business outside the ordinary course.

While a buyer might gripe about the unreasonableness of such restrictions, perhaps a fair argument can be made by the seller that the buyer shouldn't be allowed to run hog-wild with his or her money. Again, it is a question of appreciating the competing interests of different family members.

Miscellaneous Considerations in Drafting a Buy-Sell Agreement

Every family needs to consider its unique situation when preparing its buy-sell agreement. As emphasized in Chapter 10, boilerplate documents often spell trouble and that may particularly be the case with a document as important as this one. The following suggestions (which should be discussed with your professional advisers) may be useful to help your family customize its buy-sell agreement.

Consider the merits of using different payment terms and conditions for different trigger events.   For example, if an employee, having reached retirement age, is required to sell his or her ownership interest in the family business, it may be appropriate to pay that owner generously and quickly. If, however, an employee is required to sell his or her ownership interest because he or she has been fired for cause (e.g., for stealing from the family business), it may be equally appropriate to pay the owner less generously and over a longer period of time. Because complex estate-planning considerations may be involved in making such distinctions, they should be carefully reviewed with competent professional advisers.

Family members should agree on who should remain liable for financial obligations that may have been incurred prior to the occurrence of a trigger event but have not yet matured into actual claims or judgments against the business.   In some cases, the family business or individual owners may wish to indemnify the seller for all potential liabilities arising out of business operations. In other instances, the seller may fairly be required to indemnify the buyers. In still other instances, it may even be appropriate for the buyers to indemnify the seller for certain matters and the seller to indemnify the buyers for other matters. However this allocation of risk is resolved, it can be useful to address these subjects somewhere (and what better place than a buy-sell agreement?) in order to provide a measure of closure to a family's business relationship.

Provide ways in which certain outstanding financial issues should be resolved.   For instance, are unpaid loans to be repaid or treated as compensation? Are declared but unpaid bonuses or dividends to be paid or waived? These and related subjects should be put to bed, informally or more formally, through the family's agreement. The added degree of certainty and finality with respect to family relationships can enhance the likelihood of mutual satisfaction with the agreement.

Miscellaneous Provisions for a Shareholder Agreement

As noted earlier, shareholder agreements can be designed to accommodate a variety of interests relating to buy-sell provisions. This same flexibility also can be creatively used to accommodate a variety of other interests that a family might have. Some of the creative uses that families have found helpful to include in their shareholder agreements are briefly reviewed in this section. As with other suggestions, consider these suggestions in consultation with your professional advisers.

Management of the Family Business

It may be possible to use a shareholder agreement to spell out how managerial control in a family business is to be allocated among owners. This could be accomplished either by broadly referencing the subject of control or by specifically defining how certain issues should be determined by which manager or management group. It is even possible for agreements to ratify the election of certain individuals to specific positions, in order to have certain titles and control. Such management control, of course, should dovetail with the philosophy, if not moral agreement, held or reached by the family council. To the extent necessary, agreements can include powers of attorney or similar powers to vest legal control in designated individuals. It is, of course, equally possible to spell out specific limitations on management control in an agreement. Such limitations also can be broadly or specifically covered. For example, a shareholder agreement might provide that the family business's management team cannot borrow or spend money in excess of a specified dollar amount without the approval of all or a specified percentage of the owners. Because of complex estate planning considerations, provisions that allocate control of a family business on the basis of something other than on the basis of ownership interests should be reviewed with competent professional advisers.

Financial Policies

It may be useful for a family to spell out certain agreements relating to financial policies of its business operations. For example, an agreement might be reached that additional capital contributions will not be required unless all family members unanimously consent to make the contemplated contribution. A similar provision could provide that capital improvements in excess of a specified dollar amount will not be undertaken unless a specified percentage of family owners consent to the expenditure. Indeed, many other financial decisions, ranging from compensation, fringe benefits, dividends, etc., could be included in a shareholder agreement in order to minimize opportunity for disagreement and maximize consensus.

Confidentiality

Many employment agreements are prepared with provisions requiring employees to keep certain proprietary information confidential. This information will vary from business to business and could range from such different information as customer names to sale prices to manufacturing techniques. The obvious purpose is to ensure that a business is not later adversely affected by employees who leave and, armed with such confidential information, are able to more effectively compete against their former employer. While it may be a family's practice to require employees to sign a written employment agreement, a confidentiality provision can easily be included in a shareholders agreement to provide similar protection.

Covenants Not to Compete

Many employment agreements also contain provisions that preclude key employees from using the knowledge and skill they acquire from their employers in a competitive manner following termination of their employment. Although courts construe these covenants not to compete narrowly, since their effect is to restrain trade, they are enforceable if narrowly drafted. As with confidentiality provisions, such covenants might not be routinely secured from family members in formal employment agreements but might be appropriately included in a shareholder agreement.

S Corporation Planning

Subchapter S of the Internal Revenue Code permits qualifying corporations to be treated as small business corporations. Many family businesses have taken advantage of the benefits offered under these provisions and operate as *S corporations*. Because of the code's qualification requirements for treatment under S corporation rules, safeguards should be established to ensure that disgruntled shareholders cannot terminate the S election by, for example, transferring their shares to a nonqualifying shareholder or to multiple other owners in order to raise the number of owners beyond the permitted number of 75. It is therefore commonplace for shareholders of S corporation stock to reach an agreement that any attempted transfer of stock in violation of the S corporation qualification rules is void and without any legal effect. Some agreements provide that the nonbreaching shareholders or the corporation have the right to acquire the shares from the owner who attempted to violate the shareholders agreement.

Securities Regulation

Businesses must comply with applicable federal and state securities law restrictions. While this complex body of law is beyond the scope of this book, it should be noted that ownership interests in a business (like stock in a corporation) generally cannot be freely sold unless the stock is registered under applicable law or there is an available exemption from otherwise applicable registration requirements. Because significant penalties may be imposed for violating securities laws, it is a good idea to include a provision in a shareholder agreement that confirms applicable restrictions. Competent professional advice should, of course, be sought if there are any questions about such matters.

An agreement might provide, for example, that each stock certificate of the corporation shall be inscribed with the following notation (or "legend"):

The shares represented by this certificate have not been registered under the Securities Act of 1933, as amended. These shares may not be sold or transferred in the absence of such registration or an exemption therefrom under said Act.

The shares represented by this stock certificate are subject to a stockholder agreement, a copy of which is on file at the office of the Corporation and will be furnished to any prospective purchaser upon request. Such stockholder agreement provides, among other things, for certain restrictions on the sale, transfer, pledge, hypothecation, or other disposition of the shares represented by this certificate.

Miscellaneous

Three other subjects can be extremely important to the prosperity of family and, so, merit inclusion in a family's shareholder agreement:

1. Agreement that disputes within a family can be peacefully resolved through, if necessary, application of an agreed on dispute resolution mechanism
2. Succession planning
3. Estate planning

Because of their respective importance, these subjects are addressed in detail in the following chapters.

Recommendations

Family businesses can benefit by adopting a fair and equitable buy-sell agreement. Such an agreement should be designed to ensure that sellers receive, and the buyers pay, fair value for the ownership interests being exchanged. Consideration should be given to including at least three key provisions that are not always found in traditional buy-sell agreements:

1. Family members must agree on a method for determining the fair market value of the business on the occurrence of a triggering event. This value should be determined only after making appropriate adjustments for such matters as above-market compensation, fringe benefits, etc.

2. The agreement should include a provision that, in the event of a sale by the buyer at a later date to an unrelated party for a premium price beyond that reached as part of the underlying intra-family sale, a fair portion of that premium should be shared with the former family owner (or his or her heirs). The purpose of such a provision is to provide confidence (and, so, an incentive to sell) to the selling family members that the sale price is fair and that they have minimized the risk that the family buyer, in turn, will resell their former interest almost immediately thereafter for a premium price. Such a provision, often referred to as a look-back provision, should provide an ever-decreasing share of that premium to the original seller, since presumably the longer the period of time between the intrafamily sale and the interfamily sale, the more likely it is that the premium is due to the efforts of the remaining family members in growing and nurturing the family business.

3. Finally, the agreement might include a provision to the effect that if the family buyer cannot fund the entire purchase price at a reasonably timely closing date, the buyer will not unreasonably use or invest family business capital to expand operations of the family business until such time as the purchase price has been paid in full. Various refinements to this general proposition might be useful, including reasonable limitations on compensation and benefits arrangements during this period and an agreement that excess capital can be used to maintain, but not expand, operations until the buyout is completed and the purchase price paid in full. In effect, the seller fills the role of a traditional lender. Therefore, traditional negative and affirmative covenants that are typically included in a credit agreement

might then be made applicable to the buyer. In the event all parties agree to otherwise use capital of the family business for expansion and growth opportunities, the selling party may even be entitled to an incremental return since the seller, who essentially is acting as a lender or even a venture capitalist in that situation, might fairly be entitled to benefit from the incremental risk that may be associated with the buyer's new use of funds.

Family Business Audit

1. Does your family business have a written shareholder agreement including, as applicable, a partnership agreement, membership agreement, or other agreement among all the business owners?

2. Does your shareholder agreement regulate the entry into, and exit out of, your family business?

3. Is your buy-sell agreement properly designed as a redemption agreement, a cross-purchase agreement, or a hybrid agreement?

4. Does your buy-sell agreement include all appropriate trigger events for your family, such as death, divorce, bankruptcy, etc.?

5. Is the buy-sell price fair to both buyer and seller? Does the agreement have a look-back provision?

6. Are sufficient funds available to the buyer to pay the purchase price of a seller's ownership interest on the occurrence of a trigger event?

7. Does your shareholder agreement specify the control of management power within the family business?

8. Does your shareholder agreement address critical financial issues relating to your family business?

CHAPTER 5

What Can You Do If Conflict Erupts?

Establish a Dispute Resolution Process

*A*lthough business owners typically spend countless hours agonizing over their business plans, they often fail to give even the slightest consideration to the prospect of how an internal dispute among family members may affect their businesses. It is almost as if such owners keep their fingers crossed and hope for the best. The odds of avoiding a damaging dispute without preplanning, however, are small. Even utilizing the planning techniques suggested throughout this book, disputes (perhaps less frequently and less severe) are bound to occur in most families. There are too many events, too many personalities, too many decisions to disagree over for the typical family business to exist without suffering some type of dispute among its principals. This is the essence of conflict dynamics, and the bloody history of many family business breakups confirms its validity.

Given its predictability, families are well advised to assume conflict will occur in their business and to develop a plan for resolving it when it does occur. Sensitively and intelligently handled, conflict can actually serve productive purposes and help clear the air from time to time. Without such a plan, conflict may be left unresolved to fester within pockets of increasingly disgruntled family members. When unresolved emotions and feelings feed into a cycle of sustained conflict, it becomes nearly impossible for families to effectively resolve any issue, since, by then, the real cause of their surface disagreements and battles probably lies several layers below the stated problem.

The premise of this chapter is simple: Those families that hold their breath and hope to avoid conflict are putting their family relationships as well as their family businesses on the line. This consequence stems from the fact that all states have legislation that authorizes a court, in appropriate circumstances, to intervene in a family conflict and force a liquidation of the business. Instead, families should consider how to minimize the destructive effects of conflict so they can spend more time on productive endeavors such as growing their businesses and enjoying life. The suggestions offered in this chapter are offered in this spirit.

Why Planning Techniques Cannot Eliminate Dissension

Many, maybe even most, disputes can be avoided by careful planning and consensus building well in advance of the occurrence of an actual dispute. The planning techniques offered throughout this book are designed to help build such consensus within a family. By reaching an understanding in advance of how certain decisions will be made, families are better able to guide their conduct while remaining sensitive to the concerns of all family members. For example, if two brothers in business together had a shareholder agreement that expressly permitted them to establish a competitive business on their own, the possibility that one of the brothers would later argue that the other brother unfairly competed with the family business would be all but eliminated. Similarly, if these brothers formed a corporation and caused their corporation to enter into employment agreements with each of them, one brother could not later arbitrarily fire the other without facing a substantial lawsuit.

Notwithstanding this premise, it is theoretically and practically impossible for families to reach an agreement on all matters and all future decisions. Common sense suggests that it would take too long (and would cost too much money) to retain a lawyer to write a contract that sought to anticipate how all possible subjects of dispute should be resolved. There are simply too many decisions required to cover them all in a contract. Moreover, business circumstances change, family dynamics change, and individuals change. Therefore, trying to draft an all-inclusive agreement on every possible subject is like trying to hit a moving target. Even if an all-inclusive agreement could be reached, it would probably be outdated by the end of the day! In short, it is impossible to anticipate all possible theoretical subjects of dispute and decide in advance how to avoid an actual dispute. As a result, it is imperative for a family to understand how it will face conflict when it does arrive. This chapter offers some suggestions in this regard that each family should consider in consultation with its own professional advisers.

The Failure of Traditional Dispute Resolution Techniques

Historically, it has been common practice for many families to resolve internal family disputes by relying on some form of dispute resolution that has been included in their shareholder agreement. The agreement may specify that a dispute is to be resolved by mediation, arbitration, or even by litigation in a specified court in a specified community. Some agreements I have seen even contain provisions that provide that, in the event a family dispute remains unresolved for a specified period (say 30 or 60 days), one of the disgruntled family members can force a sale of the entire family business! The theory behind such a provision, presumably, is that the remedy of a forced sale is so draconian that no one would use it. Of course, that doesn't otherwise help a family actually resolve its problems and, in the event an embittered family member did elect to rely on such a provision, the result could be disastrous.

I believe that family plans that are designed to resolve a dispute by relying on a provision in an agreement are ineffective. Plain and simple. Why? In my experience, conflict in family businesses ordinarily does not result from a single discrete event but, instead, results from a series of events, some of which may occur over a lengthy period of time. Left unresolved, these have erupted in family hostility. As a result, application of a single technique, a quick fix, usually is ineffective. Indeed, by relying on a particular dispute resolution mechanism, traditional family plans may only function to blow up a dispute into a catastrophic event and, so, may well be counterproductive!

To effectively prevent and resolve internal disputes when they do occur, families must recognize that dispute resolution is not simply about choosing and applying the correct technique or legal mechanism to the particular circumstance. It is, rather, a process that has the following qualities:

- Begins with good communication.
- Continues by providing family members with an opportunity to resolve certain disputes at a meeting of the family council.
- Continues thereafter by requiring certain decisions within the business to be made by a preapproved level of agreement (e.g., majority, supermajority, and unanimous agreement requirements on particular issues).
- Continues, perhaps, by providing family members with an opportunity to resolve certain business disputes by the vote of disinterested advisers or directors.
- Continues, perhaps, by seeking to resolve the dispute through a more formal mechanism such as mediation or arbitration.
- Only after these or other mechanisms have failed, looks to solutions that include the buying and selling of family members' ownership interests.

By viewing dispute resolution as a process and not an event, families are more likely to learn how to work together constructively to resolve their differences in an atmosphere characterized more by cooperation than threats. If families can't learn to work together and trust each other, they surely will be unable to trust a decision of a mediator or arbitrator and ultimately may only feel comfortable seeking to resolve their disputes by threat of receivership, court-ordered liquidation, or sale of the family business. To help families avoid such a tragedy, the balance of this chapter considers two stages of the dispute resolution process in more detail: Stage 1 reviews a variety of informal dispute resolution processes, and stage 2 reviews more formal processes. Intelligently applied, these techniques equip families to avoid the unhealthy consequences of dissension and conflict in their family businesses.

Stage 1: Informal Dispute Resolution Mechanisms

Study and Utilize Good Communication Techniques

Many arguments that begin because of poor communication can just as easily end through good communication. Unfortunately, good communication is as much a skill and talent as is understanding financial statements. Many people might look at a cash-flow statement; fewer can understand its real significance. So too it is with communication. Many know how to talk, fewer know how to listen, and fewer still know how to effectively communicate. Many books and articles have been written on this subject, which I commend for your consideration. Professional consultants, including psychologists, can be excellent instructors on how this skill can be improved. Since a study of the mechanics of communication is beyond the scope of this book, I offer only a few observations.

Many of us are reluctant to communicate with each other on uncomfortable subjects.   Perhaps we dislike confrontation. Perhaps we are uncomfortable criticizing another family member. Perhaps we are concerned that, by criticizing another, we, in turn, will be criticized for the things we have said or done in the past. Whatever the reason, many of us keep quiet and stuff our feelings inside of us instead of venting them. Like anything else, however, when there's no more room inside to stuff our feelings, they come exploding out.

Unfortunately, our explosive response is often totally inappropriate to the circumstance at the time, and, had we not previously stuffed so many feelings inside of us, we might otherwise have offered a properly reasoned and balanced response. It therefore becomes imperative that family members be encouraged to communicate freely and openly (yet sensitively) to minimize stuffing and maximize reasoned and balanced communication.

Many of us think we have "communicated," even when we share concerns or displeasure with a person who is not the direct cause of such displeasure.   In such cases, the communication is happening with the wrong person! For example, a brother and sister may have a disagreement over whether the family business should spend $250,000 to advertise the family business on television and, hopefully, attract new customers as a result. Instead of talking with each other and explaining their respective opinions, they might both independently talk with their parents, explaining to them what a great idea they have and why their sibling's idea is so stupid. Professionals refer to this communication dynamic as *triangulation.* Instead on having a two-way dialogue, the dialogue is expanded to include a third person who becomes an intermediary. In appropriate and limited circumstances it may be useful to have a family member serve as an intermediary or mediator; however, such conversation usually is much less effective in resolving disputes and often serves to "Band-Aid" the problem instead of healing it. Moreover, if that third person is no longer available for some reason to serve as an intermediary, the two disagreeing parties may be unsure as to how (and so unable!) to resolve their dispute on their own.

Remember to treat your own family at least as well as you treat others. It is a strange phenomenon that, while many people may be perfectly prepared to show respect for strangers, they often show no respect for members of their own family. Basic communication and interpersonal skills such as showing respect, expressing concern, apologizing when appropriate, etc., are skills that should be valued and encouraged, not only in the outside world but in the world of our families as well. Family members can always agree to disagree with each other in a manner that preserves mutual respect, instead of destroying it.

Use the Family Council to Help Resolve Disputes

As discussed in Chapter 2, family disputes can be brought to the family council in appropriate instances and often resolved through family communication and dialogue. For example, if the brother mentioned earlier wanted to spend $250,000 to advertise on television but the sister thinks the decision is unwise and the money, instead, should be used to pay dividends or higher salaries, a family council meeting might be an effective venue to address underlying issues such as qualifications to make or review advertising decisions, forecast profits for the year based on a new advertising campaign, etc. Often, a family member may only be looking for an opportunity to express an opinion or ask a question and, once done, is content to accept another's opinion or decision.

Utilize Customized Decision-Making Standards

Families that are able to customize their decision-making process are often more successful in resolving disputes than are families who give the subject of dispute resolution little or no thought. For example, assume our hypothetical brother and sister belong to a family that has the following agreement on advertising expenditures:

- The president of the family business can spend up to $50,000 a year on advertising without obtaining the consent of the directors.
- Expenditures between $50,000 and $200,000 require the consent of a majority of the directors.
- Expenditures between $200,000 and $300,000 require the consent of at least 80 percent of the directors.
- Expenditures over $300,000 require the unanimous consent of all of the directors.

In this case, the brother would have to demonstrate to at least 80 percent of the directors that the advertising campaign is merited.

If the board includes competent outsiders in addition to family members, a vote to proceed with the campaign should, presumably, give the sister in this case a level of comfort that the campaign has, after all, been carefully conceived and is appropriate.

In some instances, it may even be advisable to have certain decisions made only by a group that is mainly or exclusively comprised of non-family advisers. For instance, if the brother wanted to spend $250,000 to advertise on a television station of which he is the sole owner, he has an obvious conflict of interest, since company funds would be used in a manner that disproportionately benefits him. On the other hand, his station may have the most popular programming in town and may truly be the most suitable place to advertise. Sometimes in situations like this, a decision by disinterested advisers can bring not only business competence, but also a useful level of impartiality to the equation.

Stage 2: Formal Dispute Resolution Mechanisms

Negotiation with Professional Advisers

In some instances, professional advisers can play a useful role in helping families resolve conflicts. Lawyers, for example, may be able to explain why certain decisions are advantageous or required, either as a matter of law or as part of the family's long-term estate or business plan. In other instances, professional consultants can act as facilitators, assisting families who are unable to effectively communicate with each other, perhaps because of egos, jealousies, repressed feelings, etc.

Almost without exception, negotiating a dispute through a trusted family adviser is the best formal dispute resolution mechanism. Such negotiations can proceed with almost unlimited flexibility, can be kept private, and are comparatively inexpensive to the alternatives discussed later in this section. Most important, a resolution to a dispute through this process is based on a decision by the parties to the dispute themselves, not some outsider. In certain cases, it may be useful to reflect the agreement reached in appropriate documents, such as a shareholder agreement.

The disadvantage of the negotiation process is that individuals cannot be forced to accept a proposal, even if it is a reasonable one. In other words, there is typically no coercive influence backing up the negotiation except the business and family interests of the individuals involved. If hostility is extreme and families have no interest in working together to resolve their differences, this mechanism ultimately will be unsuccessful. Any resolution to a dispute through a negotiation is later enforceable only if the parties have signed off on a written agreement.

Mediation

Mediation is a process by which neutral persons seek to help individuals resolve their disputes. The process is ordinarily entered into voluntarily by the parties, and the mediator has no power to impose a settlement. Most mediators seek to facilitate the communication process that, for a variety of reasons, may have gotten off track. This process can assist family members who may have lost sight of their family and financial interests and, instead, are hung up with their more emotional concerns.

Effective mediation practices often share the following characteristics:

- Both sides agree to give the process a fair chance.
- The mediator is selected on the basis of specific skills and experience in resolving family business disputes.
- Each side has the opportunity to caucus with the mediator in private, since there may be an unwillingness to speak openly.
- The parties agree that information relayed in the mediation cannot be brought out in a lawsuit unless it would have been available in the absence of a mediation. (This also means that the parties agree not to subpoena the mediator to testify as a witness in such a lawsuit.)
- Both sides have set—and agree to stick to—deadlines.
- Mediation encourages parties to brainstorm for novel solutions to old problems.
- The parties should avoid focusing on who is right and who is wrong; the focus instead is on the interests that can be served by different decisions.
- The parties should consider minimizing the role of lawyers, who can impede the resolution process if they look at family peace as the end of a gravy train of expensive litigation.
- If resolutions can be reached through mediation, the resolution should be recorded in a written agreement.

Arbitration

Arbitration is another popular alternative dispute resolution mechanism. It is a process in which parties select one or more neutral person(s) to hear, evaluate, and resolve a dispute by rendering either an advisory opinion (*nonbinding arbitration*) or a binding opinion (*binding arbitration*). The process can be flexibly designed in an almost infinite variety of ways, although a family is advised, at a minimum, to agree in advance on the following subjects:

- How the arbitrator is to be selected
- When the arbitration is to be scheduled

- What information can be discovered in preparation of the arbitration hearing
- What "rules of evidence" will be applied
- What state's law will be applied

The arbitration process offers a variety of advantages over the more formal litigation process. For example, arbitration is typically faster and cheaper than litigation, abusive discovery proceedings can be limited, and the process is usually private. Perhaps most important, the process can be customized, which sometimes makes it easier for family members to surmount potential obstacles to a resolution of the dispute. Of course, there are potential disadvantages with arbitration as well that should be considered. For example, in nonbinding arbitration, there may be an inadequate level of coercive influence to force parties to resolve their dispute. Indeed, the process can be inappropriately manipulated by disgruntled family members to hinder the timely resolution of legitimate claims.

Litigation

In exceptional cases, family members may be able to resolve their disagreements with other family members only through the coercive power of a court order. Probably the most common claims asserted in family business–related litigation involve claims for breach of fiduciary duty, oppression, fraud, and corporate waste. A variety of different remedies may be available to successful claimants, including monetary damages, appointment of a receiver or custodian, and a forced buyout. Litigation offers a party a formal and structured procedure for resolving a dispute, and court decisions (subject to rights of appeal) are binding. There is no more coercive form of relief than a court order, which even the most egotistical and recalcitrant individuals are forced to accept. On the other hand, litigation tends to be expensive, time consuming, highly public, and, above everything else, highly adversarial. As a result, there is often little hope that family members can work together again after warring with each other in court. Victory, if it can be called that, is usually claimed by a winner who is left standing on a pile of ashes.

Buy-Sell Agreements

If a dispute has risen to the level of litigation among family members, the only meaningful dispute resolution mechanism may be for either particular individuals or the entire family to sell their ownership interests in the family business. While a court may order such a sale as part of the litigation process, it may be reluctant to impose such a draconian solution and is more likely to provide limited (i.e., interim or partial) relief to successful claimants. For example, in our hypothetical dispute, if a court determined that the brother's advertising campaign was designed to unfairly benefit him, a court order might simply direct the brother to share with his sister the advertising profits his television station made on the $250,000 ad campaign.

Such limited relief is unsatisfactory in most instances, since the hatred and venom within a family rises to unacceptable levels during, and as a result of, litigation. As a result, following litigation, family members can usually no longer work together and are often better off realizing that their respective interests are better served if some family members stay in the business and others, or perhaps all family members, leave. In that instance, a buy-sell agreement that has a mechanism that determines who the buyers or sellers should be, along with the terms and conditions for such sale, can be extremely helpful. If the family doesn't have a buy-sell agreement that addresses this circumstance, the parties are, of course, free to negotiate a buyout arrangement at that time on mutually acceptable terms. The sooner family members realize that this is the only real alternative, the better off everyone will be.

Recommendations

Given the certainty of conflict, families must learn to do several things well:

- When possible, families should reach agreement on how they will handle certain critical decisions that must be made or events that are either certain to occur (e.g., an owner's death) or statistically likely to occur (e.g., an owner's interest in cashing out). Shareholder agreements can be useful in recording these agreements.

- Families are well served by focusing and improving the *process* of communicating with each other. By developing effective listening, communication, and conflict resolution skills, as well as a dose of sensitivity, families will have the tools they need to resolve conflicts when they inevitably occur.

- Anticipating that conflict will occur at some time, a prudent family will decide ahead of time how it will seek to resolve conflict in its family business in the easiest, fastest, cheapest, and friendliest method possible. Selecting one or more dispute resolution mechanisms, which can be incorporated in your written family agreements, may be the ultimate salvation technique. Revisit these written agreements from time to time to ensure that their terms remain relevant and acceptable. If necessary, amend the agreements as appropriate.

- Hold formal meetings of shareholders and directors to address routine and extraordinary issues and avoid reaching decisions informally and executing corporate minutes on the basis of "written consents" without meetings.

- Design your own family charters to serve as a family business contract. As noted in Chapter 2, such a document might establish, among other things, the guidelines for entering and remaining in your family business, and a code of conduct expected from all family members when disagreement exists.

- Because the likelihood of conflict increases as increasing numbers of family members work together, consider the best way to "prune" your family business tree to avoid too many family members working in the business. Share your thoughts with everyone on how "inactive" members will be compensated so as to provide incentives to work elsewhere.

- Consider other legal mechanisms that can help regulate relationships between business partners to promote stability. For example, in drafting your corporation's articles of incorporation, consider including provisions that accomplish the following:
    - Provide high quorum and voting requirements for shareholder and director action.
    - Deny directors the power to fix their own compensation.

- Deny directors the power to pledge corporate assets without shareholder consent.
- Recognize the occasional necessity for resolving family disputes through the legal process. Litigation can force family members to abandon arrogant positions and produce a resolution when all else fails. This may be especially true if the family is lucky enough to wind up in front of a capable judge who can use the influence of the legal system to mediate a solution.
- Recognize that there are usually no winners in litigation except, perhaps, the Internal Revenue Service, who may become aware of previously undisclosed taxable perks. Most family lawsuits wind up in state courts, which, as a rule, are more equipped to resolve criminal matters than complex business claims. Litigation is expensive, and capable lawyers who are able to make some allegations stick are not hard to find. Lawyers, moreover, are not always well trained to solve family emotional problems and, instead, view their role as that of a champion for individual family members (a role which, if litigation is prolonged, can become quite lucrative!).
- Never forget the value of love, mutual respect, and the fact that, sometimes, an apology is more important than money! Remember, any partnership requires care and nurturing. Good communication and sensitivity to the reasonable expectations of your partners is essential to fostering good relationships. Practiced in combination with the suggestions set forth earlier, you will improve the odds that your business can avoid a premature and unnecessary demise.

Family Business Audit

1. Have your family's business agreements been prepared in a manner designed to minimize or avoid unhealthy conflict? Do these agreements view dispute resolution as a process or a discrete event?

2. Are good communication skills emphasized and rewarded in your family business, or do you engage in unhealthy communication patterns (e.g., stuffing, triangulation, etc.)?

3. Do you show your family the same respect you show nonfamily members?

4. Do you use customized decision-making standards to help minimize the occurrence of conflict?

5. Do your family agreements explicitly provide for mediation or arbitration in the event all informal attempts to resolve conflict are unsuccessful?

6. Does your buy-sell agreement provide a mechanism for parties to a dispute to exit from the business at a fair price and on fair terms?

CHAPTER 6

You're Ready to Pass the Leadership Baton?

Here's How to Plan a Smooth Transition!

*T*here probably is no more critical challenge for any family business than succession planning—the process of identifying and transferring management authority to the next leader of the family business. In spite of its importance, most families fail to plan for succession from one generation to the next. The most common succession technique seems to be for a family leader to ignore the subject altogether and hope he or she lives forever. This reluctance is no doubt due to the inherent difficulty of the succession process, which is evidenced by the fact that, statistically, most family businesses are unable to continue after even one such transfer and the odds of continuing after a second transfer may be only slightly better than finding a needle in a haystack!

In spite of its difficulty, the transfer of control and authority in every family business is (short of a sale or closure of the business) a biological certainty. A business leader, no matter how extraordinary and talented, can only work and live so long. A family that wants to continue its business, therefore, has two choices:

1. It can ignore the subject of succession and wait to decide who should run the business until the current leader is unable to do so.
2. It can plan ahead and try to ensure a coordinated and smooth transfer of leadership authority.

Without an acceptable plan, some family members will inevitably answer the succession question (and the future course the family business should take) quite differently than other family members will. Without the former leader available to help mediate any differences of opinions between family members on such questions, the eruption of conflict is virtually inevitable. Without, in short, a smooth and orderly transition of authority and control, the vacuum in leadership is sure to unleash rivalries between family members who each stake their claim to the family throne.

Aside from increasing the likelihood of family conflict, the failure to smoothly transfer leadership authority from one generation to the next is bad business, which can create critical problems and inefficiencies for any business. For example, valuable proprietary information that a business leader had may be lost on his or her death or disability; so too may his or her important relationships with customers, suppliers, clients, bankers, and other key contacts. A well-planned transition of leadership authority helps preserve such information, relationships, and contacts.

In light of the inevitability of conflict and inefficiency that results when families fail to plan for the transfer of leadership, the alternative option, developing a succession plan, is the only real choice for a family that sincerely wishes to perpetuate its business. Make no mistake, however; this option is not an easy one either! It is an option that forces a family to embark on a long journey over unpaved and poorly marked roads. Inevitably, most families find that this road's many detours and wrong turns make it difficult to arrive at the intended destination of family peace and business prosperity. Nevertheless, this is the only real road for a family to take if it wants to remain in business.

Since every family's membership and business interest is unique, so every succession plan must be different as well. There are no fixed solutions, no boilerplate succession plans, no succession plan forms that a family can clone from a word processor or business-form book. A family's failure to consider its uniqueness in developing its own succession plan will almost surely spell failure. Indeed, some families may even conclude that they are unable to develop a traditional succession plan, since they have no qualified successor. The succession plan for these families may be to hire professional managers to run the business upon the retirement or demise of a leader or, in some cases, to sell the family business. While this succession plan may be fraught with hard feelings and regret, a decision to pass on the leadership reins of a family business to an unqualified family member risks financial disaster or ruin for the entire family.

While there is no such thing as a generic succession plan, there are, nevertheless, experience and judgment that suggest certain features of the succession planning process are important for most family businesses. Sensitively utilized and intelligently applied, the following six features can enhance the likelihood of a smooth transition of leadership authority and become the cornerstone for your family's unique succession plan:

1. Develop clear and sensible criteria that can be used to select a successor.
2. Clearly communicate what the succession plan is and how the successor has been selected.
3. Utilize outside directors to help manage the succession process.
4. Provide a designated successor with appropriate training.
5. Develop a succession time frame and stick to it.
6. Provide the exiting leader with an opportunity to exit gracefully into some other activity that he or she enjoys.

Because of their respective importance to the succession planning process, each of these subjects will be addressed in detail in the balance of this chapter.

Develop Clear and Sensible Criteria to Select a Successor

One of the first steps to take in planning for succession in a family business is for the family or its existing business leaders to articulate clear and sensible criteria that a potential successor must meet in order to be considered for a leadership position. Such criteria helps ensure that a qualified successor is ultimately selected while conveying to family members a sense that the selection process is not only sensible and fair but can be neutrally and fairly applied as well. As a result, family members are more likely to support the successor who is eventually chosen to lead the family business and less likely to complain that a successor's selection was arbitrarily made in order to favor either a particular branch of the family or a particular family member. This sense of fairness ultimately minimizes the likelihood of conflict that can result from the selection of a successor. Without appropriate selection standards, the process often otherwise results in a virtual free-for-all where multiple family members each think that they are the best qualified candidate for the next leadership position and anyone who disagrees with them is ignorant, spiteful, or jealous.

A number of other advantages may arise from the use of appropriate criteria when selecting a successor:

- All family members are guaranteed due consideration for leadership positions, and frustration and resentment that results from not being considered is minimized.
- By ensuring that only competent family members are eligible for top leadership positions, the family minimizes the negative effects of nepotism, which often results in the excessive employment of unqualified sycophants.
- The selection of a qualified successor enhances the business's ability to attract and retain more capable nonfamily employees, who might find working for an incapable successor intolerable.

The selection criteria should ideally include the following:

- A specified level of formal education
- Requisite job experience outside the family business
- Requisite job experience of increasing responsibility within the family business

These criteria are examined below.

Educational Qualifications

The importance of setting criteria that include formal and continuing education requirements may be best understood by reference to the sheer complexity and difficulty of running almost any substantial business today. For example, negotiating with a bank for an extension of a line of credit, with a labor union for a new contract, or with a customer who wants three shipments of goods separately delivered FOB, FAS, and CIF, are all complex matters. Determining whether to establish (and how to fund) a pension plan or how to comply with regulations and statutes as complex as OSHA, ERISA, FMLA, ADA, much less the Internal Revenue Code, are not easy tasks. And these are but a few of the many complex subjects a leader may be forced to address every day when running a family business!

To competently address such matters, a business leader must have a broad background in a variety of areas, including business, economics, and negotiation skills. This background is usually most effectively acquired by individuals who have received a formal education through college, if not graduate school. Beyond technical information, the study habits and discipline acquired in college, the ability to identify and articulate appropriate questions, and the skill of determining how to research and investigate new subjects, are essential by-products of a good education and are nothing less than requisite skills for a business leader in today's global and ever-changing economy.

Exceptions to compliance with established educational criteria may, in extraordinary circumstances, be justified. Clearly, a number of talented and successful business leaders have had no formal college or university education—a small number. These individuals are increasingly the exception in today's complex society and a prudent succession plan should not be designed around such exceptions. Indeed, a decision to disregard educational criteria when selecting a potential successor should be carefully and only reluctantly made. It may even be a good idea to get the blessings of outside directors to support a waiver of such criteria in order to ensure that making an exception is properly justifiable on the basis of merit, not family bias.

Because of ongoing changes in the world, from technology, management strategies, new accounting policies, and beyond, the education of a potential successor shouldn't end when a degree is conferred. Instead, a potential successor should demonstrate commitment to a lifelong process of education. A family may be wise to formally establish, or informally encourage, appropriate continuing education requirements.

Job Experience Outside the Family Business

The importance of having family employees spend a minimum amount of time working outside the family business is hard to overestimate and, for a number of reasons, often is another useful criterion to establish for potential successors. Children who have worked outside the family business are more likely to have higher self-esteem, knowing that they can hold a job because they earned it, than are children who have only worked for the family and wonder how they would have fared if the position hadn't been "given" to them. Children who have earned a position also tend to have a high level of self-confidence, which is an important leadership characteristic. By contrast, children who have been given a position may have an unhealthy lack of confidence, resulting in undue dependence on their parents or, perhaps, paralysis when their parents are no longer around as a result of death or retirement.

Appropriate training outside the family business also helps a successor establish respect with other family members, key employees, and the community with whom the successor must later work. People are more apt to respect those leaders who have earned their positions. When a family member does enter the family business after having first worked somewhere else, it will be easier for him or her to gain the respect, confidence, and support of coworkers and others. In addition, I believe outside work experience usually helps people learn how to better get along with others, including by developing an appreciation for the importance of compromise, sensitivity to others' feelings, and common courtesy. Experience perhaps enables one to intuitively understand the road to family peace and prosperity and how to enhance it!

By contrast, I believe family members whose positions have been assumed as a result of unbridled nepotism tend to be less sensitive to the feelings of others, less appreciative of the need for compromise, and even less courteous. Such family members tend to contribute to high turnover of talented employees who resent working with incompetent leadership. Less sensitive to the feelings of nonfamily employees (never having been one), family members without job experience in another business may be more likely to fuel intrafamily conflict.

Finally, requiring family members to first work outside the family business makes sense from a pure business perspective as well. Such employees can acquire important skills and experience by working for other businesses that can later be productively applied to the family business. Moreover, such experience outside the family business also enables family members to make mistakes on someone else's nickel.

Mistakes made by young and inexperienced family members can not only be costly but can aggravate other family members as well. Depending on the significance of the mistakes, an inexperienced family employee can really foul up the family business.

Increasing Job Responsibility within the Family Business

Of all the possible criteria that a family may wish to consider when selecting a successor, undoubtedly the most important is requiring a potential successor to work his or her way up the corporate ladder by holding positions of increasing responsibility within the family business. The importance of this criterion is based on the self-evident truth that respect can only be earned, not demanded. A family employee will have a difficult time gaining the respect and confidence of nonfamily members, including employees, customers, suppliers, and bankers. Nonfamily employees in particular may not only be suspicious of a family employee's competence but may resent being ordered about by a young kid, still wet behind the ears, who comes into the business and thinks he or she knows everything. In most instances, the assumption will be that such family employees not only don't know everything, they know almost nothing! Without proving over time and through holding different positions that such family members are competent, unhealthy resentment among nonfamily employees tends to build, to the detriment of the family business.

The value of requiring family employees to climb their way up the corporate ladder also provides an important measure of comfort to other family owners, who may be even more suspicious of such employees' competence, motives, and self-interest. This suspicion manifests itself in an untested employee's decisions and actions being challenged and second-guessed. Their motives for taking action are often questioned. Concerns of expertise, let alone impartiality, tend to enhance the likelihood of conflict. Family members can't simply be promised that an employee is competent and fair; they need evidence that this is the case.

As in other situations, actions by family members speak louder than their words. If an employee works in the business for many years and demonstrates business competence and sensitivity to family issues in a variety of positions of increasing responsibility, the other family members will have more positive feelings about that employee than if he or she walks into the business without any experience or history of treating the family fairly, and, from the beginning, is in charge of a substantial budget and the direction of the business. In such cases, the family employee's authority, which has been given, not earned, may even be counterproductive, since the other members of the family may be unwilling to accept the merit of his or her decisions and more likely to challenge such decisions as unwise or unfairly biased to promote that employee's personal interests.

As with anything else, there is no substitute for experience, and most people are only able to take comfort in entrusting matters of importance to someone who has appropriate experience and has demonstrated a commitment to treating all members of the family fairly. From a business point of view, requiring family employees to start off in junior positions also makes sense. If mistakes are going to be made on the family's nickel (and they will be), at least they will be small mistakes.

A textbook example of how succession in a family business can be smoothly orchestrated is provided by the case of Comcast Corporation, one of the largest cable television operators in the country and controlled by its founder, Ralph Roberts and his five children. In an interview with *The New York Times,* Roberts observed that "[t]he most dangerous thing [in planning succession] is a son or daughter coming into a business where they think they get special treatment. . . . They drag the business down because it kills the morale of everybody in the company." In this family business, leadership is being transferred to Roberts' son Brian, who, according to the report, graduated from the University of Pennsylvania's Wharton School of Business and was then encouraged to work in another family business. When Brian decided to go directly to work in Comcast, his father started him off stringing cables. As a result of this training, Brian is respected by his peers and supported by his family, a good combination of ingredients to improve the likelihood of family peace and business prosperity!

Communicate the Succession Plan to the Family

To accomplish many of its key objectives, a succession plan can't simply be tucked away inside a few family members' heads; it must be shared with all family members. The communication process fulfills a valuable role in minimizing family conflict. Family members can take comfort that a rational plan has been developed and the selection of a competent successor can be ensured. There will be an enhanced sense of fairness as well, a sense that any family member can ultimately assume a leadership role—not only, for example, the oldest son. Through good communication, potential successors will also know that they can't assume that the leadership mantle will be passed to them by mere dint of the passage of time. Instead, such candidates will know (with plenty of time to prepare) that they must satisfy high standards of education, training, and appropriate experience and can't later complain that new "job requirements" have been unfairly sprung on them.

A family council can play an important role in managing the family business succession process by providing a forum within which family members can share their feelings, concerns, and interests about the process. It can provide a vehicle for individuals to express what the family business means to them now, what they expect from the business in the future, including jobs, perks, dividends, and liquidity, and ask questions about how a potential successor might view these interests. A council also can serve as a forum within which different family members can express their opinions and perspectives on all aspects of the family and the family business. This type of communication, among other things, may help the current leader and successor understand the visions of the other family members and so better equip them to work with such individuals in a sensitive manner.

Utilize Outside Directors to Help Manage the Succession Process

Part of the difficulty families have in initiating the succession planning process is no doubt due to the fact that it often requires parents to judge the worthiness of one or more of their children to take over the family company. In many instances, this process requires a parent to select one successor from several children who are potential candidates. It can be very difficult for any parent to acknowledge that one child is more capable than another. It may be more difficult still for a parent to acknowledge that no child is fully capable of running the family business. Perhaps this difficulty helps explain the remarkable talent many parents have for overlooking their children's obvious business-related weaknesses!

While it is difficult for a business leader to select his or her own successor because of the inherent conflict of interest between being a parent and being a businessperson, most family businesses are unable to afford the luxury of selecting an incompetent successor. A successor who is uneducated, insensitive, or simply lazy can ruin a long-established and successful family business in no time at all.

If a business leader genuinely wants the family business to succeed beyond his or her tenure, succession criteria must be carefully developed and rigorously applied. In order to help minimize parents' angst in evaluating their children, the company's nonfamily directors should play an active role in the selection process. Such outsiders can help ensure that the established succession criteria is, indeed, neutrally and appropriately applied. Without the parents' conflicts of interest, such outsiders are better able to fairly evaluate a potential successor's competence to take over the leadership reins of a particular business. Moreover, the outsider's lack of bias will give other family members confidence that the successor has indeed been chosen on the basis of merit, not lineage. Among other things, such confidence improves the likelihood that the designated successor will be supported by the rest of the family.

Provide a Designated Successor with Appropriate Training

A well-crafted succession plan also should be designed to provide a designated successor with appropriate leadership training. Such training should help ensure that the successor will, when in control, be both a capable and a fair business and family leader. Leadership skills are often acquired over time and can almost always be improved in the right environment. Therefore, as part of the grooming process, the successor's skills and weaknesses should be assessed and a customized program designed to shore up the weaknesses. The program should include continuing education, mentoring by key employees and family advisers, and a broad range of experiences where appropriate feedback can be provided.

In some instances, potential successors are simply not prepared to assume a leadership role in the family business when family circumstances require some successor to step into a leadership role. It may be that a potential successor is too young or too inexperienced. Whatever the reason, it usually is a mistake to force the issue and prematurely empower that individual in a leadership role. Instead, it may make more sense to appoint an interim successor who, through previous experience, is sufficiently qualified to assume the leadership mantle. Such an appointment may provide the family with an opportunity to get used to fact that its prior leader is gone and a new era has begun. Over time, the family can continually revisit the leadership structure and, if appropriate, eventually move a family member back into the leadership position.

In a family business, it often is difficult for family members to receive constructive, unbiased feedback. Either the family members don't really want such feedback or the nonfamily employees and advisers are afraid to provide it. Nevertheless, a family that is truly committed to its succession plan must develop a meaningful system for providing feedback to all their employees, particularly its heir apparent. Without a functioning appraisal system, an employee who needs to improve job performance in one or more areas may never do so. If helpful information can be provided, shouldn't it be? A designated successor is more likely to succeed if he or she continually seeks to learn. Formal and informal education is important, but in the business world, there may be nothing more important to the success of a future leader than a meaningful opportunity to learn from mentors and coworkers.

Develop a Succession Time Frame and Stick to It!

A good succession plan also requires family members to agree on an appropriate time frame for when leadership power will be transferred and stick to it. Otherwise, the plan moves from something the family can count on to, at best, a mere aspirational goal, which, in the opinion of some family members, ultimately may or may not be followed. In that instance, the plan loses validity, and the integrity of the plan's individual components lose their credibility as well. After all, if the family can delay or disregard implementation of the entire succession plan, it certainly can delay or disregard particular aspects of that same plan.

Adhering to a timetable can also help ensure that the outgoing leader is around to support and affirm the incoming leader's assumption of authority. Criticisms such as "That's not how Dad would have done it" or "Mom wouldn't approve" can quickly be rejected if Dad or Mom is around to say, "It's time to listen to your new leader, who has my full support."

Finally, adhering to a timetable helps reduce the risk that a family is caught unprepared by a plan glitch that requires a sudden transition in leadership authority. If a plan is well designed, all contingencies, such as the unexpected illness or death of the current leader, are covered. If, on the other hand, the family has abandoned its adherence to a timetable, a contingency plan may, as a practical matter, become irrelevant in the opinion of the leader. If the leader is unlucky, a successor may then be forced to assume a role he or she is not completely prepared to assume.

Develop a Retirement Plan for the Outgoing Leader

Many leaders of family businesses find that their biggest career challenge is letting go of their business. To many leaders, the act of turning over control of a family business to a successor is tantamount to signing their death warrant. Over a long career, the family business inevitably becomes a central part of a leader's core identity. The leader's self-esteem often is tied up and largely based on this leadership position. In such cases, it is very difficult for a leader to let go because there is nothing to let go to. To many leaders, life without the family business is no life at all. In extreme cases, an aging or retiring leader may even consciously or subconsciously want the designated successor to fail so that the leader's role as the indispensable linchpin in the family's success can be publicly confirmed and, perhaps, the leader brought out of retirement to rescue the family business. "Our financial success wasn't due to the business," the leader might like to say, "it was my leadership skills."

To avoid such difficulties, it is important that the succession plan be developed with an eye toward ensuring that a retiring leader has an emotionally satisfying retirement plan to which he or she looks forward, rather than merely accepting. Whether the plan is to move to a sunny climate and play golf or read books by the pool, write memoirs, or go fishing, the business leader must be comfortable moving on to the next stage of life and not "hanging on" to a leadership position in the family business.

If a satisfactory retirement plan is not developed, family conflict becomes very predictable. Indeed, one of the most commonly recurring conflict scenarios within a family business is between an aged leader, who is unprepared to relinquish control of the business, and the successor, who seeks to wrestle that control from the leader. The retiring leader and the new leader are likely to bump heads with each other over a variety of issues, perhaps each other's compensation, the company's dividend policy, or the merits of an aggressive expansion program. While the aged leader must inevitably relinquish authority, he or she can make a successor's career in the family business intolerable. For example, if the retired leader is constantly second-guessing the decisions being made by the new leader, the successor may have a very difficult time gaining the respect and confidence of the other employees. Such action can sabotage any chance the successor may have had for a successful career at the family business.

"Mesh" a Leader's Retirement Plan with an Estate Plan

A retiring leader must make sure a retirement plan is coordinated and meshes with a well-designed estate plan. Ideally, retirement leaves a leader with enough income to satisfy his or her lifestyle requirements. At the same time, however, because of the extremely high estate and gift taxes, the best estate plan may be for the retiring owner of a family business to die without any income or assets and, so, avoid having to pay taxes! Failure to coordinate and balance these competing objectives can be disastrous.

The national media has recently reported that Harold C. Simmons, a Texas billionaire, was being sued by members of his family in a case that was splashed across the nation's newspapers. It appears that Simmons had decided that the best way to reduce his estate taxes was to transfer much of his wealth to trusts established for his daughters. Two of his daughters maintained, however, that his luxurious lifestyle was improperly being supported by these trusts which was "their" inheritance to preserve, not his to spend. Obviously, Simmons' retirement plan bumped head-on into his estate plan!

How a leader transfers both ownership and control in a family business needs to be carefully considered. The challenge of balancing ownership and control is made difficult by the fact that what may be good from a retirement plan perspective (holding onto as much money as possible) is often prohibitively expensive from an estate planning perspective (where the goal, in order to minimize taxes, is to get rid of as much money as possible!). This, perhaps, is the ultimate source of conflict in many family businesses. Fortunately, certain planning techniques are available to family business owners. These techniques are the subjects of the next three chapters.

Retaining Key Employees—A Footnote

Family businesses must be ever-vigilant that they are doing all they can to retain their key nonfamily employees. On a regular basis, this means providing such employees with adequate compensation; good benefits, such as a pension or profit-sharing plan; and related perks. It also means being particularly sensitive to such employees during the transition of leadership from one generation to another. Many key employees are prepared to work in a family business because they are confident that the current leader will "do right" by them. After the leadership baton has been passed, however, such employees may wonder whether the new leader will share that same loyalty. If excessive concern develops, nonfamily employees may feel more secure leaving the family business to start their own (competitive) business or simply going to work directly for an existing competitor.

The succession process must come to grips with this business reality. The process must be developed in a manner that provides the nonfamily employees with a level of comfort that the chosen successor is well equipped to take over the leadership helm and their future is as secure, if not more secure, than ever before. Presumably, the selection criteria and process that will satisfy family members should also satisfy nonfamily employees as well. If it doesn't, the process should be reworked.

Recommendations

Human mortality (a reality that many business leaders seem to ignore) dictates that a family business must, eventually, transition leadership authority within the business from one individual to another. Absent a smooth transition, the business will either close its doors or be sold, in whole or part. By ignoring these simple facts, too many family businesses are forced to accept these unpleasant consequences.

Because conflict in a family business is inevitable, efforts must be made to reduce family tension and struggle by establishing intelligent and neutral criteria for selecting a successor—and then fairly applying such criteria to make the actual selection. Decisions based on all other criteria will, eventually, create problems. For example, a successor selected on the basis of age will be resented by younger siblings who are more qualified. A successor selected on the basis of sex will be resented by a member of the opposite sex who was not seriously considered for the leadership role. Finally, a successor chosen only by dint of being active in the business will be resented by those family members who are not active in the business.

Instead, family members can ultimately feel comfortable about a succession decision only if the chosen successor has demonstrated qualifications to assume the leadership mantle. Such qualifications ordinarily include minimal educational achievement, outside work experience, and experience within the family business in positions of gradually increasing responsibility. The degree of comfort is enhanced if the decision is made in conjunction with input from neutral nonfamily directors. If there is no capable successor within the family, the family should consider hiring a nonfamily member to fill the leadership position or, if that alternative is unacceptable, consider selling the business. In the long run, these are the only sensible options.

Family Business Audit

1. Has your family developed clear and sensible criteria that can be used to select a successor?

2. Do the members of your family understand what the succession plan is and how a successor will be selected?

3. Is your family utilizing outside advisers or directors to help manage the succession process?

4. Is the designated successor for your family business receiving continuing education and training?

5. Does your family have a succession time frame and are you sticking with it?

6. Does your family's existing business leader have a retirement plan? Does he or she have sufficient financial resources with which to retire in accordance with that plan without support from the family business?

CHAPTER 7

You're Worried about Estate Taxes?

Here's What You Can Do!

*T*he process of planning an estate is an inherently unique one, since individuals have different financial resources; personal and family needs; and objectives. One person may strive to leave each of his children with $100,000, while another may strive to leave her children with five, ten, or twenty times that amount. One person may choose to leave most of his money to charity, another may leave no money to charity. In spite of the many differences that exist between individual estate plans, there are at least two assumptions commonly shared by most people:

1. It is better to leave one's heirs with more wealth than less.
2. It is preferable to select who those heirs should be rather than have someone else make that decision.

These two basic observations lie at the very root of the much-heralded estate planning crisis. It is a crisis because an individual's lifetime savings may be involuntarily shared with the government, which can significantly deplete the wealth that can be left to one's chosen heirs.

Many Americans work and save all their lives, planning and hoping to leave an inheritance to their children, other heirs, or even their favorite charities. For many, the cost of attaining this goal is personal sacrifice. Vacations are shorter, homes are smaller, cars are used a little longer. In spite of these lifelong efforts, the largest beneficiary of these efforts is often the federal government, which alone imposes a tax on estates at rates that currently range from a "low" of 37 percent to as high as 55 percent of the total taxable estate! State governments may also impose a separate estate tax, an inheritance tax, or a "pick-up" tax. These taxes vary from state to state and can rise as high as 32 percent for property passing to nonfamily members in some states. And, let us not forget, these taxes are on top of administrative expenses, which are ordinarily incurred on someone's death, such as legal and accounting fees, appraisal fees, probate fees, and the like. All told, most financially successful Americans wind up making substantial "involuntary payments" when they die.

As bad as this problem is for the typical successful American, owners of successful family businesses have it even worse. Here's why: With one significant exception (discussed later), payment of the federal estate tax alone is due within six months of the owner's death. Paying this tax is painful enough when one's assets are comprised of cash, publicly traded stocks and bonds, and other forms of "liquid assets." Raising money to make this payment, however, can be much more difficult when a decedent's assets are tied up in family business stock, which cannot be sold easily to raise money through a stockbroker in the public market. Ironically, the more successful an owner of a family business has been, the more difficult it becomes for survivors to raise sufficient money to pay applicable estate taxes on his or her death! As a result, it is not uncommon for many successful family businesses to be sold upon an owner's death simply to raise the cash necessary to satisfy applicable estate tax obligations.

Financial success does not, however, have to come at the ultimate expense of the family business. With careful planning, salvation techniques are available that often permit the family to maintain its wealth, pay required estate taxes, and retain the family business.

An Overview of the Estate Tax

The federal government imposes its estate tax on all of the assets an individual owns at death, including cash, securities, homes, jewelry, furnishings, and automobiles. The technical term the IRS gives to all of these assets is *gross estate,* and its definition is, well, gross. The IRS is not content to level its tax on what most normal people would typically consider estate assets, such as the foregoing. Instead, it has determined that a wide variety of other assets are subject to its estate tax as well. For example, property that an individual held in joint tenancy is included in the estate. So too are the value of certain annuity payments that are payable to a survivor. Proceeds from insurance policies are also includable if payable to the estate or if the individual retained "incidents of ownership" over the policy, by, for example, having the right to change the beneficiary of the policy. Other assets over which an individual exercises a certain level of control through such devices as testamentary powers of appointment, might also be included in that individual's estate.

The taxable estate, in turn, is determined by subtracting certain authorized deductions from a decedent's gross estate. These deductions include expenses incurred in winding up an individual's affairs, charitable deductions, and distributions to a spouse, whether outright or through a qualifying trust. The mathematical calculations for determining the amount of estate tax due can be summarized as follows:

Gross estate (Individually owned and miscellaneous property)
- **Deductions** (Expenses, income taxes, charitable bequests, debts, certain losses, and bequests to a surviving spouse, etc.)
= **Taxable Estate**
× **Federal Estate Tax** (see Figure 7.1)
+ **Adjusted Taxable Gifts**
- **Gift Tax Paid After 1976,** *except* for gifts made within three years of death
= **Tentative Estate Tax**
- **Unified credit, state death tax credit, and other credits**
= **Net Estate Tax**

The estate tax itself is then computed by applying the applicable tax rate to the taxable estate. The graduated tax brackets as this book went to publication in late 1997 are set forth in Figure 7.1.

FIGURE 7.1 Unified Rates for Federal Estate and Gift Taxes

Taxable Amount (Cumulative)	Federal Tax after Unified Credit* ($192,800)	Tax Rate on Next Block
$ 600,000	$ –0–	37%
750,000	55,550	39
1,000,000	153,000	41
1,250,000	255,500	43
1,500,000	363,000	45
2,000,000	588,000	49
2,500,000	833,000	53
3,000,000	1,098,000	55
5,000,000	2,198,000	55
7,500,000	3,573,000	55
10,000,000	4,948,000	55

*The unified credit is phased out for taxable cumulative gifts exceeding $10 million. This is accomplished by adding to the tax an amount equal to 5 percent of so much of the cumulative gifts as exceeds $10 million, but does not exceed $21.04 million. This credit is adjusted under the Taxpayer Relief Act of 1997.

The Taxpayer Relief Act of 1997

On August 5, 1997, President Clinton signed the Taxpayer Relief Act of 1997 into law. This Act revised the estate and gift tax section of the Internal Revenue Code in several important respects, which are noted throughout this chapter.

Gift tax. To prevent individuals from avoiding payment of estate tax by simply gifting away all of their assets, either over a period of years or on their deathbeds, the federal government also imposes a tax on gifts except if the gift is

- $10,000 or less per year, per donee,
- a payment directly to a school on behalf of a beneficiary's tuition, or
- a payment to a health care provider of a beneficiary's medical expenses.

This Act provides that the $10,000 annual gift tax exclusion is indexed to increase by the cost of living, based on 1997 figures, for gifts made after December 31, 1998, rounded to the next lowest multiple of $1,000. Certain states also impose their own gift taxes on certain transfers, which should be considered with your advisers.

The federal gift tax is imposed by Section 2501 of the Internal Revenue Code on the "transfer of property by gift." Property, in turn, has been broadly defined in the code, tax regulations, and other applicable legal precedents. As a result, cash, securities, real estate, artwork, jewelry, and other tangible property are all considered property that can be gifted. In addition, certain intangible rights and claims are considered property that can be gifted. For example, an irrevocable right to receive income can be the subject of a gift. So too can be uncompensated services, wealth-producing opportunities, interest-free loans, and the below-market or free use of assets. The gift tax and estate tax, although referred to separately, are actually part of one global transfer tax system. The following section explains how this global system works.

Unified estate and gift tax.   Prior to 1977, lifetime gifts of property were viewed separately from transfers of property at death, and a gift tax would be imposed by reference to a separate gift tax rate schedule in the year a gift was completed. As a result, wealthy individuals were able to gift property, otherwise taxable at the highest estate tax rate, to beneficiaries and take advantage of the lowest gift tax rate. While it lasted, this was a tremendous loophole for wealthy individuals, since only they would be subject to the highest estate tax rate but could afford to transfer by gift substantial wealth during their lifetimes and still have plenty of additional assets to live on. Everyone else either would not be subject to the highest estate tax rate or, if they were, couldn't afford to give away sufficient assets during their lifetimes to significantly reduce estate taxes and maintain their lifestyle.

To close this loophole, the federal government combined the estate tax and the gift tax into one tax system in 1977. As a result, these taxes are designed to work in conjunction with each other as part of a unified tax system. Here's how: Since 1977, any taxable gift, except gifts includable in the gross estate, are called adjusted taxable gifts. Adjusted taxable gifts are included in the donor's tax base when he or she dies. By including the amount of the gifts in this tax base, the donor's estate may be taxed at a higher marginal estate tax rate! Such gifts, however, are still only taxed once. In the year the gift was completed, the donor pays a gift tax based on the fair market value of the gift that year. The gift taxes paid are later subtracted in determining estate tax liability.

As part of this unified system, the federal government gives each citizen a credit that is currently set at $192,800. This credit (called the *unified credit,* since it applies to both lifetime gifts and taxable estates under the unified tax system) currently offsets taxes on estates of less than $600,000, which, as a result, should wind up paying no federal estate tax (although they may be subject to applicable state tax). Thereafter, the estate tax kicks in, taxing estates in the graduated rate brackets set forth in Figure 7.1. The Taxpayer Relief Act of 1997 provides that the $600,000 exemption from estate and gift taxes will be gradually increased to $1 million, in accordance with the following schedule:

Year of Death or Gift	*Amount of Unified Credit*
1997	$ 600,000
1998	625,000
1999	650,000
2000–2001	675,000
2002–2003	700,000
2004	850,000
2005	950,000
2006 and thereafter	1,000,000

This all sounds pretty complicated, but an example will help. Let's consider the case of Bob Jones, a widower, who has one son, Peter Jones. Bob makes a cash gift to Peter of $300,000 in 1994. In 1998, Bob dies, leaving an estate valued at $500,000. Bob might be exempt from having to pay gift tax on the 1994 transfer because of the unified credit. Moreover, he was able to give away up to $10,000 tax-free every year of his life, including 1994. However, when Bob dies, his estate tax will be computed as if he owned $790,000 (i.e., $500,000 plus $300,000, less $10,000), not as if he owned $500,000. What's the difference? The estate tax rate for $790,000 will be higher than the rates that otherwise would have been separately imposed on the $300,000 gift and a $500,000 estate! The net effect of the unified system, in short, is to close the gap between the effect of lifetime gifts and deathtime transfers.

Additional Exemption for Family Businesses

The Taxpayer Relief Act of 1997 provides additional (although highly complex) tax relief provisions aimed at owners of family-owned and closely held businesses. Under these new rules, owners of family businesses can exclude up to $1.3 million of an interest in a family business from taxes. With careful planning, therefore, a husband and wife can pass an interest in a family business up to a total of $2.6 million free of estate taxes. The $1.3 million exclusion, however, is reduced by the unified credit (which is now $600,000 and scheduled to increase to $1 million by 2006). Generally, in order to qualify for this special exemption, you must meet all of the following rules:

- The business must be worth at least 50 percent of your estate.
- The business must be owned by you or a member of your family for five out of the eight years proceeding your death.
- A family member must be active in the business ("passive investments" don't qualify for this exemption).
- The family business interests in your estate must be left to a spouse or other close relative.
- Your family must own at least 50 percent of the business (if two families own the business, they must collectively own at least 70 percent of the business and if three families own the business, they must collectively own at least 90 percent of the business).
- The business must be located within the United States.
- If, within ten years of your death, your heir is no longer active in the business, the business is sold, your heir loses his or her U.S. citizenship, or the principal place of business ceases to be located within the United States, the tax saved as a result of this exemption, plus applicable interest, is "recaptured" and must be paid to the IRS.

As an owner of a family business, you should be certain to review this new provision with your business's advisers to determine its possible impact on your estate plan.

The generation skipping transfer tax (GST). Because the federal estate and gift taxes are so substantial, it occurred to many families and their advisers over the years to try to skip the tax by "passing over children" and, instead, transferring assets to grandchildren or even great-grandchildren. The plan may have provided children with income from those assets during their lifetime although, since they never legally "controlled" those assets, the estate tax that would otherwise have later been imposed when their child dies would have been completely eliminated! This, too, was a great planning tool while it lasted. In order to curtail what the IRS perceived to be an abuse of the estate tax system, it now imposes another tax on transfers of property to a beneficiary (or a trust on his or her behalf) who is two or more generations junior to the individual making the transfer. This generation skipping tax (or GST) now prevents people from avoiding a layer of estate tax that would otherwise have been imposed on the member of the skipped generation's death. This was obviously one big loophole the IRS decided it could do without! The GST tax rate is a flat 55 percent, although there is an exemption that permits each person to transfer up to $1 million free of this tax. As a result, married couples can give up to a total of $2 million (plus other exempt gifts, like annual gifts of $10,000 or less) before a GST tax is levied. Payments of medical expenses and school tuitions also are exempted from this tax. Under the Taxpayer Relief Act of 1997, the $1 million exemption is indexed to increase in accordance with the cost of living, based on 1997 figures, for gifts or deaths occurring after December 31, 1998, rounded to the next lowest multiple of $10,000.

Although the GST restricts the usefulness of gifts to grandchildren or great-grandchildren, this may still be a useful planning opportunity that should not be overlooked. For example, assume an owner of a family business has an estate that will be taxed in the 55 percent tax bracket. Therefore, the $1 million that he or she was planning to leave to a child will really be worth only $450,000 after taxes to the child. If that child later passes that money on to his or her child, and assuming the same 55 percent tax bracket for the child, additional estate tax will be due in the amount of $247,500. Thus, only $202,500 of the $450,000 will be left to the grandchild. If, however, the $1 million is left to the grandchild through a generation skipping transfer, the grandchild will receive $450,000, or an additional $247,500! Thus, substantial tax savings can be accomplished through this technique.

Permissible tax deductions.   In addition to the unified credit, Congress has taken several other steps to ameliorate the harsh effects of the federal estate tax:

- It has provided that spouses can leave all of their assets to each other tax-free, with the estate tax being imposed only when the second spouse has died. This is the so called unlimited marital deduction.
- It has provided that individuals can make tax-free gifts every year to as many people as they want to as long as the gifts do not exceed $10,000 per person (or, in estate planning jargon, per donee). Individual gifts above this level get taxed at applicable gift tax rates. This is the annual exclusion gift, so-called because annual gifts of $10,000 or less are excluded from taxation.
- Congress has provided that certain charitable contributions entitle a donor to specified deductions off otherwise applicable estate tax obligations.
- Estates of owners with qualifying interests in family businesses have an option to pay estate taxes in installments over a ten-year period, although the IRS does impose a substantial interest charge for this privilege.

These ameliorative features are often incorporated into many well-crafted estate plans. We'll see how shortly, but first it is necessary to examine the role business valuation plays in the estate planning process.

Tax reform.   The confiscatory nature of the federal estate tax, and the unique problems it creates for family businesses, has not escaped the attention of Congress and business lobbies. A variety of reforms are regularly introduced in Congress to reduce these problems and minimize the pain to family business owners. The Taxpayer Relief Act of 1997 is a step in the right direction, although this new law is extremely complex and still leaves many problems unresolved. One day, it is hoped, the estate tax crisis may be eliminated completely. Business owners, in conjunction with their professional advisers, should continue to monitor how changes in the law might affect their unique transfer plans.

Valuation of a Family Business

Since the IRS imposes its taxes on an individual's gross estate, the value of a family business must be determined so its allocable tax can also be assessed. Determining this value may be the single most important issue for many owners of family businesses as they plan their estate. At the 55 percent tax rate, differences in the final value of a business can have a huge effect on the tax bill. As important as this determination is, however, the valuation process is wrought with difficulty and uncertainty and can prove incredibly frustrating to the owners of a family business and their advisers. While a review of the mechanics of the valuation process is beyond the scope of this book, several observations relevant to family businesses are in order.

The frustration often experienced in valuing family businesses arises from the fact that the valuation process is an art, not a science. There are no correct answers, only accepted approaches. Also, since every family and every business is unique, the approaches followed must accommodate these unique features or the value will be arbitrarily high or low. For example, two businesses with the same financial statement might have a vastly different value if one business depends on a single customer that is on the verge of bankruptcy, while the other business has more than 50 customers, none of which accounts for more than 5 percent of its business. The adjustments to a valuation made in connection with establishing the value of a business pursuant to a buy-sell agreement, discussed in Chapter 5, are often equally applicable in determining a value for estate tax purposes. Consider this subject with your advisers. Since circumstances change, the value of a business can (and usually does) change as well. A value determined at a particular point in time may be outdated within weeks, months, or, certainly, years. Finally, because of the flexibility that is available in determining value, multiple valuations are often commissioned and used for different purposes. For example, owners of a business may want to establish the following:

- A high value when seeking to obtain outside financing or when making a charitable contribution of company stock
- A low value to minimize applicable estate taxes or settlement on a family member's divorce

- A fair market value when seeking to determine the price at which family members transfer ownership interests to each other pursuant to a buy-sell agreement

In recognition of the fact that family and other nonpublic businesses cannot be mechanically valued through application of a single formula, the IRS has established guidelines that should be followed as closely and appropriately as possible. The most significant guideline is found in IRS Revenue Ruling 59-60. In this ruling, the IRS lists the following eight critical factors to consider in valuing a business:

1. The nature of the business and the history of the enterprise from its inception
2. The economic outlook in general and the condition and outlook of the specific industry in particular
3. The book value of the stock and the financial condition of the business
4. The earnings capacity of the business
5. The dividend-paying capacity of the business
6. Whether the business has goodwill or other intangible value
7. Sales of stock and the size of the block of stock to be valued
8. The market price of stocks of businesses engaged in the same or similar line of business, whose stock is publicly traded, either on an exchange or over the counter

Given the combination of facts and circumstances that must be considered in valuing a private business, it is often helpful to combine individual valuation techniques as well to get a blended average value. This may set the stage for either convincing the IRS that the determined value is acceptable, since it is based on multiple approaches, or, at least, that the value should be strongly relied on in reaching an acceptable compromise valuation.

"Discounting" the Value of a Family Business

The valuation process is not finished simply because the value of a family business has been determined. That would make life too easy! Instead, the IRS recognizes that this value may need to be adjusted to reflect certain factors that distinguish a family-owned or closely held business from a publicly traded business. Fortunately for the taxpayer, most of these adjustments decrease the value of ownership interests in a family business resulting, of course, in reduced tax obligations. The two most common adjustments are a discount for lack of marketability and a discount for owning a minority interest in a business.

The IRS has accepted the notion that there is a difference between owning an interest in a public company, which can be sold by simply directing a stockbroker to complete a trade, and owning an interest in a private company, like a family business. For the latter type of business, there is no easily identifiable market in which the owner can sell his or her ownership interest. The difficulty of selling an interest in a private business makes it less attractive than owning an interest in a public business. In recognition of this difficulty, the IRS acknowledges that it may be appropriate to discount the value of a privately held business.

The IRS has also acknowledged that there is an important difference between owning a majority interest in a private business and owning a minority interest (i.e., control of less than 50 percent of the ownership interest of a business). Not only are minority interest owners generally unable to determine business policy, such as, for example, whether profits should be reinvested or paid out in dividends, or even whether the business should be sold, but they are also ordinarily unable to guarantee even being hired by the business, much less determine their salary if a position is made available to them. As a result of the disadvantageous position in which minority owners often find themselves by comparison to the position of majority owners, a discount off the value of their ownership interests is often available.

A corollary to the discount given for transfers of minority interests is that owners of majority interests in family businesses may be charged with a "control premium" on their ownership interests, raising the value of those interests to reflect their desired status. The possibility of being hit with a control premium should be considered with your professional advisers.

Until recently, the IRS took the position that a discount for minority interest would not be allowed in valuing a family business if the entire family continued to own a controlling interest in the business. This position was reversed in Revenue Ruling 93-12, where the IRS conceded that family control should be disregarded when valuing the transfer of a minority interest in a business to a family member.

If a discount for lack of marketability or minority control is justified, a decision also must be made as to how big a discount should be taken. At this time, no simple answer can be provided here. The range of discounts taken by owners and their advisers may range from 5 percent to 15 percent, on the low end, to 45 percent to 50 percent, on the high end. This can be a highly arbitrary decision, and is probably based as much on an owner's tolerance for risk or philosophy on how to best negotiate with the IRS as anything else. It is another decision that the owners of a family business should make in close consultation with their professional advisers.

Estate Planning Techniques

Having considered the broad structure of the estate, gift, and generation skipping taxes (which, for ease of reference, will be generally referred to below simply as the *estate tax* unless otherwise noted), and the significance of determining the value of a family business in order to calculate the tax that is assessable against that business, the "enemy" has been identified and the battle plan can be developed. The table is now set to consider how these taxes can be avoided or minimized. While an entire treatise could easily be written on this subject alone, this section provides an overview of some of the most important estate planning techniques that owners of family businesses can consider with their professional advisers.

Accumulate Assets in Junior Generations

Since estate tax will only be imposed on assets that an individual owns at death, assets that aren't then owned, aren't subject to estate tax. The implication of this fact is often ignored as a planning technique by owners of family businesses. Here's how this technique works. At a certain point, a senior family member (particularly a successful one) might comfortably feel wealthy enough. At that point, the family should determine how to slow down the senior family member's accumulation of even more assets. This can often easily be accomplished by providing that ownership of new business opportunities resides in junior family members. This ensures the wealth created through the success of those opportunities belongs to those junior family members and never even enters the taxable estate of the senior family member.

Deflecting new assets, or the growth in existing assets, away from the senior family member's estate may be the single most important estate planning technique for owners of family businesses and can often be accomplished with very little difficulty. For example, if a family owns a dry cleaning operation with six separate locations, it might simply decide that the seventh location should be owned by the junior generation. If outside financing is required with respect to the new business, the preexisting family business(es) may serve as collateral, or the senior family member may even provide a personal guarantee. Financing the new business, however, can often be accomplished in a manner that shouldn't alter the family's plan to channel ownership of new business interests to members of the junior generation. Channeling new business opportunities away from members of the senior generation can be an easy and effective estate planning tool for family business owners, since it keeps assets out of a senior family member's gross estate.

Similarly, if the family owns a business that is rapidly appreciating in value, transferring all or a portion of that business to junior family members can be a terrific estate planning technique, since the appreciation following the transfer no longer belongs to the senior family member and, therefore, escapes estate tax on that member's death.

An example may be helpful. Assume Mr. Senior has a rapidly expanding dairy business that is currently valued at $250,000. If he sells that business today to his son, Junior, in exchange for $250,000 cash, Senior's "wealth" has remained identical, only its "form" has changed. Assume the dairy business continues to grow, and, when Senior dies five years later, is valued at $1 million. Senior's estate will be obligated to pay estate tax on the $250,000 cash (if he hasn't spent it and assuming he hasn't otherwise profitably invested this money) but the incremental $750,000 in value in the dairy business has been kept out of his estate and avoids estate tax completely!

While it is easier to avoid estate taxes by channeling new businesses away from the senior family members, a variety of techniques can be used to minimize or even avoid such taxes by transferring ownership interests in existing businesses within the family. Some of the more commonly used transfer techniques are discussed in the following sections.

Transfers by Intrafamily Gifts

Estate taxes can be minimized by taking advantage of the opportunity to make certain gifts with little or no tax:

- Annual exclusion gifts
- Unified credit gifts
- Net gifts
- Gifts to spouses

This section considers these planning opportunities.

Annual exclusion gifts.   The Internal Revenue Code exempts transfers of assets in amounts of $10,000 or less per person per year from its otherwise applicable gift tax. As noted above, the Taxpayer Relief Act of 1997 increases this amount after December 31, 1998, based on a cost-of-living change. This exemption is drafted in a manner that permits a spouse to "join" in making the gift, even if the gifted assets are in the other spouse's name, by providing his or her consent to the gift. As a result, married couples can collectively give up to $20,000, or more after December 31, 1998, tax-free to each of their children or other beneficiaries every year. As long as the gifts are made to separate beneficiaries, there is no limit to the number of annual tax-free gifts that can be made under this provision. So, for example, parents with six children could choose to make tax-free gifts totaling up to $120,000 each year to their children.

Families can take advantage of this annual gift tax exemption regardless of the form of the gift. Thus, gifts can be made not only in cash, but in the form of anything else of value, including ownership interests in a family business! The amount of a parent's wealth that can be transferred out of his or her estate by means of annual exclusion gifts to avoid otherwise applicable estate tax depends on the following:

- The value of the business
- The number of beneficiaries who receive gifts each year
- The number of years over which the gifting program continues

In certain instances, this gifting technique alone may be sufficient to transfer ownership in a family business from one generation to the next, tax-free.

Unified credit transfers.   As noted above, the federal government provides each citizen with a credit (the unified credit), which can be taken against the federal tax due on their estate. This credit currently amounts to $192,800, which is enough to offset the tax that would otherwise be due on an estate valued at $600,000. As a result of the unified credit, estates that are valued at $600,000 (or $1.2 million between two spouses) or less should escape federal estate tax completely. As noted earlier, this amount is gradually increased under the Taxpayer Relief Act of 1997.

The unified credit can be used at any time during one's life by making tax-free gifts or, at death, by passing assets valued up to the unified credit amount estate tax-free. Lifetime use of the credit can be made through either a lump-sum gift or multiple gifts over multiple years. For the reasons noted earlier, owners of family businesses (particularly businesses whose value is rapidly appreciating) are wise to consider the merits of using their unified credit by making gifts of their business interests to their family during their lifetime. For example, if a senior family member is able to use the unified credit today to transfer a business worth $600,000 to his children, and that business is worth $5 million five years later on his death, he will have managed to keep $4.4 million worth of value out of his gross estate and, so, avoid estate tax on that amount (roughly $2.42 million assuming a 55 percent tax rate).

Net gifts.   The term *net gift* refers to the sale of an ownership interest in a business for less than fair market value. The seller then uses the proceeds from that sale to pay the gift tax resulting from the bargain element of the sale. By leveraging the gift portion of the transaction with the sale portion, the amount of gift tax is reduced while providing a source to pay such tax at the same time. For example, if a share of corporate stock is valued at $100 and, assuming a 50 percent applicable gift tax rate, the share could be sold by the senior-generation owner for $50. The gift element of this transaction would therefore be equal to $50, which the seller could pay with the proceeds from the sale! The principal disadvantage of a net gift is that the purchase consideration for the ownership interest being transferred must be immediately payable in cash, instead of financed over time, since the senior family member will incur a gift tax, which will be due in the tax year that the transfer was made.

Transfers to spouses.   If the combination of annual exclusion gifts and, perhaps, the unified credit and net gifts by a member of the senior generation is insufficient to complete the transfer of ownership in a family business to members of the junior generation, it is possible to enlist the help of the senior generation member's spouse to assist the cause. Here's how: The Economic Recovery Tax Act of 1981 established the unlimited marital deduction. This deduction permits one spouse to transfer all of his or her assets to the other spouse tax-free— no gift tax, no estate tax. Whether the assets being transferred are $100 or $100 million, the transfer is tax-free.

The ability to pass assets to a spouse tax-free provides several important estate planning opportunities to owners of family businesses. The spouse, of course, can help maximize the tax-free transfers of ownership interests to junior family members by joining or independently making annual exclusion gifts or through the use of his or her unified credit to transfer an additional $600,000 of value tax-free (or a total of $1.2 million between both spouses). Since one spouse typically outlives the other spouse, the transfer of assets to the surviving spouse also provides that spouse with additional time to "solve" the estate tax problem. This may be as simple as continuing the annual exclusion gifts of ownership interests in the business valued at $10,000 or less for the remainder of that surviving spouse's life. It may involve application of some of the other techniques reviewed later in this section. Generally, the longer taxes can be deferred, the better off the family is.

While the additional time to pay the estate tax provided by the unlimited marital deduction can often be helpful, several caveats are in order:

- There may be highly technical tax or other reasons why deferring estate taxes may be inappropriate.

- This deduction is more like a deferral than a classic deduction. Estate tax is not eliminated; it is only delayed until the death of the surviving spouse.
- Many owners are uncomfortable transferring complete ownership interest of their business to a spouse for a number of reasons. For example, owners may be concerned that their spouse will later remarry and their business, ultimately, will wind up benefiting members of another family. An owner also may be concerned that the spouse is incapable of prudently managing the business or its ownership interest. These kinds of concerns do have some solutions, which are considered in the following chapter. Alternatively, however, an owner may feel that the value of the family business is appreciating so rapidly that it may be wiser to bite the bullet and pay applicable estate taxes today rather than risk paying even higher estate taxes on the death of the surviving spouse. Consult your professional advisers to determine whether and how to take advantage of the unlimited marital deduction.

Transferring ownership of a family business through a combination of unified credit transfers, annual exclusion gifts of $10,000, and, perhaps, net gifts, can solve the estate and gift tax problems for many family businesses. If, however, the business is substantial, these transfer techniques may barely make a dent in the transfer of ownership interests. Indeed, if the business is appreciating rapidly in value, the relative percentage of ownership that can be transferred through these techniques alone may be relatively small or negligible. This scenario may be true even if gifts of ownership interests in a family business are continued following an owner's death by a surviving spouse. In that case, other planning techniques must be considered. Some of the more important of these techniques are considered later in this section.

Transfers by Intrafamily Sale

Transferring ownership in a family business by a gifting strategy alone may be inappropriate for at least two important reasons:

1. It may be impossible to transfer complete ownership of a family business from the senior to the junior generation simply through

the use of annual exclusion gifts or the unified credit, since the business is more valuable than the value of transfers that can be made through these techniques.

2. In other instances, the senior family member may not be able to afford to simply gift the ownership away, since that would deplete him or her of a level of wealth necessary to finance the retirement years.

Fortunately, additional estate planning techniques permit ownership interests to be transferred to junior family members by way of sale, not gift. These techniques have the advantage of providing the senior family member with financial liquidity in exchange for an illiquid ownership interest, which can be used to fund retirement needs while facilitating the transfer process. Because of applicable tax consequences, these techniques should be developed in consultation with your professional advisers. An overview of some of the more important of these techniques follows. It is assumed that the price of the ownership interest being sold at least equals its fair market value, so that the family avoids exposure to otherwise applicable gift tax.

Repurchase of ownership interest by the family business.
One possible buyer of the senior family member's ownership interest in the family business is the business itself, which may have deep pockets, while members of the junior generation may not. The purchase can be completed in one lump sum or, to defer taxes on a ratable basis as payments are received, on an installment basis. Because the junior family members hold onto their ownership shares while taking advantage of the family business cash flow, this method is essentially the equivalent of a leveraged buyout, or LBO. At the end of the day, the junior family members are the sole owners of the family business.

If the buyer is a corporation, the purchase is technically referred to as a *redemption*. Unless a redemption meets certain requirements set forth in the Internal Revenue Code, the entire sale proceeds paid to the seller are taxable as ordinary income (a so-called *dividend redemption*). If these limited exceptions can be met, the sale proceeds qualify as a so-called *exchange transaction,* which permits the seller to limit his or her tax to the capital gain on the amount the sale proceeds exceed the basis in the shares sold. Since the maximum capital gains tax is currently 20 percent, while the maximum income tax is currently 39.6 percent, it can be extremely important to structure a redemption sale to qualify as an exchange transaction. Consider this subject with your advisers.

There are four common methods that a business can use to finance its purchase of an individual's ownership interest in the business:

1. Use available cash.
2. Secure bank or other financing.
3. Pay over time pursuant to a "corporate note."
4. Distribute property of the business to the seller in lieu of either cash or notes (ideally through a tax-free split-off).

These techniques need to be considered in light of a family's unique circumstances and, perhaps, even used in combination with each other.

Sale of ownership interests to family members. Individual family members may also be possible candidates to purchase a senior family member's ownership interest in the family business. Such sales (at a fair market price to avoid gift tax) not only remove the appreciation potential of that ownership interest from the senior family member's estate, but they also provide the senior family member with cash that can be used, among other things, to help fund retirement expenses. From a financial perspective, the desirability of a senior member's selling part or all of his or her ownership interest to a junior family member depends, in part, on comparing the current income tax cost of the sale with the potential to minimize estate taxes by removing potential appreciation on the value of that ownership interest from the senior family member's estate. Consider such factors with your advisers. The junior members could fund their purchase obligations either by using their available savings or by borrowing money. Payments might even be made over time, evidenced by a note. Deferred payments may permit the senior family member to defer applicable income taxes under the tax code's installment sales provisions.

Funding a buyout by having the family business distribute additional money directly to the junior family members who, in turn, would use such money to finance the buyout can be extremely tax inefficient, since the funds are taxed on distribution to the junior family members and again on payment to the senior family member. Certain techniques, such as the private annuity and the self-canceling installment note (SCIN), offer a number of tax advantages to intrafamily sales of ownership interests. Consider such techniques with your advisers.

Private annuities.   A private annuity is a legal arrangement in which the owner of a business transfers ownership interest in the business to a family member in exchange for a promise to make specified payments to the seller for life. Properly structured, this annuity can offer a number of advantages. For example, the junior family member is able to finance the purchase of the senior family member's ownership interest over a period of time. Because the annuity payments are calculated based on the annuitant's life expectancy, no payment is due to the annuitant on his or her death and, so, the entire value of the annuity is excludable from the annuitant's estate (and so avoids estate tax!). As a result, the family is able to transfer the business without incurring a gift or estate tax on the future appreciation in the value of the business.

The amount of the annuity payments is determined by reference to actuarial tables set forth in the Internal Revenue Code as well as the fair market value of the ownership interests being transferred. Depending on the seller's actual mortality, this technique can be very attractive. Consider this technique only in conjunction with professional advisers.

Self-canceling installment notes.   Another technique combines the private annuity with an installment sale pursuant to a promise by a junior family member to pay the senior family member for his or her ownership interest over a period of years. The junior member provides the senior member with a note that provides for specific payments over a fixed period of years. In the event the senior member dies before the note is completely paid off, payments are canceled, hence the term *self-canceling* installment note.

A SCIN offers family business owners several advantages:

- It removes the future appreciation in the family business from the seller's estate.
- It removes the unpaid principal balance of the note (which is canceled at the noteholder's death) from the estate.

- It reduces the seller's taxable estate by the amount of capital gains tax paid (on an installment basis) on the sale of the ownership interest.

Because the rules applicable to SCINs are also extremely complex, this technique should be used only in conjunction with professional advice.

Transfers by Sales to Nonfamily Members

It may be desirable for a family to sell all or part of its business to nonfamily members in anticipation of future estate taxes or following the death of a family leader. This decision can be tied to the lack of an otherwise acceptable succession plan or can be part of the estate tax solution.

The most common form of sale involves a straight sale to one or more nonfamily members. As before, this technique may be particularly useful if structured so that the purchase payments are made in installments to help defer applicable capital gains taxes to the selling family members. Obviously, if the family decides to accept payment over time, it not only will want to receive a fair rate of interest, but also will want to be comfortable with the buyer's credit to minimize the risk of default on nonpayment.

Two less common techniques involving the sale of all or part of a family business to outsiders, but as potentially important, are the employee stock ownership plan (ESOP) and the initial public stock offering (IPO).

The employee stock ownership plan. An ESOP is a technique designed to transfer all or part of an ownership interest in a closely held business to the employees of that business. This technique can be extremely attractive because the owners are given substantial tax incentives in connection with that transfer. For example, an owner may sell stock in a corporation to an ESOP established for employees and then reinvest those proceeds in another corporation. Attractive financing is also available to ESOPs. Use of ESOPs requires compliance with complex rules and regulations and should be used only in conjunction with professional advice.

The initial public stock offering.   In certain exceptional cir-cumstances, a family business may be both large and successful enough to go public. By making an IPO of its stock, a family may be able to raise cash to help pay estate taxes and raise substantial funds to grow the business as well. This technique usually provides the best exit strat-egy for family members who would like to cash out of the business, since a public market for the ownership interests is established, which not only facilitates the sale of such interests but establishes the price of the interests as well. Unfortunately, this technique is available to only the most successful family businesses. Applicable securities laws are extremely complex and professional assistance will be required for a family that wishes to have its business go public.

Estate Freezing Techniques

One of the most complex of all estate planning techniques involves what estate planning experts commonly refer to as the *estate freeze*. An estate freeze is designed around a recapitalization of ownership inter-ests in order to

- convert the senior family member's interest to "preferred shares" so that
- the value of the "common shares" is diluted, thus
- permitting the future appreciation in the business's value (which belongs to the common shareholder) to be more easily passed to the junior generation owners.

Let's consider an example. Assume a family business is valued at $2 million, of which $400,000 is currently represented by preferred stock and $1.6 million is represented by common stock. If an additional $500,000 of preferred stock were issued, $900,000 of the total equity would then be represented by preferred stock and only $1.1 million by common stock. Using available transfer techniques, it will be easier to pass $1.1 million to the junior generation than it would be to pass $1.6 million. For instance, a husband and wife could collectively use their unified credit (totaling at least $1.2 million) and transfer all of their common ownership interest to their children tax-free and still have a portion of their credit leftover!

If the preferred stock is distributed pro rata to owners of the family business, the ownership interests are diluted in the same manner so no freezing of value is accomplished without also using available transfer techniques to reduce the senior family members' common interests (which represent the future growth potential of the business). If, on the other hand, only the senior family members trade their common stock for preferred stock (a non–pro-rata recapitalization), the value of the senior members' ownership interests have been independently frozen, since any future appreciation in the value of the business will automatically accrue to members of the junior generation, who own all of the common stock! Because of applicable laws, the estate freeze should be considered only in conjunction with your professional advisers.

Reducing Taxes through Charitable Donations

As noted earlier, the Internal Revenue Code provides a deduction from both gift and estate taxes for qualified charitable donations. As a result, a senior family member can reduce his or her other taxable estate by making the following types of gifts:

- An outright gift of cash or other liquid assets to a charity
- An outright gift of an ownership interest in the family business to a charity
- A gift of an ownership interest in the family business pursuant to a trust

The first option is self-explanatory and the third option is reviewed in detail in the next chapter. The second option is reviewed in the following paragraphs.

A family business owner who contributes stock in the business to a qualified charity, instead of simply cash, may recognize certain tangible benefits, especially if the value of the stock has increased above its tax basis. Donations of such appreciated stock often are referred to as stock bail-outs. Here's how it works. The business owner first makes a contribution of the stock to an approved charity. After the contribution has been completed, the family business then purchases (or redeems) the stock back from the charity. The charity then has an asset it can use (cash) and the family has (again) complete ownership of its business back! Not only does the family member accomplish his or her charitable objectives, but, as a tax-exempt organization, the charity avoids capital gains tax on the redemption even if the redemption price exceeds the basis of the ownership interest. If members of the junior generation already own an interest in the family business, the repurchase of the charity's interest proportionately increases the ownership interest of the junior members. This increase is the equivalent of letting senior family members pass part of their ownership interests to the junior members free of gift or estate taxes. In a very real sense, a gift to charity can very tangibly affect the family as well! Because of complex tax rules, including changes made under the Taxpayer Relief Act of 1997, consult your advisers.

Deflecting Insurance away from the Estate

Another estate planning technique relates to the ownership of insurance. Under the Internal Revenue Code, life insurance that an individual owns is part of his or her gross estate, regardless of who the named beneficiary might be. So, for example, if an individual has assets worth $2 million and a life insurance policy worth an additional $1 million, the total estate would be worth $3 million. After subtracting the $600,000 current unified credit, the taxable estate would be $2.4 million. Assuming a tax rate of 50 percent, the federal estate tax would be $1.2 million.

Alternatively, if this same individual doesn't own that $1 million policy, the taxable estate would be only $1.4 million ($2 million less the $600,000 current unified credit) and, again assuming the same 50 percent tax rate, the federal tax would be only $700,000, a savings of $500,000. That's a lot of money that even the wealthiest Americans would typically prefer to pass on to their heirs or favorite charities!

By contrast to many other estate planning techniques, avoiding tax on insurance policies can be easily accomplished in several ways. For example, an individual can simply give a spouse or child an insurance policy instead of owning the policy on his or her own. Some people are reluctant to adopt this approach, however, because they are concerned that the insurance benefits might not ultimately be used for their intended purpose, such as to satisfy estate tax obligations. An alternative approach that permits a spouse or parent to procure insurance benefits outside his or her estate is to establish a trust to own the insurance policy. Since the trust "owns" the policy, the insurance is exempt from the owner's gross estate. A number of requirements must be met to ensure that the policy's death benefits remain exempt from estate tax, and professional advice should be secured when using this technique.

Miscellaneous Planning Techniques

Myriad other useful estate planning techniques can be used effectively by family members to transition ownership of a family business in an affordable and tax-efficient manner. Without attempting to exhaustively chronicle all of these techniques, this section reviews some of the techniques that many families have found useful.

The "sale-leaseback" technique.   In this technique, the family business distributes designated business assets to a family member who, in turn, leases those assets back to the family business in exchange for rental payments. The technique offers a number of advantages:

- The lease payments made by the business are deductible.
- The distribution is made in exchange for all or part of the senior family member's ownership interest in the business, which increases the ownership interest of the junior family members.
- The sale-leaseback technique can provide a cash stream to a retiring family member. This same technique can be used to provide economic benefits to a family member who is otherwise inactive in the business.

Consulting pay.   This technique is also designed to provide a family member with additional cash, ordinarily to fund retirement expenses. A senior family member who has been active in the business is retained by the business to provide consulting services. A written consulting contract can be helpful in seeking to establish that the consulting fees are deductible by the business. By ensuring that a senior family member receives a continuing stream of income, it is often financially and psychologically easier for that family member to transfer a greater percentage of his or her ownership interest in the family business to junior family members.

Business spin-offs, split-offs, and split-ups. In certain circumstances, it may be possible for owners of a single family business to split that business among different family members by creating multiple businesses. While there are a variety of ways to accomplish this objective, perhaps the most typical is for a family business to transfer one of its divisions to a new subsidiary, which in turn is distributed to a shareholder in exchange for that shareholder's stock in the family business. Consult your advisers in order to ensure compliance with the technical requirements that must be satisfied to accomplish this technique tax-free. This technique also can be used to resolve family conflict if it is possible to equitably split up the family business among the family factions.

Stock bonuses and options. It may be emotionally difficult for senior family members to give up their ownership in a business by use of the techniques earlier in this chapter. An alternative estate planning strategy is based, therefore, not on the transfer of the senior member's ownership interest, but instead on the creation of new ownership interests earmarked for junior family members only. Such ownership interests can be created with a minimum of adverse tax consequences through the award of stock bonuses or stock options. Stock options can be structured in a variety of ways, but typically, provide that a family employee has a right (or option) to purchase additional shares of the family business at a price equal to the fair value of those shares at the time the option was granted. This technique offers two important benefits to a family:

1. It provides junior family members with an incentive to work hard and increase the value of the business without having to worry that such efforts will later prove counterproductive by having to pay higher estate or gift taxes.
2. The senior family member may feel less like he or she is giving up the ownership interest and more like the junior family member is earning his or her new ownership interest.

This strategy may not eliminate the estate tax on the demise of the senior family member but (depending on the aggressiveness of the program) it may substantially diminish its impact.

Life insurance. One of the best estate planning techniques for family business owners often is based on the intelligent use of life insurance. Why? Because there are only a few options available to pay estate taxes. First, the estate may have available cash that could be used. The use of estate cash, however, reduces the amount of cash otherwise available to be passed to your chosen beneficiaries on a dollar-for-dollar basis: Every dollar paid to Uncle Sam is one less dollar that can go to your children or other heirs!

The estate could borrow cash; however, this strategy requires the estate to pay interest on the borrowed money as well, making a bad problem even worse!

The family could decide to liquidate its family business, but the sale might be considered by potential buyers as a liquidation sale and fair market value may be a pipe dream. More likely, the proceeds realized on such a sale will be at a steep discount from fair value, which, of course, adds to the cost of the estate. Moreover, the business is gone forever and, if there was an interest in maintaining family ownership, that objective is gone forever as well.

As a result of these various shortcomings, life insurance has become a welcome planning tool in the hands of capable planners. With appropriate planning, life insurance can be

- inexpensive,
- income tax–free,
- estate tax–free, and
- available when you need it the most to satisfy tax obligations without reducing the value of the estate or requiring the forced sale of the family business.

A good estate plan for a family business usually incorporates one or more life insurance policies. Consider this tool with competent planners.

Deferring Payment of Estate Taxes

The Internal Revenue Code contains several provisions that permit deferring payment of estate taxes, two of which are relatively significant and deserve mention. First, Section 6161 permits a deferral of up to 6 months for gift tax and up to 12 months for estate tax. The extension is requested by filing an application on IRS form 4768 (Application for Extension of Time to File U.S. Estate Tax Return and/or Pay Estate Tax). If an extension is granted, applicable interest on the tax is compounded daily.

By far the most significant deferral provision in the Internal Revenue Code for family business owners is found in Section 6166, which provides, in part:

> If the value of an interest in a closely held business which is includable in determining the gross estate of a decedent who was (at the time of his death) a citizen or resident of the United States exceeds 35% of the adjusted gross estate, the executor may elect to pay part or all of the (applicable estate tax) in 2 or more (but not exceeding 10) equal installments.

The portion of estate tax that can be deferred under Section 6166 is the ratio of the value of the closely held (e.g., family-owned) business to the value of the adjusted gross estate. The first installment on the estate tax payable under this section can generally be deferred for up to five years after the due date of the return. This effectively permits the deferral to actually be spread over a period of up to 15 years. While this might provide a family with much needed relief, the deferral comes at a cost of interest that must be paid annually, even during the first five years when principal is being deferred! Deferring estate tax under Section 6166 involves a variety of considerations, including changes incorporated in the Taxpayer Relief Act of 1997, that should be carefully examined with your advisers.

Retirement Planning: A Footnote

No estate plan is complete without an acceptable retirement plan. Just because a senior family member retires from a family business doesn't mean he or she no longer has expenses! Whether it means owning a second home in a sunny climate, traveling around the world, helping to pay education expenses for a grandchild, or affording more basic expenses such as food, shelter, and utilities, retirement certainly does not mean the end to expenses. Unless the senior family member is able to pay for those expenses without the income that the family business had previously provided, the entire estate plan may be worth little more than the paper it's written on.

While some of the techniques reviewed in this chapter are designed to ensure the continuation of some business-related income to the retiring family member, there are other techniques that should be a part of every family member's plan. These techniques, referred to generically as *benefit plans,* come in a variety of different forms, such as defined pension plans, target pension plans, and profit-sharing plans. Benefit planning also may encompass a variety of deferred compensation arrangements, and the creative use of life insurance to provide retirement benefits. Review of these very important planning techniques is beyond the scope of this book but the reader should consider these matters with qualified advisers.

Relinquishing Ownership without Relinquishing Control

Estate planning for family business owners is unusually complex because it may require the following:

- The application of complex techniques
- Balancing of the need to minimize estate taxes by making lifetime transfers of ownership interests in the family business (and, perhaps, other assets as well) against the need many owners have to retain control of their business, whether for financial, psychological, or other reasons

Let's consider this second requirement. The unlimited marital deduction, for example, is great in theory, since estate taxes can be deferred for the remainder of the surviving spouse's life. Nevertheless, many individuals might be reluctant to simply transfer all of their assets to their spouse on their death. This reluctance may be due to a fear that the surviving spouse is incapable of responsibly managing those assets or, perhaps, that the spouse might later remarry and use those assets to disproportionately benefit another person's family. Similarly, while annual tax-free gifts of $10,000 or less (as adjusted by the Taxpayer Relief Act of 1997) in the form of ownership interests in the family business may help reduce the tax bill, a senior family member may be concerned that his or her children have not yet demonstrated sufficient maturity and competence to manage the business on their own.

As a result of these and numerous other concerns, a variety of ownership transfer techniques have been developed that permit senior family members to retain desired levels of control of a business while beginning the process of transferring ownership interests to their heirs in order to minimize future estate taxes. These techniques can often be blended together with the techniques discussed in the following two chapters to create a plan tailor-made to satisfy each family's unique circumstances. These techniques should be reviewed and updated in recognition of the fact that the life of a family business, much like life itself, is dynamic and ever-changing.

Recommendations

Planning an estate can be quite intimidating because there is so much to do, so many difficult decisions to make, and so many complex tax rules that need to be considered. It often seems better to do little or nothing in the hopes that eventually these concerns will sort themselves out. In fact, procrastination inevitably makes the estate tax liability even worse and prevents a family from strategically transferring ownership of its business in a manner designed to maximize family harmony. As a result, many estates are "planned" in a haphazard manner that eventually contributes to unhealthy family conflict.

Under current tax law, estate tax can always be minimized and often avoided by application of the estate planning techniques considered in this chapter. The estate plan, however, must be sensitively developed to address not simply the goal of tax minimization but personal and family interests as well. The techniques reviewed in this chapter can all be employed to minimize estate taxes and enhance the likelihood of prosperity. In order to accomplish these twin objectives, the family must do the following:

- Forge ahead with its estate plan, and not procrastinate.
- Design its estate plan in a manner that is compatible with the family succession plan.

- Utilize techniques in a manner that looks not just to the short-term goal of minimizing taxes but also to the long-term goal of maximizing family peace. Judicious estate planning, used in combination with the techniques discussed throughout this book, can help a family accomplish these twin objectives.

Family Business Audit

1. Have you estimated the state, federal, and estate taxes due on your death? Have you set aside sufficient liquid assets to pay those taxes and expenses?

2. Have you considered whether to take advantage of the generation skipping tax exemption?

3. Has your family business been professionally valued? Have you considered the possibility of discounting this value for lack of free transferability, minority interest, etc.?

4. Does it make sense to accumulate assets in junior generations of family members?

5. Are you taking advantage of the annual exclusion from gift tax?

6. Have you considered the merits of utilizing your unified credit by making a lifetime transfer of all or part of your family business to members of your family?

7. Have you considered how the unlimited marital deduction fits into your estate plan?

8. Have you considered how to transfer all or part of your family business to family members through techniques that include installment sales, private annuities, SCINs, etc.?

9. Have you considered how to transfer all or part of your family business to nonfamily members through techniques that include sales, ESOPS, IPOs, etc.?

10. Have you considered the merits of an estate freeze for your family business?

11. Have you considered the merits of making a charitable donation or bequest? Have you considered the tax benefits of doing so?

12. Have you considered how to avoid having life insurance taxed in your estate?

13. Have you considered the variety of other available estate planning techniques?

14. Have you considered how your estate plan meshes with your retirement plan?

CHAPTER 8

You're Worried about Losing Control When You Transfer Assets to Family Members?

Here's What You Can Do!

*I*n order to work effectively, the estate planning salvation techniques reviewed in the preceding chapter must be applied intelligently and sensitively. Intelligently, because the techniques have been developed to enable Americans to comply with, but keep to an absolute minimum, the myriad applicable income, estate, gift, and generation skipping taxes imposed by the federal (and, to a lesser extent, state) government, all of which are complex, confusing, and, sometimes, even contradictory. Application of these techniques to secure tax compliance and tax minimization in this environment is never an easy task. Sensitivity in applying the estate planning techniques is also important because a family's unique composition, interests, and dynamics, as well as ongoing changes in the lives of the family members themselves, will make some of these techniques better for some families than for others. Techniques that one family finds wonderful may prove disastrous for another. For example, an estate planning technique that would require a middle-aged owner with young children to transfer control of the business to those children would be silly, although an estate plan for an elderly owner with adult children that did not contemplate such a transfer might be equally as silly. Therefore, the estate plan must be sensitively designed to reflect each family's unique circumstances and adjusted from time to time to reflect the changes in these circumstances; otherwise, what may be a great estate plan today may create a family nightmare tomorrow.

The dynamic nature of the estate planning process can make it difficult to plan today for contingencies that may or may not happen tomorrow. As a result, taking advantage of a technique such as the unlimited marital deduction may be a great tax strategy for an owner of a family business, although he or she may be understandably reluctant to transfer complete ownership of the business to a spouse who may remarry after the owner's death and use the business assets to disproportionately benefit another's family. Similarly, transferring ownership interests in the family business by making annual exclusion gifts worth $10,000 (or more as adjusted by the Taxpayer Relief Act of 1997) to members of a family's junior generation(s) may offer excellent tax savings opportunities but, if those members are young children or adults who have yet to demonstrate financial responsibility, the tax savings may come at a high price.

As a result of the changes in the lives of individual family members and their business, brought by the mere passage of time, estate planning techniques applied without due consideration of a family's particular and dynamically changing circumstances and composition will likely fail. Essentially, such plans go awry because they are made without due consideration of the possibility of conflicts inherent in the estate planning process, which can include the following:

- The conflict between an owner's interest in minimizing taxes, accomplished by transferring the family business and other assets to junior family members.
- The owner's interest in maintaining as much control as possible over the business and other assets until the occurrence of certain events. Among these events might be a qualified successor taking over the leadership helm, a spouse dying without having remarried, or the owner recognizing that he or she has sufficient resources to fund retirement without requiring financial support from other family members or the family business.

I believe that an owner's failure to acknowledge the many inherent conflicts of interest at work in the estate planning process, and the attendant failure to modify his or her estate plan as family circumstances change, are ultimately responsible for precipitating conflict within many families. Indeed, I believe an owner's failure to acknowledge the existence of such conflicts helps explain why families with elaborate and expensive estate plans (if made without regard to the causes of conflict) can be as prone to ruinous family conflict as those that have completely ignored the planning process. Thus, a family leader's final test of greatness, passing on the family business while positioning the family to maintain peace, is one that many leaders fail to pass. All too often, such leaders are dead before the results of their inadequate or ill-conceived estate plans are apparent and they never know the havoc they have wreaked on beloved members of their family.

Fortunately, a variety of techniques have been developed over the years to permit owners to sensitively apply many of the estate planning techniques considered in the preceding chapter in a manner that permits the transfer of assets to proceed while allowing the owner to maintain a measure of control over those assets. These additional techniques can permit a family business owner to accomplish the objectives of minimizing applicable taxes while preserving a degree of control over the family business that, over time, can gradually be relinquished. The more sensitively these techniques are applied and modified over the years, the greater, I believe, is the likelihood that the objectives of reduced taxes and family peace can be secured. In the context of the estate planning process, this is the real objective. Some of the more important techniques that allow a family business owner to wisely "manage" the transition of both wealth and control in a family business in pursuit of family peace and prosperity are the subject of this chapter.

Managing Control through the Family Business

Family businesses can easily adapt a number of voting mechanisms to allow ownership to be transferred to junior generations (to help minimize future estate taxes) while permitting members of the senior generation to retain voting control of the business. Some of these more commonly used mechanisms are reviewed in the following sections.

Voting and Nonvoting Stock

The most common mechanism to manage control in a corporation may be to create two classes of stock, voting and nonvoting. These classes of stock can be created tax-free, and are permitted by S corporation rules as well (which otherwise can only have one class of stock). The stock is distributed as part of the recapitalization in a manner that permits senior generation member(s) to retain all or most of the voting stock and the junior generation to be issued all or most of the nonvoting stock. This permits the value of the business to appreciate in the hands of the junior generation without transferring control. As the junior generation matures and demonstrates its capability to responsibly manage the business, voting control can be transferred. In more complex family businesses, voting stock can be further subdivided into multiple classes, with each class having different voting rights. For example, one share of a Class A stock might be created to provide the equivalent of one vote to its owner, while one share of a Class B stock might be created to provide the equivalent of ten votes to its owner. Consider these possible refinements with your advisers.

Voting Preferred and Nonvoting Common Stock

An offshoot of the foregoing stock recapitalization technique is for the family to create two different classes of stock: a preferred stock, which has voting rights, and a common stock, which does not have voting rights. The senior generation transfers its common stock in exchange for an equal value of the voting preferred, which permits it to retain management control of the business as well as the right to receive a fixed annual dividend payment as required by the terms of the preferred stock. The tradeoff for receiving this fixed payment is that the value of this preferred stock is "locked in" by its terms and the preferred stockholder does not share or participate in any future growth in the business. The junior generation, in turn, transfers its common stock in exchange for an equivalent value of nonvoting common stock. By its terms, this stock has no management control, although any future growth in the value of the business will accrue to the benefit of the common stockholders. As a result, this technique permits the value of a senior generation's interest in a family business to be frozen and any growth in the business escapes estate taxation on the death of the senior stockholders.

Recapitalizing a corporation's stock with preferred and common shares may secure more estate planning benefits than a recapitalization with voting and nonvoting common stock only, since a senior family member who owns voting common stock ordinarily shares in the equity growth of the corporation as a common stockholder. If a business is taxed as an S corporation, however, it is not permitted to have two different classes of stock. As noted earlier, while voting and nonvoting common stock are considered the same class under these rules, common and preferred stock are not. Therefore, a preferred stock recapitalization can only be accomplished in a regular or C corporation. A family operating its business through an S corporation should consider how the respective tradeoffs in these options affect their unique situation to ensure selection of an optimal plan. Analogous techniques may be available in other entities, such as partnerships and limited liability companies, which are able to create both preferred membership interests and common membership interests. These opportunities are considered in the following section.

Freezing Partnership Interests

While many people may think that estate freezes like the two described earlier can only be accomplished in the corporate environment, the same plan can be developed even more efficiently in entities taxed as partnerships, including general partnerships, limited liability companies, and limited liability partnerships. To accomplish the freeze, a partnership agreement is used to create two classes of partnership interests, analogous to common and preferred stock. Holders of the preferred partnership interests (preferred partners) are entitled to receive a specified distribution of cash each year. Holders of the common partnership interests, members of the junior generation, benefit from any future growth in the value of the partnership. Under the terms of the partnership agreement, management resides in the hands of the preferred partners. Unlike corporations, which have a separate level of tax, there is no tax on the partnership itself, only on the partners. Eliminating this layer of tax can be extremely advantageous. While S corporations avoid this entity level tax, they are not permitted to have different classes of stock (only voting and nonvoting stock) so a preferred recapitalization cannot work in that context.

Voting Trusts

Corporation law recognizes that shareholders may transfer all or part of their shares to another person (a trustee) for the purpose of vesting in such a person the voting rights that pertain to those shares. The transfer is ordinarily made pursuant to a written agreement, called a voting trust, which establishes the terms and conditions of the transfer, including the period for which the shares are held in the trust. Essentially, the beneficial ownership of the shares remains with the shareholder, with only the voting control being transferred. Voting trusts can be used to permit members of the senior generation to transfer ownership of a corporation to junior generation members, while placing voting control in the hands of a capable trustee. This permits estate taxes to be minimized while retaining control! Applicable contractual and other restrictions may apply to ensure that this tool is not abused. For example, a well-known estate planning limitation, known as the rule against perpetuities, prevents this trust (as well as all other restrictions on the transfer of assets) from continuing beyond a certain length of time. Discuss such limitations with your advisers.

Using Ownership Agreements to Maintain Control

Senior family members can often insist that the terms of their shareholder, partnership, or membership agreement, as applicable, provide them with a specified level of control over the family business. Such agreements, for example, may give senior family members rights to make certain business decisions, rights to veto other specified business decisions the other owners might make, and even rights to hold specified titles and fill designated positions in the family business. These agreements can provide a measured level of control to the senior family members, while permitting the transfer of ownership interests to junior family members to help minimize otherwise applicable estate taxes. Because estate tax rules are complex and business laws may vary from state to state, consult your professional adviser to determine how such an agreement can be structured for your family business.

Managing Control through Trusts

Trusts are remarkably effective planning techniques that have a respected and long tradition of use by estate planners to help manage the transfer of wealth from one generation to the next. In order to understand how trusts can be effectively used by owners of family businesses, a basic background in terminology is important. Trusts are separate legal entities, created by *grantors,* to hold title to assets, which are referred to as the *corpus.* The trust assets are managed by *trustees* for the benefit of designated individuals, referred to as *beneficiaries,* pursuant to an agreement between the grantor and trustee, called the *trust.*

Trust law has evolved over time to permit the delegation of broad power by a grantor to a trustee to make decisions on behalf of the beneficiary. As a result, many trusts are drafted to permit the trustee to exercise wide discretion in managing the trust assets as well as to retain outside professional advisers, including lawyers, accountants, and investment counsel.

Historically, trusts have been widely used by family members to protect the interests of incompetent, disabled, or young family members by making sure a competent manager (the trustee) is available to manage assets on their behalf. Trusts can also offer owners of family businesses the following:

- An opportunity to eliminate or minimize estate taxes
- Protection from creditors
- Protection against claims arising out of a family member's divorce

Estate Tax Savings

Under current estate tax law, individuals pay taxes not only on property that they own when they die, but also on certain other property, including that which has been transferred but over which the individual has retained control or in which he or she has maintained a beneficial interest. This provision creates an important distinction between two types of trusts: the revocable trust and the irrevocable trust.

Revocable trust. Also commonly referred to as a *living trust,* the revocable trust is simply a device that many advisers tout as the greatest way to avoid the costs and expenses of probate. The assets in the living trust are intended to be used by the grantor who, retaining the right to use those assets, is also a beneficiary. Since the grantor has retained a very meaningful beneficial interest in the trust property, living trusts, contrary to popular misconception, do not reduce estate taxes. Indeed, all of the assets the grantor places in a living trust are subject to applicable estate taxes on his or her death.

Irrevocable trust.   By contrast, the irrevocable trust is designed to transfer property out of the control of the grantor for the benefit of another party, the beneficiary. In order to satisfy the requirement that the grantor not retain control over assets in order to keep such assets out of his or her estate, the trust is made irrevocable. This designation essentially means that the grantor cannot change or revoke the terms of the trust at any time in the future. By providing that the terms of the trust are irrevocable, the IRS cannot argue that the grantor has control, which rests only in the hands of an independent trustee. A variety of different forms of irrevocable trusts have been developed in order to permit grantors to transfer assets out of their estate while maintaining a degree of practical if not legal control over those assets through both the terms of the trust agreement and the selection of independent, yet friendly, trustees. Some of the more commonly used types of trusts are considered later in this chapter.

Protection from Creditors

Asset protection, long a popular subject among business owners, has become a buzzword of the 1990s. With the cost of litigation skyrocketing, astronomical jury awards, and the propensity for Americans to sue each other, a family business without a modicum of asset protection strategies in place is a sitting duck. As a result, the asset protection benefits of trusts are quite popular among many family business advisers.

This popularity is largely due to the fact that state trust law protects beneficiaries of irrevocable trusts from claims of creditors. While laws vary from state to state, creditors are often unable to assert direct claims against assets held in trust for a beneficiary. A trustee, moreover, may determine not to distribute trust income or principal to a beneficiary, which usually means that the creditor has no right to such income or principal either. Some states even permit trusts to be drafted with mandatory forfeiture clauses, which terminate a beneficiary's interest in a trust in the event a creditor attempts to assert a claim against the trust. State laws do, however, prevent trusts from being established with the intent to hinder or defraud creditors. This essentially precludes individuals from transferring their assets to a trust on the eve of litigation or bankruptcy. Discuss these limitations with your advisers.

Protection from Matrimonial Claims

Irrevocable trusts can also protect the trust beneficiary from claims against the trust assets that might arise in the case of the beneficiary's divorce, particularly with respect to claims against property interests. Because matrimonial law generally exempts from equitable distribution property that one spouse acquired by gift, a gift in trust helps ensure that a beneficiary's property remains separate and outside the pot of marital assets otherwise subject to distribution. Since a trust can help ensure that certain assets remain separate property, not marital property, gifts of ownership interests in a family business, for example, by senior family members to junior family members may not be subject to equitable distribution in the event of a junior family member's divorce.

Creating an Irrevocable Trust for a Spouse

As noted in the previous chapter, the unlimited marital deduction permits an individual to leave all assets to his or her spouse, either during life or at death, without incurring either gift or estate tax. This is often a tremendous tax planning opportunity for married owners of family businesses, since it allows applicable tax to be deferred until death of the surviving spouse. In the meantime, that surviving spouse may take advantage of available transfer techniques to dispose of part or all of that property from his or her estate, and, so, avoid or minimize estate taxes on that property at death. This may be as basic as continuing to transfer ownership interests in the family business to junior family members every year in amounts valued at $10,000 (or more under the Taxpayer Relief Act of 1997) under the annual gift tax exclusion.

While the tax advantages provided by the unlimited marital deduction are obvious, many people are uncomfortable transferring all of their assets to their spouse. This may be due to a variety of reasons, although the most common are (1) concern that the surviving spouse is unprepared and ill equipped to manage the money and (2) the surviving spouse may later remarry and the assets disproportionately benefit members of another family.

In order to qualify for the unlimited marital deduction, tax law provides, with few exceptions, that the property being transferred from one spouse to the other spouse must include all rights of ownership to the property and that those rights cannot terminate. Those few exceptions, however, have provided estate planners with just enough room to let their clients with sufficient assets have their cake and eat it too! The key planning tool that is generally used to accomplish these objectives are different types of trusts. Here's how.

The Marital Deduction Trust

This trust is designed to qualify for the unlimited marital deduction while permitting the management of control over assets placed in trust. While this trust can also be flexibly designed, it has two basic requirements:

1. The surviving spouse must be given the right to use all of the income generated by the trust assets for life.
2. The surviving spouse has the right to dispose of trust assets to anyone.

This right to dispose of the trust property is referred to as a *power of appointment*. The surviving spouse is not required to actually exercise that power, however, and, in his or her failure to do so, the disposition of trust assets would be made in accordance with the provisions of the will of the first spouse to die.

The QTIP Trust

Another special trust recognized by the IRS as qualifying for the unlimited marital deduction even though the surviving spouse lacks full

control and enjoyment of the transferred property is known as the qualified terminal interest trusts or QTIP. Basically, a QTIP trust provides a
surviving spouse with all of the income generated by assets of the trust
for the remainder of that spouse's life. The trust can be created to provide the trustee with a range of authority, including the right to invade
the principal of the trust for the surviving spouse's benefit. The surviving spouse, in turn, has no power to use the principal for another beneficiary during his or her lifetime, although the trust can be prepared to
give that surviving spouse authority to determine who gets that trust
property at his or her death. This option can either be limited, so that the
surviving spouse must pick among designated potential beneficiaries
(such as only the spouses' children), or not exercised, so that the grantor
spouse decides who should benefit from the trust assets after the death
of the surviving spouse. The property held in the QTIP trust is includable in the surviving spouse's estate and, so, is subject to estate tax on
their death. Although QTIP trusts are only available if the surviving
spouse is a U.S. citizen, a variation of this trust, known as the QDOT
trust (qualified domestic trust), permits similar benefits when one
spouse is not a U.S. citizen and should be considered where appropriate.

The Bypass Trust

When designing a plan to transfer assets to a spouse in order to take
advantage of the unlimited marital deduction, care should be exercised
to ensure that the benefit provided by the unified credit is not wasted!
Remember, every U.S. citizen can currently pass up to $600,000 worth
of assets tax-free to anyone during that citizen's life or at death. If this
planning option is ignored on the death of the first spouse, and all assets
are simply passed to a spouse pursuant to the unlimited marital deduction, the credit is lost forever. Fortunately, a simple technique has been
developed to let spouses take advantage of both the unlimited marital
deduction and the unified credit. This technique is implemented
through what is referred to as the *bypass trust,* often called the *credit
shelter trust.*

The bypass trust is set up so that up to $600,000 of an individual's
assets will be segregated into a separate trust for the ultimate benefit of
that person's children or other heirs on his or her death. Under the terms
of the trust, the surviving spouse can be provided with income gener-

ated by the assets held in the trust during his or her lifetime. If necessary, the trust assets themselves can also be used to provide support for the surviving spouse. On the later death of the surviving spouse, the assets held in trust are transferred to the beneficiaries of the trust. In order to ensure that an individual's unified credit can actually be used as contemplated by this strategy, it is necessary that both spouses have assets in their own names worth at least $600,000 (for a total of at least $1.2 million), adjusted upward under the Taxpayer Relief Act of 1997. This sometimes requires one spouse to transfer assets to the other spouse (which is a tax-free transfer) so that the entire value of the unified credit can be used. Otherwise, a spouse who owns assets valued at less than this amount can only take advantage of the tax-free transfer opportunity up to the value of the assets actually owned. The difference between that value and the unified credit exemption permitted is wasted.

Spousal Planning Summary

The unlimited marital deduction provides a business owner with the next best option to not paying estate tax: to defer it. As a result, it is often desirable to transfer assets to the surviving spouse and delay the payment of otherwise applicable taxes. This tax savings strategy can be accomplished by either transferring the assets with no strings attached or transferring the assets with strings attached, pursuant to the terms of a QTIP or marital deduction trust. A family's unique circumstances should be considered when developing this plan so the terms of the trusts, if any, can be appropriately prepared. Whether assets are transferred outright or through one of these trusts, the spouses should both be certain to utilize the full amount of their unified credit through use of a bypass trust. A business owner can help ensure a strategic transfer of management power in a family business, if necessary, by giving careful consideration to the terms of the trust instrument(s) as well as the selection of the trustee(s).

Creating an Irrevocable Trust for a Child

As noted in the previous chapter, senior family members can transfer ownership interests to junior members of the family to both reduce their assets to minimize their taxable estate and eliminate the future appreciation in value on those transferred assets from their estate. Typically, such transfers are accomplished by taking advantage of the annual exclusion from gift tax and making gifts of ownership interests in the family business valued each year and, on occasion, transferring ownership interests by using up all or part of the senior family member's unified credit. A commonly used technique that permits these transfers to be made without ceding control over those ownership interests to the junior family members—who may be minors, inexperienced or incompetent businesspersons, or spendthrifts—is to transfer the ownership interests in trust for the benefit of the junior family members. Here's how.

The senior family member creates a trust, pursuant to a trust agreement, and names a member of the junior generation as the beneficiary of the trust. In order to guarantee that the senior family member does not retain control over the assets held in trust or incidents of ownership over the trust, the trust is made irrevocable and an independent trustee is selected. Instead of making annual exclusion (tax-free) gifts directly to the junior family member, the senior family member instead makes such gifts directly to the trust. In order to satisfy the requirement that the gift is a "present interest" in the assets being gifted, a "Crummey Notice" is then sent to the beneficiary of the trust, advising him or her that a gift has been made to the trust, which, if the beneficiary desires, can be withdrawn from the trust for his or her direct enjoyment.

Crummey Notices are usually drafted to limit a beneficiary's right to make a withdrawal from the trust for a limited time period. After that time period expires, the gift in trust becomes final. While the junior family member has a theoretical legal right to exercise the withdrawal rights, this is seldom done in practice because the junior member is anxious to cooperate with the senior member's estate plan and may tacitly understand that if the right is exercised, no additional gifts will be given in the future! As a result of these and other practical limitations on a beneficiary's withdrawal rights, the IRS closely scrutinizes gifts made in Crummey trusts. Nevertheless, in spite of repeated criticisms, the gift-in-trust program continues to withstand challenge if properly executed and permits the transfer of ownership to proceed in conjunction with the exercise of control by an independent trustee.

"Split-Interest Trusts" that Benefit Parents and Children

As previously discussed, it may be tax-efficient to remove an asset from a parent's estate to avoid future estate tax, yet financially unrealistic or unwise for that parent to do so, since a complete transfer of an asset to a child may deprive the parent of funds needed for retirement years. A number of creative solutions, which involve using the trust vehicle to split the ownership interests of assets between different beneficiaries, have helped solve this problem for many families. Here's how.

Parents can contribute assets to a trust (including ownership interests in family businesses!) for the benefit of their children. Unlike the classic trust, for which there is only one beneficiary, this trust has two beneficiaries, the parent and the child! This is accomplished by preparing the trust in a manner that permits the parent to receive a payment for a specified period (say five, ten, or fifteen years). At the end of the chosen time period, the assets in trust pass to the children. This type of trust is commonly referred to as a grantor retained annuity trust (GRAT), since the grantor of the trust receives an annuity payment for a specified time period. Alternatively, the trust can be prepared so that the parent receives a payment for the balance of his or her life, with the assets then passing on to the children. This trust is commonly referred to as a grantor retained unitrust (GRUT).

One of the principal advantages of such trusts is that only the actuarial value of the assets placed in trust that will eventually pass to the children or other trust beneficiary is deemed to be a gift for gift tax purposes. Since these beneficiaries are receiving a future gift (i.e., the right to receive trust assets after the established time period during which the assets are used for the benefit of the parent), a gift with a high fair market value can be transferred at a discounted gift tax rate! The precise value of the gift is determined by reference to a number of factors:

- The term for which the grantor is retaining an interest in the assets
- The interest being retained by the grantor

- The percentage of assets being paid each year, if applicable
- Actuarial tables under the Internal Revenue Code
- The current applicable federal interest rate

The value of the future gift to the children or other beneficiaries is subject to gift tax, although the grantor's estate receives a credit on the federal estate tax in the amount of gift tax paid.

The transfer of assets to a GRAT or a GRUT provides a parent with an opportunity to retain necessary income during the balance of his or her life, while locking out any appreciation in the value of the transferred asset from the estate. These trusts can also be structured so that the assets are not gifted to the children but instead are sold, perhaps through financing techniques, which include installment notes or self-canceling installment notes.

Let's consider an example of how a GRAT could be used to help transfer ownership of a family business. Assume Mr. Senior owns 70 percent of a family business worth $2 million. His three children each own 10 percent. Senior transfers his 70 percent interest into a GRAT, in return for which he gets a 70 percent interest of the business profits for, say, ten years. Based on historical performance, this return will amount to approximately $150,000 each year. After the trust expires in ten years, Senior's 70 percent ownership interest is transferred to his children. Let's assume that, based on the factors noted earlier, Senior's interest in the trust is worth $1 million ($150,000 times ten years, less applicable discount rate). The gift (without any discounting of the business for minority interest or lack of transferability, etc.) is worth $1 million, not $1.4 million, a savings of $400,000! Even using a conservative discount on the business interest, this savings could grow even bigger. Moreover, unlike a sale of the business from Senior to his children, in which he would realize a capital gains tax on the sale, the transfer of the interest through the GRAT is accomplished without any capital gains tax. As a result, Senior has accomplished the following:

- Provided himself with an income stream for ten years
- Avoided capital gains tax
- Transferred his business to his children at a discounted value and, so, saved substantial gift tax

Because of their complexities, these trusts should be used only with the assistance of professional advisers. Properly utilized, they offer tremendous planning opportunities to many family business owners.

Creating a Generation Skipping Trust for a Grandchild

As noted in the previous chapter, individuals can reduce otherwise applicable estate and gift tax by transferring assets to grandchildren, thus bypassing the imposition of tax that would otherwise have been levied on the death of their child. Although Congress enacted the generation skipping transfer tax (GST) in 1976 to reduce the loss of the layer of tax on the child's death, an exemption to this tax permits an individual to transfer up to $1 million during his or her lifetime, or at death, to grandchildren (and great-grandchildren) free of the GST. As noted earlier, the amount of the exemption is increased under the Taxpayer Relief Act of 1997, based on the cost of living index. Generation skipping transfers that exceed this exemption are subject to a flat tax rate (equal to the maximum estate tax rate) of 55 percent.

A family member may be reluctant to transfer an ownership interest to a grandchild for the same reasons a senior family member may be reluctant to transfer an ownership interest in a family business outright to a child. Such transfers can be made into a trust for the grandchild, often referred to as a generation skipping trust. Ordinarily these trusts are designed so that the income generated by the trust assets is paid to the grandparent's child during his or her lifetime, with the assets passing to the grandchild on the child's death. A competent trustee is selected in order to help ensure a consistent management approach. Extremely wealthy families, who are already struggling to reduce estate tax obligations in junior generations, may find it desirable to not only skip a single generation but two generations at the same time! A double skip transfer would skip over children and grandchildren by transferring assets directly to great-grandchildren, or to trusts for their benefit. As long as certain limits are adhered to, trustees could include family members, perhaps the parents of the great-grandchildren. The generation skipping transfer tax is extremely complicated and the trusts described in this section should be developed only in connection with professional assistance.

Creating an Irrevocable Trust for a Charity

As noted in the previous chapter, an individual's gifts to qualified charities during that person's life or at death reduces the size of his or her gross estate. In many instances, charitable contributions are given outright; in other instances, however, a donor may be reluctant to give away an entire asset, preferring instead to retain some interest in that asset for a period of time. In order to accommodate this preference, planning techniques have been developed that allow individuals to split the ownership interests in an asset, permitting one interest to be donated while retaining the other interest. The interests are usually split into the earnings from the assets (the income portion) and the assets themselves (the principal portion). The amount of the tax deduction, in turn, depends upon a variety of factors:

- The value of the asset
- The percentage of the income interest to be paid
- The period over which the income interest is paid. If the period is based on a donor's life, with or without a spouse, the period is measured by reference to mortality tables provided by the IRS.

A discussion of several techniques that permit the splitting of interests in connection with charitable contributions follows.

Charitable Remainder Unitrust

During the donor's lifetime, he or she receives a distribution based on a fixed percentage of the fair market value of assets contributed to this trust. Therefore, if the value of the assets increases, the amount of the distribution increases as well. If the value decreases, that distribution decreases. On the donor's death, the trust assets pass outright to the designated beneficiary or beneficiaries.

Charitable Remainder Annuity Trust

This technique is almost identical to the charitable remainder unitrust except that the donor receives a fixed dollar amount from the trust every year, regardless of the value of the trust assets.

Charitable Lead Trust

Trusts have also been developed that reverse the split in the interests from those noted earlier. For example, income from assets in a charitable lead trust, or charitable income trust, is distributed to the charity for a specified period. Thereafter, the trust assets are distributed to the donor's heirs.

The Taxpayer Relief Act of 1997 has added several new requirements and provisions relating to the tax treatment of charitable trusts. Before utilizing this planning technique, you should review these requirements with your professional advisers.

Charitable Contributions of Family Business Interests

In addition to receiving a tax deduction for making a charitable contribution, there may be another important benefit for the donor if donated assets consist of appreciated stock in a family business.

Consider the following scenario: An owner donates family business stock to a qualified charity, entitling the owner to receive a tax deduction based on a variety of factors. The charity then turns around and sells the stock to a third party without incurring a capital gains tax (because it's a charity). The charity then reinvests its cash proceeds and uses the investment income to pay the donor for a specified period, perhaps the donor's life.

As a result of these various steps, the following has occurred:

- An asset has been donated to a favorite charity, which provides the donor with a tax deduction.
- The sale of the stock by the charity turns an illiquid asset into a liquid asset.
- These should provide the donor with increased cash flow for the balance of his or her life.

In many instances, the donor uses part of that cash flow to purchase life insurance (in an irrevocable trust to ensure that it is not later taxed on his or her death!) in an amount of the donated asset left to the donor's heirs on his or her death in replacement of the donated asset. As a result, the charity is better off (since it has received a donation), the donor is better off (since he or she has received a tax deduction and increased cash flow), and the donor's beneficiaries are better off (since they have the insurance proceeds tax-free instead of an asset on which they must pay tax). The rules that permit these various benefits are, not surprisingly, complicated and, again, the advice of professionals is recommended.

The Trouble with Trusts!

The creative use of trusts as a planning tool for family business owners is not without certain disadvantages. Following are the most commonly cited disadvantages:

- The loss of an unacceptable level of control (in an irrevocable trust) to a trustee
- The complexity of the trust arrangement

Let's consider these problems.

Trusts (with the exception of a living trust, which has no estate tax savings benefits and is simply a device to avoid probate) all require the grantor to appoint an independent trustee to manage trust assets. Such independence is required—under applicable tax rules, if the grantor (who establishes the trust) serves as the trustee, he or she is considered to have retained an incident of ownership over the trust assets. This essentially means the assets haven't been transferred by the grantor and so remain in his or her gross estate (and therefore are taxable on his or her death).

Make no mistake—in some instances, the selection of an independent trustee is highly desirable and there is no disadvantage in the use of a trust as an estate planning technique. For example, a marital deduction or QTIP trust is established on a grantor's death and the whole purpose of the trust is to ensure that a qualified third party is available to help the surviving spouse manage and preserve assets held in such trusts.

In other instances, however, the requirement that an independent trustee be selected can be an uncomfortable requirement for many individuals, since it requires the irrevocable relinquishment of their control over the assets they transfer to a trust. Moreover, the selection of an independent trustee may be difficult in a family where there are multiple candidates, such as siblings, and a decision to select one sibling to serve as trustee can be perceived as favoritism, while the decision to use all the siblings results in an unworkable structure where there are too many decision makers. Moreover, in a world where conflicting interests are the norm and individuals view the world in their own unique way, many people find it difficult to identify a trustee who not only possesses the requisite intelligence and prudence to serve as a trustee, but can also be trusted to carry out the grantor's desires, which may change over the years for a variety of reasons.

Aside from the problems grantors may have when establishing trusts, the trust beneficiaries often resent not having control (or even the appearance of control to the outside world) over their assets. Although trusts are often established to protect such individuals from creditors or claims asserted in a divorce, many beneficiaries believe that they are fully capable of handling their own affairs and that a trust is a tool that unnecessarily ties their hands to satisfy the unwarranted concerns of the grantor, typically a parent or grandparent. In such instances, this resentment can create difficult interpersonal dynamics between the beneficiaries and the trustees.

In addition to these control problems, trusts can suffer from another important drawback: They can be extraordinarily complex to establish, fund, and maintain. For example, a few of the requirements that trusts must ordinarily meet include establishing the following:

- Incidents of ownership are not maintained by the grantor in order to avoid unexpected estate tax problems.
- Applicable trusts meet separate and additional qualifications to own stock in S corporations.
- Restrictions such as the rule against perpetuities do not apply.
- Invasion powers are properly set up (permits the use of principal assets, not just income generated from these).
- Crummey Notices, if applicable, must be provided.

This list of requirements could be continued and, to the nonprofessional, would likely seem endless and bizarre. Thus, the challenge for owners of family businesses can sometimes come down to finding tools that

- permit their transfer of ownership interests to minimize future estate taxes, while
- preserving their control over the assets (and not relinquishing control to independent trustees), and
- minimizing complexity of the arrangement.

I believe that the challenge in finding tools that satisfy all of these requirements is so daunting that many owners of family businesses simply give up and ignore seriously addressing the estate tax problems that their children are sure to face on their demise. Instead, such owners may utilize one or even several estate planning techniques, but ultimately accomplish far less than they could if they didn't have these concerns. This phenomenon perhaps explains why so many family business owners spend most of their time working in their business, not on it.

Fortunately, this sad reality can be changed. In the past few years, a new tool has emerged that permits family business owners to minimize their estate taxes while gradually relinquishing control over the family business to junior family members at a comfortable pace, all within the framework of a relatively basic and straightforward structure. The tool, called a limited liability company, or LLC for short, is the subject of the following chapter.

Recommendations

Estate planning for owners of family businesses is often complicated by the number of competing interests. A senior owner is advised to minimize estate taxes by reducing assets, but that owner typically is concerned about retaining sufficient resources to fund his or her retirement years and, perhaps, a degree of control over operations of the family business, at least until the succession plan has been completed. Moreover, that owner may be concerned that the children or spouse who is receiving the assets may be incapable of responsibly handling those assets in a manner that is consistent with the owner's desires.

A number of estate planning techniques have been developed to permit asset to be transferred while managing the transfer of the control associated with those assets. Voting mechanisms available in business forms like corporations or limited liability companies often permit control to be managed through voting structures, agreements, etc. In addition, the trust vehicle can be creatively used for the benefit of children, spouses, charities, and (through vehicles like GRATs and GRITs) even the owners themselves. Planned in conjunction with the family business succession plan, the senior owner's estate and retirement plans can be smoothly meshed together to form an overall family transfer plan that can increase the likelihood of family prosperity.

Family Business Audit

1. Do your estate, retirement, and succession plans mesh to accomplish all of their objectives in a consistent manner? Are assets being transferred as part of these plans in a manner that sensitively manages the transition of management control of your family business as well?

2. Have you considered the merits of managing control in your family business through such tools as voting and nonvoting stock, common and preferred stock, and voting trusts?

3. Have you considered the merits of employing a freeze technique?

4. Have you considered how your business ownership agreements (e.g., shareholder agreements) can be used to manage control in your family business?

5. Have you considered how to transfer assets to a spouse, children, grandchildren, great-grandchildren, or charity through one or more different types of trusts?

6. Have you considered the advantages and disadvantages of transferring assets to a trust?

CHAPTER 9

Do You Want to Reduce Taxes and Retain Control?

Consider Establishing a Family LLC

*L*imited liability companies (LLCs) have lately received widespread attention from professional advisers in all circles. Attorneys, accountants, financial planners, and others have all heralded the arrival of the LLC as one of the most significant business and legal developments of this generation. Trade journals in many industries have trumpeted its benefits and encouraged trade members to meet with their professional advisers to explore the potential advantages of operating as an LLC. Indeed, many such advisers now presume that any new business should be established as an LLC unless the peculiar facts and circumstances of that business indicate otherwise! This exciting new business tool is explored in detail in my book, *How to Profit by Forming Your Own Limited Liability Company* (Chicago: Dearborn Financial Publishing, 1996).

LLCs can offer several particular benefits to owners of family businesses:

- Provide a vehicle for senior family members to transfer ownership interests to junior family members, often taking advantage of valuation discounts.
- Design a custom-made management arrangement that permits control to be allocated and transitioned from senior to junior generations, as appropriate.

159

- Protect owners of the LLC from claims of creditors and former spouses.
- Offer favorable tax benefits associated with its partnership tax treatment.
- Are easy to format and operate without many of the complexities associated with certain trust vehicles historically used by family business planners to accomplish these objectives.
- Are easily designed to incorporate many of the planning techniques previously considered in this book—family councils, family charters, and buy-sell agreements.

This chapter reviews these and other important benefits that a LLC might provide to your family business.

Use Your LLC to Help Transfer Ownership of the Family Business

Most family business owners struggle with their attorneys, accountants, and other professional advisers to devise mechanisms that minimize their estate tax obligations without relinquishing too much control, too quickly. The LLC is one of the newest and most exciting tools now available to help owners strike this delicate balance.

LLCs Can Be Gifted and Sold

Many of the techniques used to transfer ownership interests in family businesses (e.g., gifts, installment sales, private annuities, etc.) can be used to transfer ownership interests held in LLCs. Thus, ownership interests in a family business that are held by an LLC can be transferred to junior family members to minimize estate tax on the current value of the business as well as any future appreciation in the business. Membership certificates (much like stock certificates) can be prepared to reflect the ownership interests in an LLC and can be easily canceled and reissued to reflect changes in the ownership structure.

In many instances, the senior family owners can manage the LLC as managers with members of the junior generation initially having little or no management rights. In effect, the structure is much like one found in many corporations where all of the voting stock is held by the senior generation and the nonvoting stock is held by the junior generation. LLC laws throughout the United States tend to be extremely flexible, thus permitting perhaps even more opportunity to design creative management structures in LLCs than in corporations. Indeed, because of the ease with which a senior family member can manage the transition of control to members of the junior generation in an LLC through various provisions in an operating agreement, a senior family member may feel even more inclined to do so.

How might these planning suggestions work in real life? Let's consider an example. A senior family member may establish a family business as an LLC and thereafter make a tax-free gift of ownership interests in an LLC valued at $10,000 or less to his or her children. The interests are all subject to the LLC's operating agreement, which provides that the manager shall be the senior family member until that member decides to resign or expand the management team by naming additional managers. As a result, the gift of ownership interests in the family business can be accomplished without changing the management structure of the LLC. In addition to gifting ownership interests away, senior family members may choose to sell such interests using a variety of techniques previously considered, including by use of private annuities and self-canceling installment notes.

The transfer of ownership interests in a family business that permits management control to be creatively and flexibly allocated may provide the family with a variety of collateral planning benefits. For example, many parents have been disappointed with the results of splitting particular assets among their children because it is commonplace for the value of certain assets to increase while the value of other assets decrease, often for reasons wholly unrelated to the efforts of the children. LLCs can be used to consolidate a parent's separate assets in one entity and, by transferring membership interests (with or without management rights) to children, the children should share more fairly in the future growth of all assets. The merits of this and other opportunities will depend on each family's unique circumstances.

The Value of LLC Interests Are Subject to Discounts

As discussed in Chapter 7, certain business ownership interests are more desirable than others because of the control they afford or the comparative ease with which they can be transferred. The IRS has acknowledged that the value of ownership interests in family businesses can be reduced—or discounted—in appropriate circumstances. These discounts continue to be available to LLCs that own family businesses and can help ease the ownership transfer process by reducing the value of a gift or sale of an ownership interest in the company. For example, if there are sufficient restrictions in an LLC's operating agreement that limit members' rights to transfer their ownership interests in the company, a discount for lack of marketability should be applicable. Similarly, members who own minority membership interests in an LLC should be entitled to a minority interest discount in recognition of the often unenviable status of being a minority owner. Valuation discounts for considerations such as these in family businesses typically range from 15 percent to 45 percent. The amount of the discount is important because the estate or gift tax otherwise attributable to that discounted value is eliminated. For owners of successful family businesses, such savings can be substantial. Because of the possibility of substantially reducing estate tax obligations through the use of discounts, the IRS is extremely sensitive not only to the amount of the discount but to the circumstances surrounding the discount as well. For example, a family LLC (or family limited partnership) that is formed by a business owner on his or her deathbed may be disregarded as lacking a business purpose, and, instead, be deemed to have been improperly formed, since it was formed solely to avoid estate taxes. The amount of a discount and the existence of a business purpose, therefore, should be carefully considered with professional advisers.

Use an LLC to Help Reduce the Struggle for Control

Some of the most difficult issues in the estate and transfer planning process concern control. As we have discussed in previous chapters, everybody seems to want it! Parents, children, spouses, in-laws . . . the list goes on. In addition to control, everybody wants their fair share of the income, profits, and value of the family business. Although it is not always possible to satisfy these competing demands, LLCs can help. First, an LLC's operating agreement can be prepared to tailor-fit the particular objectives of its members. Under applicable partnership tax law, profits and losses can be creatively and flexibly allocated in a variety of ways. The management of a business can also be structured in almost any manner that satisfies the interests of its members; there is no limit to the number of different ownership and management classes that can be created to serve the best interests of an LLC's members. For example, an LLC can be structured so that the younger generation benefits from the appreciation in value of the business while the senior generation retains all or part of the management control. Unlike S corporations, which only permit one class of stock, there are no limits on the variety of ownership classes that can coexist in a single LLC.

Because of an LLC's flexibility, a variety of techniques can be used to transfer ownership interests in a family business (and so minimize estate taxes) while managing the struggle for control. This objective, for example, might be easily accomplished by creating two classes of membership interests, one with management rights and the other without. The children get the latter and the parent gets the former. Alternatively, the parents could relinquish all of their ownership interest in an LLC but require their children, as a condition of becoming members, to sign an operating agreement that appoints the parents as managers of the family business for life, until their retirement, or on any other specified event the parents may choose. Because of applicable estate tax considerations, any member's control should be restricted in conjunction with competent professional assistance.

LLCs Can Be Used to Help Treat Children Equitably

Parents routinely struggle with the dilemma of trying to devise an estate and business succession plan that fairly treats children who are active in the family business and their other children who are not active in the business. This struggle is particularly acute when the bulk of the parent's wealth is locked up in the business. This dilemma is routed in the inherent conflict of interest between, on the one hand, wishing to treat all children equally but at the same time not wishing to leave the child who is active in the family business in what often becomes an intolerable situation where his or her hands are tied, and decisions second-guessed, by siblings who know little, if anything, about the business. The same flexibility that permits a parent to retain management control over assets or business interests within the LLC also permits that parent to allocate the same control to a child active in the family business while transferring actual ownership in the business to all children and so, perhaps, devising a more equitable estate plan than otherwise would be possible! For example, a parent could give all of his or her children equal ownership interests in an LLC but provide that only the child active in the family business would have management rights. As suggested in earlier chapters, the LLC's operating agreement could easily be drafted to require the inactive children's approval for specified decisions and permit or require the removal of the active child as manager on the occurrence of specified events such as bankruptcy, fraud, willful neglect, or disability.

LLCs Can Be Used to Limit Children's Access to Assets

Parents may wish to transfer ownership interests in their family business and other valuable assets to their children as part of their estate plan but, at the same time, be concerned that their children are too young, too irresponsible, or too inactive in the family business to responsibly manage that wealth.

LLCs to the rescue! The parents can put their valuable assets, including a family business, into an LLC and then gift (or sell) membership interests in the LLC to their children. The LLC's operating agreement can be drafted to provide that the children cannot require a distribution of LLC profits or assets without the consent of the parent-manager. As manager of the LLC, the parent also can retain exclusive control over the LLC's operations and business decisions through the terms and conditions of the operating agreement. Among other things, such control may include retaining complete control over such decisions as whether to distribute excess cash to children and, if so, how much and to whom. In instances where the parent determines that the child's best interests are not best served by making such distributions, the parent can simply decide that such cash should be reinvested into the family business. As the family matures, the management control can be adjusted as desired, with the parent ultimately relinquishing control in accordance with the terms of the family's succession plan.

Senior family members may be able to transfer ownership interests in an existing family business to an LLC in exchange for an interest in that LLC without incurring a tax, since Section 721(a) of the Internal Revenue Code provides that gain or loss is not ordinarily recognized as a result of a transfer of property to a partnership (which includes LLCs) in exchange for an ownership interest in that partnership (or LLC). This tax-free exchange may be particularly easy to accomplish when the family business is established as a proprietorship, general partnership, or C corporation. Because restrictions apply as to who can own stock in an S corporation, owners of such entities face additional hurdles that should be considered with professional advisers.

There are, not surprisingly, exceptions to the nonrecognition of tax on the transfer of assets into an LLC that should be considered to determine their applicability. For example, if the IRS considers an LLC an investment company (defined as a company with 80 percent of its value, excluding cash and certain debt obligations, in readily marketable securities held for investment purposes), tax may be recognized on the exchange of assets for an ownership interest in the LLC. If, however, the transfer does not result in asset diversification, this exception may not apply. In other instances, certain sales within a two-year period following the exchange of assets for a ownership interest in the LLC may be considered a disguised sale, again requiring the imposition of tax. In order to avoid unpleasant surprises, these and other applicable tax consequences should be reviewed with your professional advisers prior to implementing a strategy based on the exchange of existing ownership interests in a family business for new ownership interests in a family LLC.

Tax complications that may result when a family seeks to transfer existing ownership interests in a family business can often be avoided altogether when the family simply channels new business opportunities into LLCs. As discussed in Chapter 7, establishing ownership interests for junior generations in the first instance is often the most efficient estate planning technique, since it avoids the need to engage in later transfer techniques to remove those interests from senior members' estates. A parent can often insist, however, on retaining significant management control over even these new LLCs until a transfer of such control is appropriate.

LLCs Can Be Used to Provide Protection from Creditors

A common concern shared by parents who are transferring assets to their children is how those assets can be protected against the possible claims of their children's creditors in the future. By restricting the free transferability of ownership interests, LLCs can help minimize the need for such concern. The rule is well established in most states that creditors of an LLC member cannot satisfy their claims by seizing property of the LLC. Instead, creditors are usually only able to secure a "charging order" against the member's LLC interest. A charging order ordinarily only gives a creditor the status of an assignee of the membership interest, and not of a member. The result? The creditor will neither acquire a governance interest in the family business (and, so, will be unable to impair the member's managerial control over the business) nor will the creditor be able to force a distribution of cash or other property to satisfy the claim.

Since the creditor may only wind up with a charging order against a member's LLC interest, the creditor may be in the undesirable position of having to pay income tax on the allocable share of income accruing to that interest without receiving cash from the LLC to pay such tax (if no cash distributions are made). As a result, a planning technique in the face of a creditor's charging order is for the manager to determine not to make cash distributions to members until the creditor, who presumably is not anxious to pay taxes, agrees to settle the claim against the member. Because of the tax cost leverage the family may have against creditors, the family is often able to help the family member settle his or her claim with the creditor at a substantial discount.

In certain instances, additional remedies may be available to creditors or, if applicable, trustees in bankruptcy, including the power to force a sale of the LLC or the ability to nullify transfers in violation of applicable fraudulent conveyance laws. As a practical matter, the remedy to force a sale may be of little value, since, other than the family itself, there may be no other interested buyers of the LLC. In addition, the LLC's operating agreement, which can function as a buy-sell agreement, also can specifically provide that the ownership interest of a bankrupt member be purchased for fair value. Fraudulent conveyance laws, which may apply when assets are transferred or concealed with an intent to hinder, delay, or defraud creditors, can result in more unpleasant situations, including criminal convictions. Consult your professional advisers for assistance.

LLCs Can Be Used to Facilitate Insurance Planning

As noted in Chapter 7, an excellent estate planning technique involves the use of irrevocable trusts to serve as "owners" of life insurance policies on a senior family member. Essentially, an individual concerned about transferring wealth to, let's say, his children, can set up an irrevocable life insurance trust (ILIT), name his children the beneficiaries of the trust, and fund the trust with an insurance policy for which he pays by gifting the requisite premiums to his children. Because the parent has relinquished all control over the cash used for the premium and never had control over the policy (because of the terms of the trust), the insurance proceeds payable on his death are not part of the parent's estate and, so, are not reduced by otherwise applicable estate taxes. This pretty neat trick has only one drawback—applicable law requires the ILIT to be irrevocable. In other words, it can't be changed for any reason whatsoever—even unforeseen circumstances such as the death or divorce of a child that might otherwise prompt a reasonable parent to seek a change. While the terms of the trust can often be drafted in a manner that ensures great flexibility for a trustee, such flexibility, nevertheless, is inherently constrained by the irrevocability of the trust instrument.

LLCs may now provide an attractive alternative to ILITs! Instead of forming an irrevocable trust, a parent may form an LLC and contribute cash that is used to purchase a life insurance policy. The parent could keep a (small) membership interest or, perhaps, have no interest in the LLC. The children, in turn, would own all or most of the LLC. The parent could name himself or herself as manager of the LLC for any period of time, including the parent's lifetime, and this appointment would be recognized in the LLC's operating agreement. The parent could even be authorized to amend the LLC's organizational documents or terminate its existence. Like an ILIT, such an LLC may be able to provide tax-free insurance benefits on the parent's death to the children because the proceeds would be distributed to the children in accordance with their pro-rata ownership interests in the LLC. Unlike the ILIT, however, the LLC is not irrevocable but rather is extremely flexible. The parent can change any aspect of the structure in light of changing circumstances. Because of the newness of the LLC, it is unclear whether certain tax-related limitations on this technique may apply, so be careful to consider this planning opportunity in conjunction with your advisers.

Creative Uses of Operating Agreements

Legislation that governs LLCs throughout the United States generally permits LLC members a substantial degree of flexibility in determining how their business is to be operated. This flexibility is often expressed in legislative provisions that contemplate wide latitude in the use of operating agreements.

Such latitude offers family business owners an ideal opportunity to creatively use their operating agreement to address more than such routine matters as how profits and losses of the business should be allocated among its members. Indeed, it is possible to creatively design an operating agreement so that it serves the function of many valuable planning tools in one simple instrument. It is, in short, possible to enter into an operating agreement that is specifically designed to enhance peace and prosperity in a family. Let's see how.

Use Your Operating Agreement to Establish a Family Council

As discussed in Chapter 2, a family council can serve as an organizational planning arm of a family, facilitating the decision-making process on a variety of important issues for the family and the business, such as family employment policies, succession criteria, and the future direction of the business. Family councils can also serve many other purposes, including providing a forum for addressing jealousies within the family, a forum for resolving conflict, a mechanism to preserve family history and tradition, and, ultimately, a tool to help build a stronger family.

An LLC offers an ideal mechanism for establishing a family council with appropriate formality. For example, a family business could include in its operating agreement the following provisions:

- Regularly scheduled meetings of all or some of its members
- The office of secretary, with the responsibility of taking minutes at all meetings of the members
  - Who attends the meetings (active family members only or inactive members as well, blood relations only or in-laws as well, employees, age limitations on members who may attend?)
  - Where the meetings will be held (homes, office, or neutral territory?)
  - What the agenda is for a meeting and how it is determined (predetermined or ad hoc, opportunity for everyone to submit ideas?)
- Who leads the meetings (senior family member, company president, anyone but the foregoing, rotating leadership?)

In short, any rules that the family establishes in connection with the formation and operation of its family council can be easily incorporated into the family's LLC operating agreement.

Use Your Operating Agreement as a Mission Statement

As noted in Chapter 2, a mission statement reflects the core purpose(s) and values of a business. A typical mission statement may address the following issues, among others:

- What the business does and what it should do
- The values of the business
- The expectations for family members
- How the business accommodates the sometimes conflicting interests of the business and the family

The benefits of establishing a mission statement are many and include providing an atmosphere of good feeling among family members, renewing confidence within the family, empowering family members who may have felt disenfranchised, and, ultimately, establishing a foundation for growth of the business and the family in a positive direction.

An LLC operating agreement can be useful in developing or restating the family mission statement. Indeed, most LLC legislation throughout the United States requires or permits each LLC to specify its purpose in its organizational document. Typically, LLC members set forth a business purpose in their articles of organization or operating agreement such as, "This LLC is established for the purpose of manufacturing and wholesaling widgets." This statement of purpose, however, may offer an ideal opportunity to incorporate the family mission statement as part of the company purpose as well.

In order to emphasize its importance, the operating agreement can even specify a mechanism for determining how the mission statement can be implemented and converted into action. For example, if the mission statement emphasizes the family's commitment to community, the operating agreement might expressly authorize the making of charitable contributions to designated institutions. Similarly, a statement offering a principled basis for resolving conflicting interests of the business and those of the family could prove an important weapon in the battle to preserve family harmony. Again, the only limitations on the use of a mission statement within an LLC's operating agreement seems to be the creativity of the family members and their advisers.

Use Your Operating Agreement as a Family Charter

Because a mission statement is ordinarily very short (and very general), a more specific set of guidelines that address important family issues and agreements, whether reached at family councils or elsewhere, can also be invaluable to the family and its business. As noted in Chapter 2, such guidelines are often referred to as family charters.

The LLC operating agreement can be an ideal place to incorporate all or part of the family charter. For example, an agreement on educational requirements could be simply set forth in an operating agreement that provides that "a four-year college degree is required of any family member who seeks a position with this company." An agreement that spouses are ineligible for employment positions at the company could be reflected in a provision that simply states that "no spouse of any family member shall be employed by the company." By incorporating the agreements and decisions of the family into the operating agreement, the family creates a clear record that can be used to avoid or resolve disputes and offer helpful guidance and precedent on the inevitable variety of difficult issues that the family is sure to face.

Use Your LLC to Help Resolve Conflict

The suggestions outlined in this book are designed to help reduce the existence and significance of disputes. Nevertheless, for the reasons set forth earlier, conflict is inevitable and will occur. The conflict resolution techniques considered in Chapter 5 are, however, all easily incorporated into an LLC's operating agreement that can help ensure the peaceful and productive management of family disputes. For example, an LLC's operating agreement can require that a dispute between two or more of its members (perhaps siblings) be resolved by majority vote of all the members, by a designated family leader, by an outsider, by an arbitrator, by a mediator, or by any other appropriate mechanism. The operating agreement can even establish ground rules for resolving the dispute—time frames, rules of evidence, the binding or nonbinding nature of a decision-maker's authority—in any manner to which the members agree. An agreement might even be drafted to require the buying and selling of family members' ownership interests on specified terms and circumstances. These mechanisms are easily incorporated into an LLC operating agreement, either singly or collectively, which the family would be required to employ on the occurrence of significant disputes!

Other, more indirect techniques can also be incorporated into an operating agreement to help manage conflict in a family business. For example, it could identify certain business actions that would only be taken on the existence of a clear level of family consensus. These actions might include the decision to enter a new market, the incurrence of more than a specified level of debt, the setting of compensation, etc. An LLC operating agreement also can be easily prepared to establish an acceptable decision-making process. Quorum requirements for members' or managers' meetings can be set uniformly for all decisions or specifically for one or more types of decisions. In addition, voting requirements can be tailor-made to fit the interests of the members. Certain issues may require a simple majority vote, other issues a "supermajority" vote, and still other issues may require membership unanimity to approve. Any understanding of the family members can be easily reduced to writing and incorporated directly into the operating agreement.

Finally, an operating agreement is an ideal tool to address virtually any miscellaneous issue that is capable of precipitating a family dispute. For example, if two siblings with ownership in the same family business had an agreement that expressly permitted them to establish a competitive business on their own, the foundation for a possible dispute over that reason would be eliminated. Agreements on the permissibility of competition between company and individual family members, the individual pursuit of company opportunities, contracts between the company and family members at above-market rates, and other such issues can all be easily addressed in an operating agreement and thereby help reduce the likelihood of debilitating conflict.

LLCs Can Outperform Family Partnerships

Family limited partnerships ("FLPs") have received considerable acclaim over the years for their contribution to the estate planning process. Once a technique reserved for only the wealthy, the use of FLPs is now a common piece of many families' estate plans, since, like a family

LLC, it permits assets to be transferred by senior family members to junior family members while permitting the senior family member to retain management control over the transferred assets. Although the acclaim is well deserved, LLCs provide many of the same advantages as do FLPs plus some extras! Consider these examples:

- In an FLP, a general partner is personally liable for the debts and obligations of the business; in an LLC, all the members, including the manager, can be afforded limited liability protection against such claims.
- In an FLP, limited partners cannot materially participate in the management of the business without losing their limited liability protection.
- In an LLC, all members can (if desired) participate in management without risk of losing their limited liability protection. Since the new "check the box" tax regulations, which enhance an LLC's ability to secure partnership tax treatment for its members, the valuation discounts available to family LLCs should be equivalent to those available in FLPs. This is a complex subject, however, and should be reviewed with your professional advisers.
- In an FLP, partnership obligations do not increase the basis of the limited partners' interests unless they personally guarantee the obligations; in an LLC, nonrecourse debt *can* increase the basis of the members' interests even without personal guarantees.

In short, careful comparison between these two alternative forms suggests that all of the advantages that made FLPs so popular, plus other benefits as well, can be secured in an LLC. The family LLC may be a technique whose time has now come!

LLCs Can Easily Respond to a Changing Environment

Families change—so do laws, tax rates, the marketplace, the competition, etc. The families and family businesses that are successful don't resist such changes. They embrace them! LLCs can prove a valuable tool in the arsenal of such achievers. The operating agreement of an LLC can be drafted with change in mind. Amendments to the agreement can be accomplished, if necessary. Centralized management can be ready to spring into action to welcome change without having its hands tied by members who may be uninformed and unprepared or unwilling to take any action without substantial delay. LLCs can also offer important tools to family business owners through the creative use of mission statements, family charters, and dispute resolution mechanisms. Such tools should prove invaluable in the ongoing effort to achieve profitability and peace in the family and its business. LLCs can also serve as superb estate planning tools, facilitating the orderly transition of the family business from generation to generation. In short, the LLC's inherent flexibility can be creatively used by its members to quickly respond to an ever-changing environment, to promote family harmony, and to facilitate succession planning. These and its many other benefits highlight the exciting possibilities LLCs now offer all family-owned businesses!

Recommendation

The competing interests that families must successfully juggle in order to secure long-term peace and prosperity in their family businesses may be no more apparent than they are in the context of developing an estate plan that transitions ownership and control from a senior generation to a junior generation. Senior members are looking to reduce their assets to minimize estate taxes but they may not be looking to proportionately reduce their control in the family business at the same time. Some children may be more active than others in the family business, but a parent may be anxious to treat all children equitably, if not equally. Individuals may recognize the need to take action now, although the prospect of irrevocably relinquishing control over assets in the process is often not desirable.

The LLC can offer important economic and psychological benefits to family business owners. Interests can be transferred, often using valuation discounts, without relinquishing any control immediately. Independent trustees are not required; the senior family member completing the transfer of ownership can "manage" the LLC for as long as he or she desires, and then gradually transition that control to a designated successor. In addition, LLCs can offer protection from creditors, an alternative to the irrevocable life insurance trust, and, particularly for young children, can be used to limit junior family members' access to assets by designing the operating agreement to provide that income distributions are made at the sole discretion of the manager (e.g., the senior family member).

The LLC's operating agreement also can be designed to incorporate many of the other planning techniques discussed elsewhere in this book. Family councils, family charters, dispute resolution mechanisms, buy-sell agreements, supermajority voting provisions, etc., also can be easily incorporated into your LLC's structure. The recent popularity of the family limited partnership, which is very similar to the family LLC, attests to the merits of the LLC's benefits. The LCC, however, can be even easier to establish and operate than the limited partnership. This may be the single most valuable planning technique for family business owners. Consider its application to your situation with your advisers!

Family Business Audit

1. Have you considered how a family LLC can be used to
   - transfer assets, including a family business, to family members?
   - take advantage of valuation discounts?
   - help reduce the struggle for control in your family business?
   - help treat children equitably?
   - limit children's access to assets and claims against those assets by creditors?
   - facilitate insurance planning?
   - help establish a family council?
   - help resolve family conflict?

2. Have you considered how a family LLC stacks up against other wealth transfer techniques?

3. Have you considered how you can use a family LLC to respond to a changing business environment and changes in your family's dynamics?

CHAPTER 10

What Else Can You Do to Keep Your Family and Business on Track?

Consider These Miscellaneous Planning Techniques

*A*lthough many family businesses are "formally" established as traditional legal entities such as partnerships, corporations, or limited liability companies (LLCs), in practice they function quite differently from their publicly or widely owned counterparts. As a result, legal, financial, and other related planning tools that may be well suited for other businesses are often misused with unfortunate consequences for family businesses. Indeed, many families fail to even consider how their family structure could best mesh with their business operations, and, so, structure such operations in a haphazard manner. As a result, traditional plans and planning tools may, ironically, sow the seeds for later problems and conflict. Specific instances of this phenomenon are considered in this chapter, along with suggestions for how such problems can be avoided in your family business, and how you can use certain conventional planning tools in a variety of creative ways for your family's benefit. Because of the high incidence of divorce in this country and the damage this can inflict on a family business, the second part of this chapter considers a particular planning technique in some detail: the prenuptial agreement.

Consider the Best Form for Your Family Business

One of the most fundamental decisions that a business owner should make is the form the business should be operated in. Traditional choices include sole proprietorships, partnerships, and corporations. More recently, LLCs and limited liability partnerships (LLPs) have become increasingly popular.

Some of these forms (e.g., LLCs, LLPs, corporations) offer their owners limited liability protection against claims made against the business. Basically, this means that someone who has a claim for monetary damages against the business can't, except under extraordinary circumstances, enforce that claim against the personal assets of the business owner. Some other popular business forms (e.g., sole proprietorships and partnerships) do not provide the same protection to their owners. As a result, proprietors and partners may be individually and personally liable for business obligations if the business has insufficient resources with which to satisfy such obligations.

The importance of selecting the best business form is highlighted in the following example. Typically, an important planning objective for most owners of family businesses is to build assets outside of the family business. Outside assets can help a business leader establish a nest egg upon retirement from the business and can also provide an eventual inheritance to those family members who are inactive in the family business and who expect to receive part of an inheritance that includes assets other than, or in addition to, an ownership interest in the family business. If, however, the family business becomes liable for a claim, the owners may be personally liable for the business obligations unless the business is in a form that provides limited liability protection. A substantial claim may prove disastrous not only for the family business but its owners as well and their plans to secure objectives like those noted earlier may be irretrievably lost. By contrast, owners of a business that offers limited liability protection may sustain the same damage to their business, but their personal assets should be safe.

In light of the relative ease with which limited liability protection can be secured today, family members should carefully reexamine their business form if they do not already have this valuable benefit. The benefits to an owner of any business are clear; the benefits to owners of family businesses may be even clearer.

Segregate Operations into Separate Legal Entities

Another common instance of inartful planning by owners of family businesses is a tendency to lump business operations together. For example, the Smith family may own two separate apartment complexes across town from each other. Instead of considering the merits of owning this real estate in two separate businesses, for example, Smith Properties One LLC and Smith Properties Two LLC, it is more common for the properties to be owned by a single business, for example, Smith Properties LLC.

Although each situation needs to be analyzed on its own merits, there are several reasons why it may be eminently sensible for family business properties to be segregated into separate and distinct legal entities:

- A liability of one business may be contained in only that business while the other business may remain unscathed.
- Segregating business operations makes it easier for the newer businesses to be owned by members of a family's younger generation, which can reduce the senior family members' estate tax obligations.
- Segregating businesses may make it easier for family members to have day-to-day job responsibilities on separate "turfs," which may help improve intrafamily relations.
- Physical distance between family members should help minimize intrafamily conflict, as it reduces the occasions when family members need to reach agreement on day-to-day decisions.
- It may be desirable one day to spin off specific business operations to some family members and other assets to others. If the businesses have already been legally and operationally segregated, such a spin-off may be easier to accomplish.

The strategic segregation of certain family business operations may also make an owner's retirement and estate planning easier to complete. For example, if Mr. Smith has built a nest egg capable of financing most of his retirement years, he may wish to transfer ownership of Smith Properties One LLC to his children but retain ownership of Smith Properties Two LLC. Owning one property, which Smith can lease to his children at a fair market rate, may satisfy his financial requirements for his retirement years. By contrast, retaining ownership of both properties may be financially unnecessary and counterproductive to his ultimate estate planning objectives. In short, taking a considered approach to building a family business today may create one or even several unforeseen advantageous opportunities tomorrow.

Customize Your Documents and Avoid "Boilerplates"

Another common mistake many owners of family businesses make is the failure to customize legal documentation such as bylaws, shareholder agreements, employment agreements, etc., to suit their family's particular circumstances and objectives. Instead, such owners (or their advisers, who might not be sensitive to the peculiar realities of family businesses) utilize boilerplate documents that are designed with the hypothetical "standard" business in mind. Because there is no such thing as a standard business, such documents are often unsuitable for the particular families who use them and, indeed, may cause more problems than if there were no document in place and the parties were left simply to sort things out from time to time. Several examples of this problem follow.

Corporate Bylaws

Bylaws are the agreed-upon ground rules that establish the ways in which corporations are governed. Among other subjects, bylaws ordinarily specify how a corporation's officers and directors are elected and the voting standards that determine when they are authorized to take action on behalf of the corporation.

Canned bylaws are frequently prepared in a manner that authorizes a board of directors to take action upon securing a simple majority vote in support of such action. As a result, stockholders in such corporations elect their directors by majority vote and the directors, in turn, elect officers (president, secretary, treasurer, etc.) by majority vote as well. Although decision making by majority vote appeals to a sense of democracy and fairness, it may well be inappropriate, unfair, or unwise in a family business. For instance, if a family business is owned by three siblings, a decision by two siblings to borrow an unprecedented amount of money to expand business operations in a whole new venture unrelated to what the family business has ever done in the past may be unfair to the third sibling, who opposes such expansion as unnecessarily risky.

A family-owned business may be better served by bylaws that provide that certain decisions can be made only by majority vote, other decisions by supermajority vote (i.e., 75 percent or 85 percent of the stockholders or directors), and still other decisions that can only be made by unanimous consent of the owners. Such decisions can be identified with any degree of specificity the parties find desirable. Common subjects for such supermajority voting standards may include borrowing money in excess of a specified sum, particular compensation agreements with family members, dividend decisions, capital improvement programs, decisions to buy new businesses or sell existing ones, etc.

Classes of Stock

Another instance where the routine use of boilerplate documents can create problems for family businesses concerns the common use of only one class of stock on the formation of a corporation, which gives all owners of the business voting rights and an attendant degree of legal control over the business based on their mathematical percentage ownership interest. By contrast, a more effective approach for a family business may be for the ownership interests to be divided between voting stock and nonvoting stock. The ownership interests are in all respects equal except only the voting stock has rights to vote on key ownership decisions. By creating two or more classes of stock, a senior family member's ownership interest in a family business may be passed along equally to all the children while vesting management control in just a few of the children. This subject is considered in more detail in Chapter 8.

The "I Love You" Will

The so-called "I love you" will is one in which a spouse simply leaves all of his or her assets to the other spouse. Although easy to draft, this type of will precludes the possibility of taking advantage of the "credit shelter trust," a critical tax planning tool that helps minimize estate tax obligations by ensuring that a couple takes full advantage of their unified credit against otherwise taxable assets. This tool is discussed in more detail in Chapter 8.

Life Insurance

A final example of the substantial problems that can be created by the unconsidered use of boilerplate documents concerns the decision to acquire life insurance outright. In such instances, the insured's estate is paid the face amount of a life insurance policy on his or her demise. Unfortunately, the estate at that time may be looking at paying estate taxes at a 55 percent marginal rate on all of its assets—which includes the life insurance proceeds. Thus, a $1 million policy could be reduced by $550,000, leaving an actual benefit of only $450,000. By contrast, if the life insurance policy were owned by an irrevocable trust, whose beneficiaries are the same as those of the insured's will, the insurance escapes the estate tax, since it is not owned by the insured (it is owned by the trust!) and the full $1 million gets paid to the trust beneficiaries with no estate tax due!

Throughout this book, I highlight those instances where tailor-made documents can be particularly beneficial to owners of family businesses. Since countless other examples of this problem may exist, my best advice is to carefully review all of your planning documents with your advisers to, first, ensure that you actually understand what they are and how they are supposed to work and, second, to ensure their maximum suitability for your specific purposes and particular family situation.

Observe Legal Formalities

Many families spend a great deal of time and money "establishing" their business operations in conjunction with their lawyers and accountants. Corporations may be formed, bylaws prepared, and shareholder agreements reached. Once this initial work is completed, however, many families tend to forget all about these "legalities" and instead go about their business as if these new organizations and related documents didn't even exist. Instead, the annual meeting of shareholders and directors exists only on the company lawyer's word processor, to be generated from time to time as the auditors or bank officer may request. Records of decisions reached (or "minutes" as they are commonly called) are created years after the actual decisions have been made, again often only as a result of an IRS auditor's request that such minutes be produced. For some families, the perceived cost of adhering to legal formalities such as these may be unwarranted; for others, the effort and inconvenience is simply too much.

The failure to attend to certain fundamental legal formalities can, however, create problems for family members and their businesses. For example, the failure to hold an annual meeting of a family business's shareholders and directors only serves to reduce communication when it should be enhanced. The failure to record agreements that have been reached and decisions made on fundamental issues may result in family members having honest (yet important) differences in their recollections as to what the "real agreement" was. Depending on the subject of the purported agreement, such differences in recollections can result in hostility and conflict. If minutes were available to refresh recollections, many arguments could be avoided entirely.

The importance of observing minimal business formalities is highlighted in the case of *Samia v. Central Oil Company of Worcester*. In this case, three sisters, who claimed to be stockholders of Central Oil Company of Worcester ("Central") sued their three brothers for failing to properly account for certain charges and expense credits. Because of a variety of complex circumstances, it was not clear that one of the siblings was actually a shareholder of the corporation and, the brothers claimed, was not entitled to assert claims for damages to the corporation that may have been caused by the brothers' actions. The evidence indicated that an agreement had been reached to make a gift of some of the stock to the sibling but that the stock certificates to reflect the gift may not have actually been prepared. The brothers argued that the failure to prepare the stock certificates supported their position.

In this case, the Massachusetts court concluded that sufficient evidence existed to support a finding that all of the siblings were stockholders in spite of the absence of stock certificates, thus permitting the suit on the merits to proceed. The court explained that the siblings all seemed to have regarded each other as stockholders upon formation of the corporation and the absence of certificates was not fatal. Acknowledging the obvious difficulty in reaching a decision in the absence of relevant documentation, the court simply commented that the factual determination on this subject was "made upon conflicting oral testimony and documentary evidence. It may well be that, in this ambiguous family situation, other [findings] would have been equally reasonable."

The easiest way to avoid an argument like the siblings had in *Central Oil* is to adhere and attend to appropriate legal formalities, including the preparation of relevant documentation. In the absence of clear documentation evidencing the terms of a purported agreement, business fortunes can be as easily won as lost on the determination of a judge or jury who, charged with the impossible task of mind-reading what a family actually agreed upon, is as likely to make an incorrect decision as a correct one!

Observe the Chain of Command

Many family businesses lack an orderly chain of command due to the difficulty, if not impossibility, of determining what capacity a family member may be acting in. For example, corporation law distinguishes the roles filled by shareholders, directors, officers, and employees. As a result of these distinctions, simply being a shareholder of a portion of a family business doesn't confer management authority, nor does it mean that the owner is entitled to make minor or routine decisions on behalf of the business. Instead, corporate law provides that shareholders elect directors who, in turn, oversee the management of the business. Directors, in turn, may elect officers (such as a president, one or more vice presidents, etc.) to run the day-to-day operations of the business. Indeed, except for a limited number of specific extraordinary decisions, such as the sale of the corporation, shareholders ordinarily have no mandated right to make decisions affecting a corporation's business operations.

Many families fail to recognize and observe these distinctions and their failure to do so often creates significant problems. For example, an owner of a family business who inherited his interest and is not employed by the business may nevertheless view his role as encompassing the responsibilities intended to be reserved for directors and officers. As a result, this owner may insist on participating in the family business's employment, compensation, and operating decisions. In effect, this owner decides to disregard the established chain of command. In another instance, a spouse who does not own an interest in a family business may not only be making decisions behind the scenes at home, but may even show up at the office and give directions to company employees!

Disregarding the chain of command has several adverse consequences to a family:

- A greater likelihood of making poor business decisions, since those with the expertise and training to make good decisions have their hands tied by those who do not
- Increased tension between owners who, for the preceding reason, would like such decisions to be made by the appropriate decision makers and those owners who believe it is their business to do as they see fit

In order to ensure that good business decisions are made, owners of family businesses must recognize the appropriate role each family member should fill and agree to respect the family business's formal chain of command. It may, of course, be desirable for certain family members to fill multiple roles in the family business, but these decisions should be made on a case-by-case basis. In order to minimize an inactive owner's concern that he or she otherwise has no voice in the family business, mechanisms like family councils can be effectively used. By providing forums for effective communication and input while maximizing the authority of capable decision makers, families can strengthen their bonds and their businesses at the same time!

Recognize That an Estate Plan Is Not a Succession Plan

Historically, many owners of family businesses have neglected the differences between estate planning (addressed in Chapters 7, 8, and 9) and succession planning (addressed in Chapter 6). As a result, many families have run amok when the two different plans fail to mesh smoothly. For example, the business succession plan may call for one of four children to take over the leadership and sole ownership of the family business, since only that child is active in the business. This succession plan may have the desired effect of ensuring the business is left in the hands of an experienced and deserving heir while simultaneously pruning the family business tree (see Chapter 11). If, however, the current business leader has failed to build sufficient assets outside of the family business, he or she may design an estate plan so that equal ownership interests in the family business are left to all four children. This, of course, may be inconsistent with the leader's long-term succession planning objectives. Accordingly, when designing your various business, estate, retirement, and succession plans, make sure they are internally consistent and work well together.

Family Business Audit

1. Does your family business provide all of its owners with limited liability protection?

2. Are your business assets all held in one company? Does it make sense to segregate such assets (or future assets) into two or more entities?

3. Are your business documents customized to fit your family's unique situation or are you using boilerplate forms?

4. Does your family business observe legal formalities by, among other things, holding regular meetings and taking written minutes of meetings?

5. Does your family business have a recognizable "chain of command" that is observed in practice?

6. Does your family have both a succession plan and an estate plan and, if so, do the plans complement each other or contradict each other?

7. Do you spend enough time working on your business, not just in it?

8. Have you considered how the wide variety of available planning tools may benefit your family business?

Prenuptial Agreements

The divorce rate in this country continues to soar, with recent statistics suggesting that almost one in every two marriages is likely to end in divorce. While some divorces are amicably resolved, many others are knock-down, drag-out, bloody affairs. The blood that is spilled usually runs over not only the divorcing parties but their families and family businesses as well. Indeed, history is replete with examples of successful family businesses that have stumbled, faltered, and even failed as a result of a matrimonial dispute between the owners (or their offspring) and their spouses.

Because of matrimonial law ramifications, family business owners are often faced with the difficult decision of whether or not to interfere with a personal relationship by insisting on an agreement that would limit the claims that the spouse might otherwise make against the owner's assets in the event of a divorce. This agreement is commonly referred to alternatively as a *prenuptial agreement,* a *premarital agreement,* or, on occasion, an *antenuptial agreement.*

What Is a Prenuptial Agreement?

A prenuptial agreement is simply an agreement between two people as to how they will divide some or all of their assets in the event their marriage ends in divorce. The agreement is designed to avoid having the division made on the basis of the variety of factors state divorce courts otherwise ordinarily consider. Because courts are obligated to examine "any relevant factor," they are required to examine the circumstances surrounding a premarital agreement. If a court finds a particular agreement unreasonable, it can choose to ignore its terms and make its award on the basis of other relevant factors. As a result of this review process, there are no guarantees that a prenuptial agreement will stand up in the event of a divorce! Because courts retain discretion to review the fairness and, ultimately, the enforceability of premarital agreements, it becomes particularly important to carefully prepare such agreements in order to maximize the likelihood that it will withstand such judicial scrutiny. A well-drafted agreement can help increase the likelihood that a family business owner's marriage will not end with an ex-spouse retaining an ownership interest in the business; a poorly drafted agreement offers virtually no protection to the family business owner. In order to maximize the possibility that a premarital agreement withstands judicial scrutiny, several suggestions are noted later in this chapter. The applicability of these suggestions to individual cases should be determined in consultation with your attorney.

The range of feelings on the merits of prenuptial agreements (as we will refer to such documents here) is quite dramatic. For instance, some family business owners may call off their marriage if their loved ones refuse to sign a prenuptial agreement before their marriages and will muster all of their influence to make sure that their children do so as well before they get married. Other owners may view the subject completely differently and, wishing to help cement a marital relationship, may even offer an ownership interest in the family business to a spouse or a child's spouse!

It is, frankly, difficult to intelligently decide whether to enter into a premarital agreement on the basis of reason and logic alone, since it is impossible to look into the future and predict whether a marriage will prosper or fail. Particularly in the event of first marriages, a family may be reluctant to ask a new family member to sign an agreement to waive any claims to his or her spouse's business assets in the event of a later divorce. In other circumstances, perhaps on a third, fourth, or (yes, they do happen) fifth marriage, such an agreement might well be expected by a prospective spouse. Finding the proper balance between sensitivity and cynicism, between romanticism and pragmatism, between a marriage created out of love and hope and one borne out of financial convenience and pessimism, is a difficult task indeed. There are, in short, no easy answers on the best approach to take on this subject, and every individual business owner ultimately must decide whether to seek such legal protection or not. Make no mistake—in the matrimonial setting, this is a frequent source of conflict!

In certain circumstances (which will vary for different individuals), it may well be appropriate for an individual to insist on protecting his or her assets in the event of a later divorce. This protection should, among other things, guard against claims brought against the spouse's ownership interest in a family business itself. The most common planning tools available to families interested in minimizing the effects of a divorce are "buy-sell" or restrictive stock agreements, and prenuptial agreements. Buy-sell and restrictive stock agreements, which are reviewed in Chapter 5, can help ensure that a former spouse is forced to sell any ownership interests held in a family business at the time of a divorce. On its own, however, a buy-sell agreement only regulates claims to ownership interests; it does not minimize the amount that a former spouse can claim for under a state's equitable distribution laws. A spouse who is forced to sell an ownership interest in a family business pursuant to a buy-sell agreement will still receive the fair market value of that interest in cash. Depending on the amount of cash required to be paid, this result may still create a financial hardship.

In order to actually limit the amount that a spouse can claim in a divorce proceeding, the other spouse must secure a written agreement consenting to such limitation. That prenuptial agreement (or, if the agreement is signed after the marriage has taken place, a *postnuptial agreement*) must meet certain conditions, which are reviewed in the balance of this chapter. Because prenuptial agreements are contracts, interpreted in accordance with state contract and matrimonial laws, their requirements will vary from state to state. Readers are encouraged to consult with their advisers, therefore, in order to ensure that their agreements meet applicable local requirements.

Divorce in the Absence of Agreement

As matrimonial law continues to develop, the rights of spouses, whose only claim to a business is by marriage to the business owner, continue to expand. Courts no longer automatically award ownership of a business to the spouse who has historically operated the business as part of its equitable distribution award. Expert testimony that a spouse can be trained to operate a business has resulted in court awards of businesses to such spouses, even if those spouses have previously not spent much time working in those businesses. Where a family owns more than one business, some courts have been prepared to sever the family empire, awarding one or more of those businesses to each spouse.

While every state has its own matrimonial law, courts usually consider many of the same factors in deciding how to distribute assets upon a divorce. In New York, for example, "marital property" is ordinarily divided according to the following factors:

- Income and property at the time of the marriage and at the commencement of the divorce
- The length of the marriage, and age and health of the parties
- Need of party with child custody to remain in the marital home
- Loss of inheritance or pension rights
- Alimony award, if any
- Contribution of each to the acquisition of the property
- Liquidity of the marital property
- Probable future financial circumstances of each property
- Difficulty in evaluating an asset or business entity
- Tax consequences
- Either party's wasteful disposition of assets
- Any transfer or encumbrance in contemplation of divorce without fair consideration
- Any other relevant factor

The havoc that divorce can wreak on a family business is apparent in the case of *Penley v. Penley*. In this case, a North Carolina couple, following their divorce, wound up struggling for many years over ownership rights to a Kentucky Fried Chicken franchise in Hendersonville,

North Carolina. According to the reported decision, the couple was married from 1949 through 1979. The former husband claimed that he had been operating an automotive tire business in 1967 when his wife became ill. The wife, who had operated the restaurant, allegedly asked her husband to work there to ensure its continued operation. The husband claimed that his wife promised him that, if he devoted his full working time to helping run the business, they would divide the profits and losses of the business, and its ownership, equally. The wife claimed that she agreed only that the salaries would be split.

In considering this claim, the North Carolina Supreme Court acknowledged the general rule that "there is a 'presumption that services rendered by a wife in her husband's business are gratuitously performed absent a special agreement to the contrary.' This presumption applies equally to a husband's services in his wife's business." In this case, however, the court found that a special agreement did exist. The court explained that:

> The first contract or special agreement was the 1967 agreement that in exchange for plaintiff devoting his full time to the Hendersonville restaurant, defendant would share the business, the money, the profits with the plaintiff. . . . Another contract or special agreement was entered into when the parties agreed to incorporate the business and split the stock "fifty-fifty," later "48-48-4," and continue to operate the restaurant as a family business. *While the jury may have concluded from plaintiff's evidence that plaintiff joined the business in Hendersonville and worked long hours solely because he was the husband of an ill wife, the jury was not required by law to so find.* [Emphasis added]

Had Ms. Penley been more careful about what she intended to give her former husband, she certainly could have avoided costly, emotional, and time-consuming litigation. According to published court records, the Penleys were still litigating their claims against each other in the North Carolina Court of Appeals in 1990. Although the Penley's corporation was being liquidated by a court-appointed receiver, Ms. Penley decided to start another Kentucky Fried Chicken franchise through a second corporation. Her ex-husband claimed that this business was being started with money that she had improperly converted for her own use from the first business that was in receivership. This time, Ms. Penley "won" and the court of appeals held that she did not misappropriate corporate funds to purchase the franchise nor did she have a duty to turn the franchise over to the other corporation that was being liquidated. A prenuptial (or, in this case, since the Penleys were already married, a postnuptial agreement) would presumably have disposed of these claims in short order and to the benefit of Ms. Penley.

Preparing a Prenuptial Agreement

In drafting a prenuptial agreement, disclosure is the most important concept. Not just ordinary, run-of-the mill disclosure: full and complete disclosure. Perhaps more than anything else, when reviewing a prenuptial agreement, courts will carefully scrutinize whether the parties were fully apprised of each other's respective financial situation and whether they understood that situation.

As a result, detailed financial information should be provided and referenced with attached financial statements in the agreement itself. The information should include complete details about each of the parties' net worth, income, assets, and liabilities. The assets should be carefully described so as to specifically identify the family business ownership interests being made subject to the agreement's provisions. Similarly, any property that is important to, yet separate from, the business should also be specifically addressed. For example, a business owner may have a personal computer at home that is used for business purposes. It may, therefore, be desirable to cover the computer in the prenuptial agreement.

When specifying the assets covered by the agreement, the business owner must provide accurate values for each asset. Failure to do so may provide an ex-spouse with a basis for invalidating the provisions on the basis of fraud. Again, the more detail, the better. In some instances, even accurately identifying particular assets on a schedule to an agreement may be insufficient. For example, in order for a spouse to waive a claim to certain pension benefits, very specific written consents to waive such benefits are required by the Employee Retirement Income Act (ERISA). Failure to obtain such consents could render the otherwise applicable provisions of a prenuptial agreement, which were intended to govern the disposition of such assets, meaningless. Again, consult your attorney when drafting a prenuptial agreement.

In order to ensure not only that disclosure is complete but that the parties understand what information is being disclosed, it is prudent for the parties to retain separate and independent counsel. Ideally, the parties and their counsel will have adequate time to review and consider the terms of the agreement prior to signing. In some instances, agreements being signed on the eve of a wedding can be later invalidated, since the circumstances suggest there was undue pressure and coercion on the spouse. Certain states even require that a minimum amount of time pass between the signing of a prenuptial agreement and the wedding in order to minimize the possibility of coercion. Again, consider such requirements with your attorney.

Judicial Review of Prenuptial Agreements

As noted earlier, courts are responsible for reviewing prenuptial agreements in order to ensure that the terms are fair and reasonable. Unconscionable agreements may be disregarded. For example, in *Del Vecchio v. Del Vecchio,* the Florida Supreme Court, in its consideration of a contested prenuptial agreement, observed:

A valid antenuptial agreement contemplates a fair and reasonable provision [for the nonmonied spouse] or, absent such provision, a full and frank disclosure to [that spouse], before the signing of the agreement, of the [monied spouse's] worth . . . .

If the provision made by the agreement is not fair and reasonable then it should be made to appear that [the non-monied spouse] . . . had some understanding of her rights to be waived by the agreement [prior to signing the agreement]. In any event she must have signed freely and voluntarily, preferably, but not necessarily a required prerequisite, upon competent and independent advice . . . .

In weighing the fairness and reasonableness of the provision for the wife the courts will consider the relative situation of the parties, their respective ages, health and experience, their respective properties, their family ties and connection, the wife's needs and such factors as tend to show whether the agreement was understandingly made.

Good Agreements May Protect Both Spouses

A prenuptial agreement that protects the family business and its owners may, at the same time, provide security to the former family member, who may otherwise be left fighting an uphill battle for fair and proper support. For example, in the absence of an agreement, a family business owner may seek to unfairly squeeze out the former spouse from the business. This could be accomplished by doing the following:

- Terminating the former spouse's employment with the family business
- Denying the former spouse dividends
- Seeking to purchase the former spouse's shares in the family business at a substantially discounted price. In situations like this, an ex-spouse may ultimately succeed in achieving fair recompense, but the battle may be long and costly.

A prenuptial agreement, by specifying a certain level of protection to the former spouse, may be much more desirable!

Recommendations

Divorce may not only represent the end of a marriage, it can sometimes represent the end of a family business. Cases like *Penley v. Penley,* where a family business winds up in receivership following divorce, are not unusual. In other cases, the business survives, but at a steep cost to the owner or the family business. Buy-sell agreements can be useful to ensure that ownership interests in a family business remain within a family following a divorce, although the interests are bought and sold at what might amount to be an expensive price. A prenuptial agreement can be helpful because it provides that an ownership agreement need not be bought or sold, since it remains at all times in the hands of the individual who entered the marriage holding the ownership interest. The other spouse, in effect, agrees to waive any claim to the business or its value in the event of a divorce.

Because premarital agreements can have harsh results in the event of a divorce on the nonmonied spouse, they will be carefully scrutinized to ensure, among other things, that there was full financial disclosure between the parties, the parties understood the financial disclosure, and there was no undue compulsion on the part of the nonmonied spouse to sign the agreement. If these and other requirements are met, and the attendant psychological difficulties of asking a fiancé or fiancée to waive his or her claims to assets in the event of a divorce, a premarital agreement can be a wonderful planning tool and family business salvation technique.

Family Business Audit

1. Is there particular reason to suspect that the likelihood of divorce is higher than ordinary? (i.e., Is this a third, fourth, or fifth marriage?)

2. Has a premarital agreement been properly prepared, with full disclosure, understanding, and lack of compulsion to sign?

3. Has each party to a premarital agreement retained his or her own attorney to advise him or her on the merits of the form of agreement?

4. Does the premarital agreement fairly treat both parties or is one party treated unconscionably, under the circumstances?

5. If it is too late to enter a premarital agreement, does it make sense to seek to enter a "postmarital agreement?"

6. Have you considered how a premarital agreement can be used to ensure that a spouse will be treated fairly in the event of a later divorce?

CHAPTER 11

Planning for the Long Term?
Prune the Family Business Tree!

*M*aintaining harmony within a family business is a constant challenge, even for the closest of families. The never-ending responsibility to make decisions that impact the family and the business can, to be sure, be invigorating and satisfying, but can also be frustrating and challenging as well. Many of the "business decisions" that are routinely made may ultimately dictate whether a business will survive another day and maybe even prosper, or fail. Should a new plant be built? Should the family expand into new territories? Should a new product be rolled out and an old product discontinued? The list of such decisions is not only complex but endless.

Frustrations within a family will inevitably develop over how these decisions are made. Why? As individuals, we view the world through our own unique lenses, and a decision that one family member may view as a smart course to follow, may be viewed as a silly one by another. A decision one family member finds acceptable may be equally unacceptable to another. The greater the number of family members involved in evaluating such decisions, the greater the likelihood for disagreement, which, I submit, explains the ever-increasing likelihood that family members working together will disagree on what course of action is good for the business and good for the family.

The Usefulness of Planning Techniques

As we have seen in a variety of instances throughout this book, the range of decisions that impact a family or its business is virtually infinite. Family members may disagree with each other over almost any or every decision—from how much money to spend on office furniture to how to fairly compensate family members; from who is eligible to work in the family business to how such employees are promoted, terminated, or designated as the future leader of the family business; from the use of business profits to expand operations or to pay dividends or whether to use business profits to better compensate employees or improve the return to the owners.

The variety of planning techniques reviewed in this book, by helping to foster an atmosphere of trust and respect among family members, can enhance the likelihood for family peace and prosperity. Family members can learn to better share their thoughts, their feelings, and their concerns with each other. Better communication among family members can help dispel an atmosphere of mistrust, replacing it instead with understanding, mutual respect, and trust. Techniques like family councils, family charters, and shareholder agreements can help a family formulate mutually acceptable policies and plans, and record them for future reference and guidance. Other techniques, like the utilization of outside advisers or directors, can serve as a compass, helping to guide the business around (or through) sometimes choppy water. Yes, the techniques considered in this book can improve the quality of decisions being made by families and their businesses and, so, reduce the likelihood for family conflict—at least in the short term.

The Limits of Planning Techniques

I believe that the model of conflict offered in Chapter 1 suggests that maintaining family harmony within a business, as the number of family members expands from generation to generation, will, over a period of time, ultimately prove impossible for any family. Family members can't help but have conflicting agendas and aspirations, as well as conflicting views about how the family can maximize the benefits from its business. As family relationships grow more distant, from parent and child, to sibling and sibling, cousin and cousin, and beyond, the conflicts tend to become more severe because business interests become more and more divergent at the same time that family unity becomes less and less meaningful. A problem that brother and sister might work out together will usually be more difficult for cousins to work out.

A family must, therefore, find a tool to vent or release the pressure that inexorably builds within its family unit before the business implodes. It must find one last technique that is capable of managing the conflict that inevitably will arise within a family business and, instead, preserve family peace. Families must find a technique that lets them pursue their unique road to peace and prosperity over the long term as well as the short!

Pruning the Family Business Tree: The Final Technique

Ultimately, the only way that pressure within a family and its business can be released is to create an exit mechanism that permits the family, or some of its members, to move on from the family business. The family must create an opportunity for its members to cash in their chips and move on to another life. Only then, without having to live with the conflict and competition created by each other's decisions, may family members once again focus principally on the pleasures and benefits of being part of a family. Only then, free from the concern of whether a niece or nephew is unfairly lining his or her pockets at the aunt's or uncle's expense, can a family focus on being a family. Only then, free from the concern whether a brother or sister is capable of succeeding to the leadership reins, can a family focus on being a family. Only then, free from the concern of whether another family member is being excessively compensated at the expense of another family member, can a family focus on being a family. The reduction of family members in a family business is often referred to as pruning the family business tree and, I submit, is the key to lasting family peace and business prosperity.

A variety of legal and business mechanisms are available to help family members peacefully prune the family business tree by exchanging ownership interests in a business for cash or other property. Some of these mechanisms, reviewed earlier, include the following:

- A straight sale of an ownership interest from one family member to another
- Splitting the business into separate divisions
- Sales pursuant to a buy-sell agreement
- A sale of the family's entire ownership interest in the business to nonfamily members, including through IPOs and ESOPs

The reduction process might happen in a natural and cooperative manner. A family member, for example, may relocate or choose to pursue an alternative career path, making the sale of ownership in a family business a desirable consequence, since it permits that family member to access cash to help maintain his or her lifestyle, whereas simply owning a piece of a business, on its own, provides no economic return to such a family member.

In other instances, a family is forced to deal with an uncooperative and disgruntled co-owner. Such a co-owner may be inexperienced in business and capable of making decisions only out of spite and jealousy. In those instances, the other family members may need to force that co-owner out. This is not always a pleasant task but, in business, sometimes unpleasant decisions need to be made.

In those instances where the family is unable to mutually agree on the terms of a sale to prune the family business tree, the sale will ultimately proceed, but usually only after life within the business has become unbearable. The exit terms at that point are as likely to be decided by cram down as by mutual agreement. In some instances, the sale will be preceded by the application of one or more of a variety of squeeze-out techniques, where one family member seeks to apply unfair tactics to force another's departure. There is no limit to the number of such techniques, which includes terminating a family member's employment, withholding dividends, and providing above-market benefits to some, but not all, family members.

These squeeze-out techniques are sometimes applied by ruthless owners seeking simply to enhance their individual positions or, in other instances, as a last-ditch measure to deal with some other equally ruthless family member who is seeking to unfairly destroy the family business and who must be dealt with. More often, I suspect, these techniques are initially applied by family members with good intentions, who simply have a different perspective on what is right or wrong than other family members, and the malice associated with the techniques comes only later after those family members have reacted negatively to such techniques.

On occasion, a business will collapse before its family owners realize that their conflict is ruining what might otherwise have been a tremendous financial opportunity for everyone. Thus, it is not uncommon for once successful family businesses to be forced into liquidation or bankruptcy. In such an event, the family's return on its investment may be nonexistent in the best case and, in others, it may lose all or part of a family fortune.

How to Prune the Family Business Tree

It is easy to recommend that the family business tree be pruned. The real difficulty arises in determining how to accomplish this objective. Again, individual family members can be expected to have a difference of opinion on the subject. If there are family members who seek to remain in the business, they will have an obvious interest in paying as little as possible for their departing family members' interests. These remaining family members will usually be interested in retaining as much money as possible within the business to fund new capital projects, business expansion, or, more simply, their personal lifestyles.

The family members considering departing will usually be looking to get at least fair value for their ownership interests, if not a premium for relinquishing their claims to a valuable birthright. Such members are typically uninterested in selling out if they are concerned that they will be selling their interest at a discount. Instead, they will generally prefer to remain in the business and seek instead to maximize their value on a sale of their interest at a later date, perhaps when all of the family members are interested in cashing out. This result, of course, contradicts the course I recommend and will, I believe, ultimately hurt the family and its business.

Fair value is, perhaps, an impossible calculation to make unless all of the owners seek to sell their interests at the same time to an outsider or, in those rare instances where it is possible to do so, the family business goes public. Only then will the entire family have either the same interest of maximizing the sale price (although disputes can still erupt over how that price should be allocated between covenants not to compete, consulting agreements, etc.) or a public market that sets the price for the ownership interests outside the context of a family decision.

Since initial public offerings are difficult to accomplish for the typical family business, a global sale of the family business to an outsider is the ideal way to prune the family tree, since it eliminates most of the arguing over whether the price is too high or too low. The family can be generally convinced that it has maximized its value.

If some family members wish to remain in the business after others have sold out, determining the sale price can be extremely tricky. In order to facilitate the pruning process, the sale price established must be high enough to provide sufficient incentive for prospective sellers to actually sell. If the price is too low, some family members may not sell out at all, while those who do are likely to resent their family members (who bought them out at an unfairly low price) for the rest of their lives. The last business transaction within the family can also be the last of the family.

Each family needs to consider its unique situation to determine what fair value means in its particular situation. Application of the look-back technique, discussed in Chapter 4, may be appropriate to provide confidence to the selling family members that the buyers won't "flip" the business and sell it to an outsider for a higher price shortly after the intrafamily sale. Application of other restrictions discussed in that chapter, such as restrictions that limit the buyers' salaries or the ability to make extraordinary capital expenditures if the sale price is being financed, may also be appropriate. At the end of the day, the sale price probably should be higher than the buyer would have liked to pay and lower than the price the seller would have liked to receive. This is a tricky decision, which should be made after much intrafamily dialogue and after securing the advice of competent professional assistance.

Recommendations

I once believed that, with proper education and sensitivity to the realities of life in a family business, family members could achieve relative peace and tranquility and, perhaps, even prosperity. Those family businesses that failed to secure such objectives simply didn't have enough family members who were smart enough and sensitive enough. After much study and representation of family businesses, however, I have come to the conclusion that this is too easy an excuse. Most individuals are sufficiently intelligent and, under the right circumstances, have sufficient goodwill for their fellow family members to corroborate this explanation. A more realistic and comprehensive explanation is required.

In light of the unceasing and significant pressures that are brought to bear on the family business, which challenge even the most sensitive and educated of families, I now believe that, at best, interim arrangements can be made to help keep the peace for a period of time. Such arrangements include the use of the planning techniques discussed earlier, including the proper use of a board of directors, development of a family council, and establishment of a family charter. In order to work effectively, such arrangements must be designed to accomplish the following:

- Involve all family members in the business.
- Encourage the education of all family members.
- Establish rules by which family members can enter the family business.
- Develop an estate plan that minimizes estate taxes while accommodating a family's succession plan as well as the retirement plan of senior family members.
- Make decisions that seek to accommodate both family and business interests.

In the right family, such arrangements may keep the peace through many years and several generations of family members. Ultimately, however, these arrangements will prove insufficient. At that time, I believe most families will be better off if they either sell the family business as a unit to an outsider or some family members sell their ownership interests to other family members pursuant to the terms of a fairly designed buyout (or buy-sell) agreement. Such an agreement can serve to ensure fairness to those family members departing from the business and those family members who remain. Only then can the family achieve lasting peace outside the pressure cooker of the family business.

Sample Family Charter

I. Smith Family Philosophy

Our family philosophy is to run our family business, to the greatest extent possible, like a business. We have prepared this family charter to reflect this philosophy in order to help guide current and future family members in this regard. Among other things, we commit to evaluating matters relating to the employment, promotion, and discipline of family members within our business from primarily a business perspective. The needs of the business will come first. By taking care of our business, we will better take care of our family.

As owners of a family business, we will be afforded benefits and opportunities to enrich our personal and professional lives. These benefits must be carefully defined and monitored so that the ultimate success of our family business is not compromised.

II. Qualifications to Enter the Family Business

In order for a family member to become employed by this company, such member must have at least the following qualifications:

- A four-year college degree
- At least three years' experience with another business
- Approval from the company's Board of Directors

When entering the business, family members agree to the following:

- Entry should occur when a need exists for a legitimate position and the family member has skills and abilities or potential that match the needs.

- No employee, including incumbent nonfamily employees, will be removed to "make room" for a new family hire.
- New positions will be based on natural attrition or expansion as a result of Board-established business goals.
- If a position does not become available to a family member within three months of Board approval under the above criteria, a job will then be created that permits the qualified family member to participate in an approved training program until an opening exists. The training program will be developed by the company's personnel manager, department manager, the chairman of the Board of Directors, and the prospective family employee.

III. Guidelines for Advancement

Family members wishing to be considered for advancement in the company must do the following:

- Have successfully performed in his or her current position for at least one year.
- Announce an interest in a specific position.
- Submit qualifications for the advancement to the employee's immediate supervisor. The family member agrees to the following:
  1. If the advancement request is approved by the supervisor, it will be sent to the Board for final approval.
  2. If the request is denied, specific reasons will be provided and tangible goals for development and progress reviews will be scheduled to assist the family member to advance at a future date; additional applications can be made when developmental areas are improved.
  3. Any move into a new position will only occur when the position is actually open.

IV. Grievances

If a family member feels unjustly treated in any manner relating to the family business, including with respect to decisions to employ, promote, or terminate such family member, he or she should advise the chairman of the Board of Directors, who shall review the process and attempt to arrive at an objective and unbiased resolution. If the chairman is unable to satisfy that family member, the matter shall be submitted to the company's Board of Directors, which shall have authority to resolve the matter in its discretion.

V. Training and Development

Family members are encouraged to take advantage of training opportunities that are a part of, or which exceed, company policy. We believe in working hard to prepare future generations for leadership.

To obtain additional training and/or development that is not a part of the company's ordinary program, family employees will do the following:

- Summarize in writing the nature of the proposed training activity, why it is desired, and how it will benefit both the individual and the company.
- Review the request with the chair of the Smith Family Council and the chairman of the Board of Directors.
- the Chair of the Smith Family Council and the chairman of the Board of Directors will jointly determine whether the request should be approved and, if so, notify appropriate people in the company.
- After the training program has been completed, the family member should share his or her experience with other members of the family.

VI. Goals and Objectives

All family members who are employed in the family business must develop specific goals and objectives as part of their jobs. These are to be set with the family member and his or her immediate supervisor. At a minimum, the goals should include the following:

- Specific expectations for the current position
- Developmental objectives for family members' advancement and training
- Expectations for continuing to build family harmony

VII. Performance Review

Performance reviews for family members are to be provided based on then-existing company guidelines and practices. Family employees will be treated the same as nonfamily employees with respect to the evaluation of job performance.

Each family employee's goals and developmental objectives will be reviewed as part of the job performance evaluation.

The Board will be apprised of each family employee's performance on at least an annual basis. If a family employee receives a negative review, the Board will be updated at least quarterly.

VIII. Disciplinary Procedures

Job-related discipline of family members will generally be handled according to existing company policies and procedures.

If a family employee's performance is so poor as to threaten his or her job, the Chair of the Smith Family Council should be notified of the situation and briefed about the problems. So too should he or she be notified if there is evidence that the family employee is in some way violating the principles of the company's Code of Conduct.

Family members are accountable to themselves for ensuring that the standards and expectations set forth in their Code of Conduct are being adhered to.

IX. Termination

Family employees will be terminated for continued violations and poor performance, after the Board has approved such termination.

X. Job Compensation

Family employees will be reasonable and fairly compensated, as determined by the company's Board of Directors.

Sample Family LLC Operating Agreement

THIS OPERATING AGREEMENT ("Agreement") is made and entered into as of the _____ day of September 1998, by and among those Persons whose names are set forth on <u>Exhibit A</u> to this Agreement.

RECITALS

WHEREAS, the parties hereto desire to form a limited liability company pursuant to and in accordance with <u>your state's</u> Limited Liability Company Law;

NOW, THEREFORE, in consideration of the foregoing and of other good and valuable consideration, the receipt and sufficiency of which is hereby acknowledged, the parties hereto do hereby agree as follows:

ARTICLE I.
FORMATION

1. ORGANIZATION. The parties have directed the Manager to act as an organizer to form the Company by filing Articles of Organization with the <u>your state's</u> Secretary of State.

2. NAME. The name of the Company is the Smith Family LLC.

3. PRINCIPAL PLACE OF BUSINESS. The principal place of business of the Company shall be located at 123 Main Street, Your City, USA.

4. PURPOSE. The purpose of the Company is to:

(1) Acquire, own, buy, sell, invest in, trade, manage, finance, re-finance, exchange, or otherwise dispose of stocks, securities, partner-ship, membership interests, limited liability company interests, CDs, mutual funds, commodities, and any and all investments whatsoever, that the Manager may, from time to time, deem to be in the best inter-ests of the Company;

(2) Own, acquire, manage, develop, operate, buy, sell, exchange, finance, refinance, and otherwise deal with real estate, personal prop-erty, and any type of business, as the Manager may from time to time deem to be in the interests of the Company; and

(3) Engage in such other activities as are related or incidental to the foregoing purposes.

ARTICLE II.
MANAGEMENT

1. MANAGEMENT.

(a) <u>General.</u> Except as otherwise specifically limited in this Agreement or any other applicable law, the Managers shall have the ex-clusive right to manage the affairs and business of the Company. The Managers shall be subject to all of the duties and liabilities of Managers that are contained in this Agreement and any other applicable law.

(b) <u>Initial Manager.</u> The Initial Managers shall be Jim Smith, Sr., and Jane Smith, who shall serve as the initial managers of the Company pursuant to the terms of this Agreement.

2. TERM. The Members agree that the Managers shall serve in such capacity as provided in subsections (a) and (b) below and there shall be no annual election of Managers.

(a) <u>Initial Managers.</u> The Initial Managers shall continue to serve as the sole Managers, until the first of the following occurs: (i) he or she is unable to serve in such capacity due to legal incompetency or permanent disability, (ii) he or she is deceased, (iii) he or she is removed as a Manager by the Members for "cause," where cause means (A) the Initial Manager's willful and repeated neglect or failure to discharge his or her duties under this Agreement, or (B) the violation by the Initial Managers of the provisions of Article X hereof; or (iv) he or she resigns by providing notice to the Members of such resignation. In addition, at such time as the Initial Manager shall, for any reason, cease at any time to be a Member of the Company, the remaining Members may, in their sole discretion, by unanimous consent, remove the Initial Manager as a Manager of the Company.

(b) <u>Subsequent Managers.</u> Each Person other than the Initial Manager who becomes a Manager after the date of this Agreement pursuant to the provisions of this Agreement, shall serve as a Manager until the first of the following occurs: (i) he or she resigns as a Manager, (ii) he or she is unable to serve in such capacity due to legal incompetency or permanent disability (a "Disabling Event"); (iii) he or she is deceased; or (iv) he or she is removed as a Manager by the Members for "cause," where cause means (A) the Initial Manager's willful and repeated neglect or failure to discharge his or her duties under this Agreement, or (B) the violation of the provisions of Article X hereof.

3. VACANCIES. In the event of the resignation of any Manager or other termination of his or her status as a Manager hereunder for any reason, and there is at least one remaining Manager, such remaining Manager(s) shall continue to serve as the Manager(s). If, however, at any time there are no remaining Managers, then all of the other Members shall serve as the Managers.

4. AUTHORITY TO BIND THE COMPANY. Unless expressly authorized to do so by the written consent of the Managers, no Member or any other Person who is not a Manager of the Company shall have any authority to act on behalf of or to bind the Company.

5. RESIGNATION. Any Manager may resign at any time by giving written notice thereof to all of the Members. The resignation of any such Manager other than the Initial Manager shall take effect at the time provided in such notice and no acceptance of the resignation shall be necessary. The resignation of any Manager other than the Initial Manager shall not affect such Manager's rights as a Member and shall not constitute a withdrawal as a Member.

6. MANAGERS SHALL ACT IN GOOD FAITH. A Manager shall perform his or her duties in good faith, in the manner he or she reasonably believes to be in the best interests of the Company, and with such degree of care as an ordinarily prudent person in a similar position would use under like circumstances.

7. INDEMNIFICATION. The Company shall indemnify, defend, and hold harmless each Manager for all costs, losses, liabilities, and damages paid or incurred by such Manager in the performance of his or her duties in such capacity, to the fullest extent provided or permitted by the Act or other applicable laws.

8. COMPENSATION; EXPENSE REIMBURSEMENT. Each Manager shall be entitled to reasonable compensation for acting in such capacity, and to be reimbursed for their expenses incurred in performing their duties in such capacity.

9. LIMITATIONS ON AUTHORITY OF MANAGERS. Notwithstanding the general authority of the Managers herein provided, no action relating to any of the following matters shall be taken by the Company unless the same shall have been approved by the unanimous vote or written consent of the Members:

(a) modifying, amending, or terminating the Company's Articles of Organization or this Operating Agreement;

(b) entering into any contract(s) or incurring any indebtedness on the part of the Company, which, individually or collectively, would require annual expenditures by the Company of more than $10,000;

(c) adopting a plan for or effecting a dissolution, liquidation, merger, or consolidation of the Company, or the sale or disposition of all or substantially all of the assets of the Company;

(d) any act in contravention of this Agreement;

(e) any act that would or could reasonably be expected to subject any Member to personal liability; and

(g) any such other actions that this Agreement specifically provides shall require the consent of the Members.

ARTICLE III.
ACCOUNTS, REPORTS AND NOTICES

1. ACCOUNTS. The Managers will maintain a system of complete and accurate books of account of the Company's affairs in accordance with generally accepted accounting principles consistently applied. Within 180 days after the end of each fiscal year of the Company, the Manager shall provide to each Member a copy of the balance sheet of the Company as at the end of such fiscal year together with statements of income, Member's equity and cash flow for such fiscal year, all in reasonable detail, prepared by the Company's accountants.

2. INSPECTION. Any Member, individually or through his or her legal or accounting representatives, shall have the right at any reasonable time during normal business hours to inspect and audit the books and records of the Company.

ARTICLE IV.
MEMBERS

1. VOTING. On each matter upon which Members are entitled to vote, each Member shall vote pro rata based upon his or her Membership Interests.

2. MEETINGS. Meetings of the Members, for any purpose or purposes, may be called by any Manager or upon the request of any Member entitled to vote thereat.

3. PLACE OF MEETINGS. Meetings of the Members shall be held at the Company's principal place of business or at such other location as the Members mutually agree upon.

4. NOTICE OF MEETINGS. Written notice, stating the place, date, and time of the meeting, indicating by or at whose direction the meeting is being called, and stating the purpose or purposes for which the meeting is being called, shall be delivered to each Member no fewer than 10 nor more than 60 days before the date of the meeting.

5. QUORUM. All of the Members entitled to vote thereat shall be required to be present in order to constitute a quorum for the transaction of business at any meeting of the Members.

6. WAIVER OF NOTICE. Notice of a meeting need not be given to any Member who submits a signed waiver of notice, whether before or after the meeting. The attendance of any Member at a meeting without protesting prior to the conclusion of the meeting the lack of notice of such meeting, shall constitute waiver of notice by such Member.

7. ACTION OF MEMBERS. If a quorum is present at any meeting of the Members, the unanimous vote or written consent of the Members entitled to vote thereat and present at the meeting shall be the act of the Members.

ARTICLE V.
MEMBERSHIP INTERESTS AND TRANSFERS THEREOF

1. GENERAL RESTRICTIONS. Except as otherwise provided in and pursuant to the provisions of this Article, no Member shall transfer any of his or her Membership Interests to another person or entity. This restriction, however, shall not apply to transfers to a Member's children or grandchildren. Any Transfer of Membership Interests in violation of this Article shall be void ab initio.

2. RIGHTS OF FIRST REFUSAL UPON THIRD PARTY OFFER.

(a) In the event that a Member desires to Transfer his or her Membership Interests to any other Person, such Member (hereinafter called the "Selling Member") shall first obtain a bona fide written offer that he or she desires to accept (hereinafter called the "Third Party Offer") to purchase all (but not less than all) of his or her Membership Interests. The Third Party Offer shall set forth its date, the price, and the other terms and conditions upon which the purchase is proposed to be made, as well as the name and address of the Prospective Purchaser.

(b) The Selling Member shall transmit a copy of the Third Party Offer to the Company and to each Member, which transmittal shall constitute offers by the Selling Member to sell all of the Offered Membership Interests first to the Company (the "Company Offer") at the price and upon the terms set forth in the Third Party Offer, and then, in the event that the Company does not accept the Company Offer, to the other Members, pro rata based upon their respective Membership Interests in the Company or in such other ratio as the Members shall unanimously agree at the price and upon the terms set forth in the Third Party Offer.

(c) The Company shall have a period of fifteen (15) days after the transmission by the Selling Member of the Company Offer in which to accept the Company Offer by providing a written notice of such acceptance to the Selling Member.

(d) If the Company accepts the Company Offer within the Company Refusal Period, then the closing of the purchase of the Offered Membership Interests by the Company shall occur within thirty (30) days following the expiration of the Company Refusal Period.

(e) If the Company does not accept the Company Offer, then the Members shall then have an additional fifteen (15) days in which to accept the Member Offers by providing a written notice of such acceptance to the Selling Member.

(f) If all of the Member Offers are accepted within the Member Refusal Period, then the closing of the purchase of the Offered Membership Interests by the Members shall occur within thirty (30) days following the expiration of the Member Refusal Period.

(g) If all of the Member Offers are not accepted within the Member Refusal Period, then the Member Offers shall terminate, and the Selling Member shall consummate, in accordance with the terms and conditions of the Third Party Offer, the Transfer to the Prospective Purchaser. Upon the consummation thereof and execution by such Prospective Purchaser of a counterpart to this Agreement as a Member, such Prospective Purchaser shall have all of the rights of a Member of the Company pursuant to this Operating Agreement, the Act, and any other applicable laws.

3. RIGHTS OF FIRST REFUSAL UPON DEFAULTING EVENT.

(a) Upon the bankruptcy or termination of a Member's employment with the Company for cause (a "Defaulting Member"), the Defaulting Member shall be required to offer to sell all of the Defaulting Membership Interests in the same manner as any proposed voluntary Transfer by such Defaulting Member governed by Section 2 of this Article, except that the purchase price of the Defaulting Membership Interests shall be an amount equal in cash to the fair value of the Defaulting Membership Interests, as reasonably determined by the Managers. Such purchase price may be paid either in cash or in sixty (60) equal monthly installments commencing on the date of the closing of the sale of the Defaulting Membership Interests to such purchaser(s) pursuant to this Section, together with interest thereon.

4. PUT RIGHT UPON DISABLING EVENT.

(a) Upon the occurrence of any Disabling Event, the Disabled Member, or his or her estate, legal representative, or other direct or indirect transferee, as applicable (each, a "Disabled Transferee"):

(i) shall, if a Manager, be deemed to have resigned as a Manager as of the date of the Disabling Event;

(ii) shall not be eligible to be a Manager or be entitled to participate in the management and affairs of the Company or to become or to exercise any rights or powers of a Member; and

(iii) shall only be entitled to receive the Distributions and allocations of Net Profits and Net Losses to which the Disabled Member would have been entitled with respect to such Disabled Membership Interests.

(b) Notwithstanding the provisions of Section 4(a) above with respect to the rights and limitations of a Disabled Member or Disabled Transferee, upon the occurrence of any Disabling Event and for a period of one (1) year thereafter (the "Put Period"), the Disabled Member or Disabled Transferee, as applicable, shall have the right to sell to the Company and the Company shall be required to purchase, all but not less than all of the Disabled Membership Interests (the "Put Right").

(c) The Put Right may be exercised at any time by providing a written notice of such exercise to the Company (the "Put Notice").

(d) The purchase price to be paid by the Company for the Disabled Membership Interests shall be an amount equal in cash to the fair value of the Disabled Membership Interests, as reasonably determined by the Managers, which determination shall be final and binding on all parties. Such purchase price may be paid by the Company either in cash or in sixty (60) equal monthly installments commencing on the date of the closing of the sale of the Disabled Membership Interests to the Company, together with interest thereon.

5. LIMITATION OF LIABILITY. No Member shall be personally liable for any indebtedness, liability, or obligation of the Company, except as otherwise expressly required by this Agreement, the Act, and any other applicable law.

ARTICLE VI.
CAPITAL CONTRIBUTIONS

1. INITIAL CONTRIBUTIONS. Each Member shall make an initial Capital Contribution to the Company as set forth opposite such Member's name on Exhibit A of this Agreement. The Members agree that any property described in Exhibit A that is other than cash, has the fair market value listed opposite such property and that each Member's Capital Account shall be credited with an initial Capital Contribution equal to the fair market value listed opposite his or her name in Exhibit A.

2. ADDITIONAL CONTRIBUTIONS. The Managers may determine, from time to time, that additional Capital Contributions are appropriate in connection with the conduct of the Company's business (including, without limitation, expansion, diversification, or to meet operating deficits). In such event, the Members shall have the opportunity, but shall not be obligated or required, to make any additional Capital Contributions to the Company.

3. CAPITAL ACCOUNTS. A Capital Account shall be maintained for each Member reflecting their initial Capital Contributions, as set forth on Exhibit A, (a) increased by the value of each additional Capital

Contribution made by such Member and allocation to such Member of Net Profits, and (b) decreased by the value of each Distribution to such Member and allocation to such Member of Net Losses.

4. DEFICIT CAPITAL ACCOUNT. Except as otherwise expressly required by the Act, this Agreement, or other applicable laws, no Member shall have any liability to restore all or any portion of a deficit balance in his or her Capital Account.

5. INTEREST ON AND RETURN OF CAPITAL CONTRIBU-TIONS. No Member shall be entitled to earn any interest on any Capital Contributions, and may only receive a return of its Capital Contributions where all indebtedness, liabilities, and obligations of the Company have been paid or there remains property of the Company that the Managers have determined is sufficient to pay them. Notwithstanding the foregoing, no Capital Contributions shall be returned to any Member unless all other Members receive a proportionate return of their Capital Contributions at the same time.

ARTICLE VII.
ALLOCATIONS AND DISTRIBUTIONS

1. ALLOCATIONS OF NET PROFITS AND NET LOSSES. Subject to the limitations of this Article, the Net Profits and the Net Losses shall be allocated to each Member pro rata in proportion to their respective Capital Accounts.

2. DISTRIBUTIONS; OFFSET. The Company shall make cash Distributions to the Members from time to time as determined by the Managers, which shall be allocated to each Member pro rata in proportion to their respective Capital Accounts. Notwithstanding the foregoing, the Company shall be required to offset all amounts owing to the Company by a Member against any Distribution to be made to such Member.

3. LIMITATION UPON DISTRIBUTIONS. Notwithstanding the foregoing, no Distribution shall be declared and paid (a) if such Distribution were to violate any applicable law, (b) unless after such Distribution were to be made, the fair market value of the assets of the Company would be in excess of all liabilities, and (c) unless such Dis-

tribution is also declared and paid simultaneously to all other Members in pro-rata proportion to their respective Capital Accounts, except where the Members unanimously approve such Distribution to less than all Members and/or in non–pro-rata proportions.

ARTICLE VIII.
TAXES

1. TAX RETURNS. The Managers shall cause to be timely prepared and filed, and shall have the authority to make all tax elections in connection therewith, all necessary federal and state income tax returns for the Company. Each Member shall cooperate in furnishing all information relating to the Company reasonably necessary with respect thereto.

2. TAX MATTERS PARTNER. The Managers shall designate one Manager to be the "tax matters partner" of the Company.

ARTICLE IX.
WITHDRAWAL; DISSOLUTION

1. WITHDRAWAL. Except as expressly provided herein, no Member may withdraw as a Member of the Company at any time prior to the dissolution and winding up of the Company. Any attempted withdrawal in violation of this Section shall be void ab initio and that Member so violating or attempting to violate this Section shall be fully liable to the Company for all damages and other costs and losses suffered by the Company or any other Member as a consequence thereof.

2. DISSOLUTION. The Company shall be dissolved and its affairs shall be wound up upon the first to occur of the following:

(a) The unanimous vote or written consent of the Members;

(b) Any event that makes it unlawful or impossible to carry on the Company's business; or

(c) The entry of a decree of judicial dissolution under the Act.

Notwithstanding any provision of the Act to the contrary, the Company shall continue and not dissolve as a result of the bankruptcy, dissolution, death, expulsion, incapacity, or withdrawal of any Member or the occurrence of any other event that terminates the continued membership of any Member.

3. WINDING UP. Upon the dissolution of the Company, the Managers shall, in the name and on behalf of the Company, take all actions reasonably necessary to wind up the Company pursuant to the Act.

4. ARTICLES OF DISSOLUTION. Within ninety (90) days following the dissolution and the commencement of winding up of the Company, or at any other time that there are no Members, articles of dissolution shall be filed with the <u>your state's</u> Secretary of State in accordance with the Act.

5. DISTRIBUTIONS UPON DISSOLUTION. Upon the winding up of the Company, the assets shall be distributed as follows:

(a) First, to creditors, including any Member who is a creditor, to the extent permitted by law, in satisfaction of liabilities of the Company;

(b) Second, to Members, pro rata, based upon such respective positive Capital Account balances.

6. NONRECOURSE TO OTHER MEMBERS. Except as otherwise expressly required by the Act or applicable law, if, upon the dissolution of the Company, the assets of the Company remaining after the payment or discharge of the Company's debts and liabilities are insufficient to return any Capital Contributions to any Member, in whole or in part, such Member shall have no recourse against any other Member or any Manager or the Company therefor.

7. TERMINATION. Upon completion of the dissolution and winding up, liquidation, and distribution of the Company's assets, the Company shall be deemed terminated.

ARTICLE X.
NONCOMPETITION; CONFLICTS

1. NONCOMPETITION; CONFLICTS. For so long as any Person is a Manager or Member of the Company, and for a period of three years thereafter, such Person will not directly or indirectly:

(a) take any action in, or participate with, or become interested in or associated with any Person (other than the Company) engaged in, or permit his or her name or goodwill to be used in connection with, any business that competes with any business engaged in by the Company;

(b) divulge to anyone, other than the Company or Persons designated by it in writing, any trade secrets or other confidential information, directly or indirectly useful in or relating to any aspect of the business of the Company as conducted from time to time, which shall not be generally known to the public or recognized as standard practice;

(c) claim to have any right, title, or interest of any kind or nature whatsoever in or to any products, methods, practices, processes, discoveries, ideas, improvements, devices, creations, or inventions relating to the business of the Company, whether created, developed, or invented by the Company or the Manager or Member during the term of this Agreement;

(d) solicit, induce, or influence any customer, supplier, lender, lessor, or any other Person who has a business relationship with the Company to discontinue or reduce the extent of such relationship with the Company; or

(e) recruit, solicit, employ, or assist any third party in employing, or otherwise induce or influence any employee, agent, or other Person with a relationship to the Company (except for the Manager or Member's spouse or immediate family member) to discontinue such employment, agency, or other relationship with the Company.

Nothing herein contained shall be deemed to prohibit ownership by Member or Manager of five percent (5%) or less of the outstanding shares of any class of any corporation whose shares are publicly traded on a regular basis.

ARTICLE XI.
FAMILY CHARTER

The members agree to adhere to the Smith Family Charter, attached as Exhibit B.

ARTICLE XIII.
MISCELLANEOUS

1. OTHER AGREEMENTS. Each of the parties covenants and agrees to take all such actions as may be reasonably required to ensure that the Company complies at all times with the terms and provisions of all agreements entered into by the Company in accordance with the terms and provisions of this Agreement that are reasonably related to accomplish the objectives of those agreements.

2. AFTER ACQUIRED MEMBERSHIP INTERESTS. Whenever any Member acquires any Membership Interests other than Membership Interests owned at the time of execution of this Agreement, such Membership Interests acquired after execution of this Agreement shall be subject to all of the terms and conditions of this Agreement, and the Membership Certificates representing such Membership Interests shall be surrendered to the Company for endorsement, unless already so endorsed.

3. ADDITIONAL ACTIONS AND DOCUMENTS. Each of the parties hereto hereby agrees to take or cause to be taken such further actions, to execute, deliver, and file or cause to be executed, delivered, and filed such further statements, assignments, agreements, proxies, and other instruments, and to use reasonable best efforts to obtain such consents, as may be necessary or as may be reasonably requested in order to fully effectuate the purposes, terms, and conditions of this Agreement.

4. NOTICES. All notices required to be given pursuant to this Agreement shall be in writing and shall be hand-delivered or mailed by first class, to the address of the appropriate Member as appears on the

Company's books and records and any notices to be given to the Company shall be sent in the same way to the Company's principal office.

5. AMENDMENT. Except as otherwise expressly provided herein, this Agreement may be amended only by written agreement duly executed by all of the parties hereto.

IN WITNESS WHEREOF, the undersigned have duly executed this Agreement, or have caused this Agreement to be duly executed on their behalf, as of the day and year first above written.

MANAGERS:

_____

MEMBERS:

A

Adjusted taxable gifts, 108–9
Advisers, negotiation with, 81
Antenuptial agreement. *See* Prenuptial
    agreement(s)
Arbitration, 82–83
Articles of incorporation, 85–86
Asset(s)
    accumulation, in junior generations,
        116–17
    building, outside of family business,
        177
    limited access to, by children,
        164–66
    protection, trusts and, 144–45
    transfer of, 15–16

B

Bankruptcy, 145
    limited liability companies and, 167
Beneficiaries
    in bypass trust, 147–48
    in QTIP trust, 147
    withdrawals from trusts by, 149–50
Benefit plans, 133
Bias, 9–10
Binding arbitration, 82
Board of directors, 34–50
    director/shareholder conflict, 39–41
    dispute resolution and, 85
    family boards, 38–41, 45–47, 49
    fiduciary duties of, 41–42
    model of, 35–38. *See also* Corporate
        model
    nonfamily members of, 34, 46–48,
        49, 96–97

Boilerplate documents, 179
Business, family
    chain of command in, 183–84
    classes of stock, 180
    customized documents in, 179–81
    form, determining, 177
    legal formalities, importance of,
        181–83
    prenuptial agreements. *See*
        Prenuptial agreement(s)
    segregated operations, 178–79
    succession plan for, 184–85
Business judgment rule, 41, 43–45
Buy-sell agreements, 14, 59–61, 67–68,
    84–86
    considerations in drafting, 67–68
    divorce and, 188, 193
    funding the purchase price, 63–65
    look-back provision, 61–63
    payment terms and conditions,
        65–66
    potential buyers, 55–57
    right of first refusal, 54–55
    structure of, 55–56
    trigger events, 57–59, 64, 67
    valuation methods, 59–61
Bylaws, 37, 179–80
Bypass trust, 147–48

C

Capital gains taxes, cross-purchase
    agreements and, 57
Capital improvements, 69
Chain of command, 183–84
Charging order, 166

Charitable donations
    estate planning and, 127–28
    of family business interests, 154–55
    irrevocable trusts and, 153–55
Charitable lead trust, 154
Charitable remainder annuity trust, 154
Charitable remainder unitrust, 153
Check the box tax regulations, 173
Children
    grandchildren, generation skipping
        trusts and, 152–53
    irrevocable trusts and, 149–50
    limited liability companies and,
        163–66
    split interest trusts and, 150–52
Classes, of stock, 140, 163, 180
Codes of conduct, 30–31
Comcast Corporation, 95
Common-law agency principles, 37
Common partnership interests, 141–42
Common stock, 126–27, 140–41
Communication, 22–23, 27
    dispute resolution and, 78, 85
    family board of directors and, 40–41
    triangulated, 30, 79
Compensation, of family employees, 46
Competition, shareholders agreements
    and, 57–59
Confidentiality, 69
Conflict
    introduction to, 1–2
    limited liability companies and,
        171–72
    origin of, 2–3
    reduction of, 5, 24–25
    resolution. *See* Dispute resolution
        process
Conflicts of interest, 39, 44, 47
Consensus, maximizing, 5–21
Continuing education, 98
Control of business, 133–34. *See also*
    Limited liability companies
    freezing partnership interests,
        141–42
    observing chain of command,
        183–84
    ownership agreements, 142
    trusts. *See* Trust(s)

    voting control, 139–41
    voting trusts, 142
Corporate bylaws, 37, 179–80
Corporate form, for family business, 177
Corporate model, 35–48, 49
    checks and balances within, 41
    conflict and, 38–41
    directors, 36–37
    effective use of, 45–48
    failure of, in practice, 43–45
    officers, 37–38
    shareholders, 35–36
Corporate ownership, 51
Covenants not to compete, 69–70
Creditors, protection against, limited
    liability companies and, 166–67
Credit shelter trust, 147–48, 181
Criticism, 39
Cross-purchase agreement, 56, 57
Crummey Notices, 149–50, 156

D

Death
    of business leader, 16–17
    shareholders agreements and, 57–59
Decision-making process, 2
    customized standards of, 80
    number of family members involved
        and, 5
Deferred payment, of estate taxes,
    131–32
Del Vecchio v. Del Vecchio, 192
Directors, 36–37. *See also* Board of
    directors
    classes of, 45
Disability, shareholder agreements and,
    57–59
Dispute resolution process, 74–87
    failure, of traditional techniques,
        76–77
    formal stage, 77, 81–84
    informal stage, 77, 78–80
    planning techniques and, 75–76
    process of, 77
Divorce
    buy-sell agreements and. *See*
        Buy-sell agreements

irrevocable trusts and, 145
ownership and, 14
prenuptial agreements. *See*
Prenuptial agreement(s)
shareholder agreements and, 57–59
Dodge v. Ford Motor Company, 37
Double skip transfer, 152
Drag-along provisions, 58
Duhon v. Slickline, Inc., 31
Duty of care, 41–42
Duty of loyalty, 42

E

Economic Recovery Tax Act of 1981, 120
Education, continuing, 97–98
Education qualifications, for leadership,
91–92
Employee Retirement Income Act, 191
Employee stock ownership plan, 125
Employment agreements, 13
Escrow agreement, 66
Estate freeze, 126–27, 141–42
Estate planning, 15–16, 104–36, 185
asset accumulation, in junior
generations, 116–17
business spin-offs, split-offs, and
split-ups, 129–30
calculating amount of tax due, 106
charitable donations and, 127–28
conflicts inherent in process of,
138–39
consulting pay and, 129
deferred payment of estate taxes,
131–32
employee stock ownership plan, 125
estate freezing techniques, 126–27
exemption, of family business, 110
generation skipping transfer tax
(GST), 110–11
gift tax and, 107–8
initial public stock offering, 126
insurance and, 128, 131
limited liability companies and, 174.
See also Limited liability
companies
permissible tax deductions, 112

recapitalizing corporate stock, 140–
41
retirement planning and, 132–33
for retiring leader, 100–101
sale-leaseback technique and, 129
stock bonuses and options, 130
tax reform, 112
transfers by intrafamily gifts,
118–21
transfers by intrafamily sale, 121–24
trusts. *See* Trust(s)
unified estate and gift tax, 108–9
valuation, of family business,
113–16
Experience, outside of family business,
92–94

F

Facilitators, 81
Family business exemption, 110
Family charters, 31–33
dispute resolution and, 85
limited liability companies and, 171
sample, 203–6
Family council, 22–33
board of directors and, 26
code of conduct, 30–31
creative uses for, 28–29
design of, 23–28
family charter, 31–33
ground rules, 27–28
limited liability companies and, 169
open membership in, 25–26
professional facilitators and, 28–29
purpose of, 23–24
succession plan and, 96
Family limited liability company, 18
and limited partnerships compared,
172–73, 175
Federal estate and gift taxes, unified rates
for, 107
Fiduciary duties, of directors, 41–42
Financial policies, nonfamily board
member and, 46
Form, for family business, 177
Fraudulent conveyance laws, 167

G

Generation skipping transfer tax (GST), 110–11
Gift-in-trust program, 149–50
Gift taxes, 107–8
limited liability companies and, 160–61
split interest trusts and, 150–51
valuation discounts and, 162
Grandchildren
generation skipping transfer tax and, 110–11
generation skipping trusts and, 152–53
Grantor retained annuity trust, 150–51
Grantor retained unitrust, 150–51
GRAT, 150–51
Gross estate, 106
GRUT, 150–51

H–I

How to Profit by Forming Your Own Limited Liability Company, 159
Hunter v. Roberts, Throp & Co., 43–44
Hybrid agreement, 56, 57
Illness, of business leader, 16–17
"I love you" will, 180–81
Initial public stock offering, 126, 200
Installment notes, 151, 161
Insurance, and estate planning, 128, 131
Internal Revenue Code
discount of ownership interests and, 162
estate taxes and, 108, 131–32
transfer of property to partnership and, 165
Intrafamily gifts, 118–21
Intrafamily sale, 121–24
private annuities, 124
repurchase of ownership by the business, 122–23
sale of ownership to family, 123
self-canceling installment notes, 124
Irrevocable life insurance trust, 167–68, 181

Irrevocable trusts, 144
for charity, 153–55
for child, 149–50
life insurance and, 167–68, 181
for spouse, 145–48

J–K

Johnston, Esther, 7
Johnston v. Livingston Nursing Home, Inc., 7
Key nonfamily employees, 101–2

L

Leadership skills, 97–98
Legal formalities, importance of, 181–83
Life insurance
buy-sell agreements and, 57, 64–65
deflecting from estate, 128
irrevocable trusts and, 155, 181
limited liability companies and, 167–68
retirement benefits and, 133
Limitation, of number of decision makers, 19
Limited liability companies, 48, 51, 157–58, 159–75, 177
benefits of, 159–60, 174–75
changing environments and, 173–74
children and, 163–66
conflict resolution and, 171–72
control and, 162–63
discounted interest value, 162
and family partnerships compared, 172–73
insurance planning and, 167–68
operating agreements and, 168–71
protection from creditors and, 166–67
transfer of ownership in, 160–62
Limited liability partnerships, 177
Liquidation sale, 131
Litigation, 83, 86
Living trusts, 143–44, 155
Look-back provision, 61–63

M

Management conflict, 6–8
Management shareholders, 39. *See also*
   Shareholders
Marital deduction trust, 146, 148, 155–56
Matrimonial claims, protection against
   irrevocable trusts and, 145
      prenuptial agreements. *See*
         Prenuptial agreement(s)
Matrimonial problems, ownership and,
   14
Mediation, 81–82
Membership certificates, 160
Miller v. Miller, 42
Minority interest discount, 162
Mission, of business, 6
Mission statement, 29
   limited liability companies and, 170

N

Nepotism, 91, 93
Net gifts, 119–20
New York, division of marital property
   in, 189
Nonbinding arbitration, 82, 83

O

Obermaier v. Obermaier, 62–63
Officers, 37–38
Operating agreement, 51
   limited liability companies and, 51,
      168–71
   sample, 207–21
Ownership agreements, 142
Ownership interests, 13–14
Ownership transfer
   intrafamily sale, 121–24
   limited liability companies and. *See*
      Limited liability companies
   maintaining control after. *See*
      Control of business
   to nonfamily members, 125
   relinquishing ownership, 133–34.
      See also Buy-sell agreements
   to spouse, 120–21

P

Partnership agreement, 51
Partnerships, 48, 177
   common, 141–42
   freezing interests, 141–42
   preferred, 141–42
Penley v. Penley, 189–90
Perks, 39–40
Planning techniques, 28–33
   family charter, 31–33, 171, 203–6
   family code of conduct, 30–31
   limits of, 196–97
   mission statement, 29, 170
   pruning family business tree,
      197–201
   strategic plan, 30
   usefulness of, 196
Postnuptial agreement, 190
Power of appointment, 146
Preferred partnership interests, 141–42
Preferred stock, 126, 140–41
Premarital agreement. *See* Prenuptial
   agreement(s)
Prenuptial agreement(s), 14, 186–93
   coercion in, 191–92
   defined, 186–88
   divorce in absence of, 189–91
   judicial review of, 192
   preparation of, 191–92
   protection of both spouses in,
      193
Private annuities, 124
Profits, reinvestment of vs. distribution
   conflict, 5–6
Psychology, of family business, 19–20

Q

Qualified domestic trust (QDOT trust),
   147
Qualified terminal interest trust (QTIP
   trust), 146–47, 148, 155–57

R

Redemption agreement, 56–57
Resolutions, 37
Resources, conflict over, 8–9

Restrictive covenants, in buy-sell agreements, 66
Retirement plan, 132–33
    development of, for outgoing leader, 99–100
    in estate plan, 132–33
    segregated operations and, 178
    shareholder agreements and, 57–59
Revocable (living) trust, 143–44
Right of first refusal, 54–55
Roberts, Brian, 95
Roberts, Ralph, 95
Rule against perpetuities, 142

S

Sale-leaseback technique, and estate planning, 129
Samia v. Central Oil Company of Worcester, 182–83
S corporations, 70
    voting and nonvoting stock, 140
Securities regulation, 70–71
Security arrangements, buy-sell agreements and, 66
Self-canceling installment notes, 124, 151, 161
Self-confidence, 93
Self-interest, appearance of, 12–13
Shareholder agreements, 51–73, 84
    buy-sell agreements. *See* Buy-sell agreements
    covenants not to compete, 69–70
    family business management, 68–69
    financial policies, 69
    S corporation planning, 70
    securities regulation, 70–71
Shareholders, 34, 35–36
    dispute resolution and, 85
    shareholder/director conflict, 39–41
    voting rights of, 36
Siblings, conflicts among, 18
Simmons, Harold C., 101
Sinking fund, 64
Sole proprietorships, 48, 177
Spin-offs, split-offs, and split-ups, 130, 178
Split interest trusts, 150–52

Spouses, estate taxes and, 112
    unlimited marital deduction, 120
Stock
    bonuses and options, 130
    classes of, 140, 163, 180
    initial public offering of, 126, 200
    limited liability companies and, 163
    preferred and common, 140–41
    types of, 35
    voting and nonvoting, 36, 140, 180
    voting rights and, 36
Stock bail-outs, 127
Stockholders. *See* Shareholders
Strategic plans, 30
Subsidiaries, 129–30
Succession of leadership, 17–18, 88–103
    communication of succession plan, 96
    estate plan, for outgoing leader, 100–101
    outside directors and, 96–97
    retaining key employees, 101–2
    retirement plan, for outgoing leader, 99–100
    selection criteria, 90–95
    time frame for, 98–99
    training of designated successor, 97–98
Supermajority vote, 180

T

Tag-along provisions, 58
Taxpayer Relief Act of 1997, 107
    charitable trusts and, 154
    deferred payment of estate taxes and, 132
    exemption for family businesses, 110
    exemption from estate/gift taxes, 109
    transfer of ownership and, 145
    unified credit transfers and, 119
Tax rules, and business valuation, 60–61
Termination, shareholder agreements and, 57–59
Term insurance, 64
Training, outside family business, 92–94

Transition of leadership, 17–18. *See also*
Succession of leadership
Triangulated communication, 30, 79
Trustees, 142, 155–56
Trust(s)
    complexities of, 156–57
    disadvantages of, 155–57
    forfeiture clauses and, 145
    generation skipping, 152–53
    irrevocable, 144. *See also*
        Irrevocable trusts
    irrevocable life insurance trusts,
        167–68
    living, 143–44, 155
    ownership of insurance policy by,
        128
    protection from creditors and,
        144–45
    protection from matrimonial claims
        and, 145
    revocable, 143–44

split interest, 150–52
voting trusts, 142

U

Unified credit, 109, 147–48
    transfers, 119
Unified estate and gift tax, 108–9
Unlimited marital deduction, 120–21,
    145–46

V–W

Valuation, of family business, 113–16,
    199–299
Valuation discounts, 162
Vick, Lessie, 7
Voting stock, 36, 140, 180
Voting trusts, 142
Wills, 180–81